—— THE ARBOR HOUSE ——
TREASURY OF NOBEL PRIZE WINNERS

THE ARBOR HOUSE

TREASURY OF NOBEL PRIZE WINNERS

EDITED BY
Martin H. Greenberg
and Charles G. Waugh

ARBOR HOUSE
NEW YORK

ACKNOWLEDGMENTS

The following constitutes an extension of the copyright page.

"You Know How Women Are" by Sinclair Lewis. From *The Man Who Knew Coolidge* by Sinclair Lewis, copyright © 1927, 1928 by Harcourt Brace Jovanovich Inc.; Renewed 1955, 1956 by Michael Lewis. Reprinted by permission of the publisher.

"The Lovers" by Pearl S. Buck from pages 189–212 of *The Lovers and Other Stories* by Pearl S. Buck (John Day). Copyright 1977 by The Pearl S. Buck Foundation, Inc. By permission of Harper & Row, Publishers, Inc.

"Barn Burning" by William Faulkner. Copyright 1939 and renewed 1967 by Estelle Faulkner and Jill Faulkner Summers. Reprinted from *The Faulkner Reader* by William Faulkner, by permission of Random House, Inc.

"The Infra-redioscope" by Bertrand Russell. By kind permission of George Allen & Unwin (Publishers) from *Satan in the Suburbs and Other Stories* by Bertrand Russell.

"The Short Happy Life of Francis Macomber" by Ernest Hemingway. Reprinted with the permission of Charles Scribner's Sons from *The Short Stories of Ernest Hemingway*. Copyright 1936 Ernest Hemingway; copyright renewed 1964 by Mary Hemingway.

"The Leader of the People" by John Steinbeck. From *The Long Valley* by John Steinbeck. Copyright 1938 by John Steinbeck. Copyright renewed 1966 by John Steinbeck. Reprinted by permission of Viking Penguin Inc.

"The Cockatoos" by Patrick White. From *The Cockatoos* by Patrick White, published by Viking Press and Penguin Books. Reprinted by permission of Curtis Brown (Aust.) Pty. Ltd., Sydney.

"The Gonzaga Manuscripts" by Saul Bellow. From *Mosby's Memoirs and Other Stories* by Saul Bellow. Copyright 1954, 1968 by Saul Bellow. Copy-

CONTENTS

PREFACE

THIS BOOK brings together for the first time all the Nobel laureates who write in English or (in the case of Isaac Bashevis Singer) who translate much of their own work into English. We have included only those honorees who have written short stories, which means that Eugene O'Neill (who received the Nobel Prize in 1936), T. S. Eliot (1948), and Sir Winston Churchill (1953) are not represented. It is our hope to bring you all non-English-language short story writers who have the prize in future volumes. Samuel Beckett is a problem, since he writes in French and then is translated into English. Although he sometimes does this translation himself, he is frequently translated by others, and we decided to save him for a subsequent book.

The Nobel Prizes were first awarded in 1901 in five fields—peace, chemistry, physics, medicine, and literature. Economics was added as a category in 1969. The prizes, named after Alfred Nobel, a Swedish industrialist who developed dynamite, were to be awarded for contributions to the "good of humanity," and the literature prize was intended to reward work of an "idealistic nature."

The literature prize is a most important one, since it helps to define greatness. However, it should be pointed out that several of the winners, especially those writing in languages other than English, are now largely forgotten, a few for good reason. Nevertheless, the prize is widely sought after and has become quite valuable in a financial sense, currently awarding over $200,000 to the winner (or split if there is more than one laureate in the same year). No award in literature was given in 1914, 1918, 1935, and 1940–1943.

The laureates are chosen by the Swedish Academy of Literature in Stockholm, working under the formal directive of seeking recipients whose work has been "proved by the test of experience or by the examination of experts," which means that literary critics and the reputations they enhance play a significant role in the final choices. In actuality, the prize contains political elements which reflect the views of the Academy, and it is clear that the selectors pay considerable attention to factors of geographical and linguistic balance. Unlike the science prizes, the literature prize almost always is awarded for the complete work of an author, rather than for a particular book, play, or poem.

The prize is awarded on December 10 of each year, the anniversary of Nobel's death. We trust that you will enjoy the great literature contained in this book as much as we enjoyed compiling it for you.

—Martin H. Greenberg and Charles G. Waugh

Rudyard Kipling

THE MAN WHO WOULD BE KING

NOBEL PRIZE 1907

Rudyard Kipling (1865–1936) was born in Bombay, India. Sent to England at the age of six, he spent an unhappy childhood being looked after by an elderly relative. In school he became interested in journalism, returning to India to work for the La- hore Civil and Military Gazette *in 1883. Indeed,* Plain Tales from the Hills *(1888), the short story collection which made his reputation, is composed of works previously contributed to this paper. In 1889 he became the London correspondent for the* Allahabad Pioneer. *Married in 1892, he traveled frequently during the next decade, publishing such classics as* Barrack- Room Ballads *(1892),* The Jungle Books *(1894–1895)* Captains Courageous *(1897), and* Kim *(1901) before settling in the Sussex countryside.*

Kipling was a master of setting and language and a persuasive advocate for patriotism, camaraderie, courage, and duty. But his literary popularity declined in later years as the public grew increasingly unhappy with war, imperialism, and chauvinism.

Brother to a Prince and fellow to a beggar if he be found worthy.

11

THE LAW, AS QUOTED, lays down a fair conduct of life, and one not easy to follow. I have been fellow to a beggar again and again under circumstances which prevented either of us finding out whether the other was worthy. I have still to be brother to a Prince, though I once came near to kinship with what might have been a veritable King and was promised the reversion of a Kingdom—army law-courts, revenue and policy all complete. But, to-day, I greatly fear that my King is dead, and if I want a crown I must go and hunt it for myself.

The beginning of everything was in a railway train upon the road to Mhow from Ajmir. There had been a Deficit in the Budget, which necessitated traveling, not Second-class, which is only half as dear as First-class, but by Intermediate, which is very awful indeed. There are no cushions in the Intermediate class, and the population are either Intermediate, which is Eurasian, or native, which for a long night journey is nasty, or Loafer, which is amusing though intoxicated. Intermediates do not patronize refreshment-rooms. They carry their food in bundles and pots, and buy sweets from the native sweetmeat-sellers, and drink the roadside water. That is why in the hot weather Intermediates are taken out of the carriages dead, and in all weathers are most properly looked down upon.

My particular Intermediate happened to be empty till I reached Nasirabad, when a huge gentleman in shirt-sleeves entered, and, following the custom of Intermediates, passed the time of day. He was a wanderer and a vagabond like myself, but with an educated taste for whiskey. He told tales of things he had seen and done, of out-of-the-way corners of the Empire into which he had penetrated, and of adventures in which he risked his life for a few days' food. "If India was filled with men like you and me, not knowing more than the crows where they'd get their next day's rations, it isn't seventy millions of revenue the land would be paying—it's seven hundred millions," said he; and as I looked at his mouth and chin I was disposed to agree with him. We talked politics—the politics of Loaferdom that sees things from the underside where the lath and plaster is not smoothed off—and we talked postal arrangements because my friend wanted to send a telegram back from the next station to Ajmir, which is the turning-off place from the Bombay to the Mhow line as you travel westward. My friend had no money beyond eight annas which he wanted for dinner, and I had no money at all, owing to the hitch in the Budget before mentioned. Further, I was going into a wilderness where, though I should resume touch with the Treasury, there were no telegraph offices. I was, therefore, unable to help him in any way.

"We might threaten a Station-master, and make him send a wire on tick," said my friend, "but that'd mean inquiries for you and for me, and I've got my hands full these days. Did you say you are traveling back along this line within any days?"

"Within ten," I said.

"Can't you make it eight?" said he. "Mine is rather urgent business."

"I can send your telegram within ten days if that will serve you," I said.

"I couldn't trust the wire to fetch him now I think of it. It's this way. He leaves Delhi on the 23d for Bombay. That means he'll be running through Ajmir about the night of the 23d."

"But I'm going into the Indian Desert," I explained.

"Well *and* good," said he. "You'll be changing at Marwar Junction to get into Jodhpore territory—you must do that—and he'll be coming through Marwar Junction in the early morning of the 24th by the Bombay Mail. Can you be at Marwar Junction on that time? 'Twon't be inconveniencing you because I know that there's precious few pickings to be got out of these Central India States— even though you pretend to be correspondent of the *Backwoodsman.*"

"Have you ever tried that trick?" I asked.

"Again and again, but the Residents finds you out, and then you get escorted to the Border before you've time to get your knife into them. But about my friend here. I *must* give him a word o' mouth to tell him what's come to me or else he won't know where to go. I would take it more than kind of you if you was to come out of Central India in time to catch him at Marwar Junction, and say to him:—'He has gone South for the week.' He'll know what that means. He's a big man with a red beard, and a great swell he is. You'll find him sleeping like a gentleman with all his luggage round him in a Second-class compartment. But don't you be afraid. Slip down the window, and say:—'He has gone South for the week,' and he'll tumble. It's only cutting your time of stay in those parts by two days. I ask you as a stranger—going to the West," he said, with emphasis.

"Where have *you* come from?" said I.

"From the East," said he, "and I am hoping that you will give him the message on the Square—for the sake of my Mother as well as your own."

Englishmen are not usually softened by appeals to the memory of their mothers, but for certain reasons, which will be fully apparent, I saw fit to agree.

"It's more than a little matter," said he, "and that's why I ask you to do it—and now I know that I can depend on you doing it. A Second-class carriage at Marwar Junction, and a redhaired man asleep in it. You'll be sure to remember. I get out at the next station, and I must hold on there till he comes or sends me what I want."

"I'll give the message if I catch him," I said, "and for the sake of your Mother as well as mine I'll give you a word of advice. Don't try to run the Central India States just now as the correspondent of the *Backwoodsman*. There's a real one knocking about here, and it might lead to trouble,"

"Thank you," said he, simply, "and when will the swine be gone? I can't starve because he's ruining my work. I wanted to get hold of the Degumber Rajah down here about his father's widow, and give him a jump."

"What did he do to his father's widow, then?"

"Filled her up with red pepper and slippered her to death as she hung from a beam. I found that out myself and I'm the only man that would dare going into the State to get hush-money for it. They'll try to poison me, same as they did in Chortumna when I went on the loot there. But you'll give the man at Marwar Junction my message?"

He got out at a little roadside station, and I reflected. I had heard, more than once, of men personating correspondents of newspapers and bleeding small Native States with threats of exposure, but I had never met any of the caste before. They lead a hard life, and generally die with great suddenness. The Native States have a wholesome horror of English newspapers, which may throw light on their peculiar methods of government, and do their best to choke correspondents with champagne, or drive them out of their mind with four-in-hand barouches. They do not understand that nobody cares a straw for the internal administration of Native States so long as oppression and crime are kept within decent limits, and the ruler is not drugged, drunk, or diseased from one end of the year to the other. Native States were created by Providence in order to supply picturesque scenery, tigers, and tall-writing. They are the dark places of the earth, full of unimaginable cruelty, touching the Railway and the Telegraph on one side, and, on the other, the days of Harun-al-Raschid. When I left the train I did business with divers Kings, and in eight days passed through many changes of life. Sometimes I wore dress-clothes and consorted with Princes and Politicals, drinking from crystal and eating from silver. Sometimes I lay out upon the ground and devoured what I could get, from a plate made of a flapjack, and drank the running water, and slept under the same rug as my servant. It was all in the day's work.

Then I headed for the Great Indian Desert upon the proper day, as I had promised, and the night Mail set me down at Marwar Junction, where a funny little, happy-go-lucky, native-managed railway runs to Jodhpore. The Bombay Mail from Delhi makes a short halt at Marwar. She arrived as I got in, and I had just time to hurry to her platform and go down the carriages. There was only one Second-class on the train. I slipped the window and looked down upon a flaming red beard, half covered by a railway rug. That was my man, fast asleep, and I dug him gently in the ribs. He woke with a grunt and I saw his face in the light of the lamps. It was a great and shining face.

"Tickets again?" said he.

"No," said I. "I am to tell you that he is gone South for the week. He is gone South for the week!"

The train had begun to move out. The red man rubbed his eyes. "He has gone South for the week," he repeated. "Now that's just like his impidence. Did he say that I was to give you anything?— 'Cause I won't."

"He didn't," I said, and dropped away, and watched the red lights die out in the dark. I was horribly cold because the wind was blowing off the sands. I climbed into my own train—not an Intermediate Carriage this time—and went to sleep.

If the man with the beard had given me a rupee I should have kept it as a memento of a rather curious affair. But the consciousness of having done my duty was my only reward.

Later on I reflected that two gentlemen like my friends could not do any good if they foregathered and personated correspondents of newspapers, and might, if they "stuck up" one of the little rat-trap states of Central India or Southern Rajputana, get themselves into serious difficulties. I therefore took some trouble to describe them as accurately as I could remember to people who would be interested in deporting them: and succeeded, so I was later informed, in having them headed back from the Degumber borders.

Then I became respectable, and returned to an Office where there were no Kings and no incidents except the daily manufacture of a newspaper. A newspaper office seems to attract every conceivable sort of person, to the prejudice of discipline. Zenana-mission ladies arrive, and beg that the Editor will instantly abandon all his duties to describe a Christian prize-giving in a back-slum of a perfectly inaccessible village; Colonels who have been overpassed for commands sit down and sketch the outline of a series of ten, twenty, or twenty-four leading articles on Seniority *versus* Selection; missionaries wish to know why they have not been permitted to escape from their regular vehicles of abuse and swear at a brother-missionary under special patronage of the editorial We; stranded theatrical companies troop up to explain that they cannot pay for their advertisements, but on their return from New Zealand or Tahiti will do so with interest; inventors of patent punkah-pulling machines, carriages couplings and unbreakable swords and axle-trees call with specifications in their pockets and hours at their disposal; tea-companies enter and elaborate their prospectuses with the office pens; secretaries of ball-committees clamor to have the glories of their last dance more fully expounded; strange ladies rustle in and say:—"I want a hundred lady's cards printed *at once,* please," which is manifestly part of an Editor's duty; and every dissolute ruffian that ever tramped the Grand Trunk Road makes it his business to ask for employment as a proof-reader. And, all the time, the telephone-bell is ringing madly, and Kings are being killed on the Continent, and Empires are saying—"You're another," and Mister Gladstone is calling down brimstone upon the British Dominions, and the little black copy-boys are whining, "*kaapi chay-ha-yeh*" (copy wanted) like tired bees, and most of the paper is as blank as Modred's shield.

But that is the amusing part of the year. There are other six months wherein none ever come to call, and the thermometer walks inch by inch up to the top of the glass, and the office is darkened to just above reading light, and the press machines are red-hot of touch, and nobody writes anything but accounts of amusements in the Hill-stations or obituary notices. Then the telephone becomes a tinkling terror, because it tells you of the sudden deaths of men and women that you knew intimately, and the prickly-heat covers you as with a garment, and you sit down and write:—"A slight increase of sickness is reported from the Khuda Janta Khan District. The outbreak is purely sporadic in its nature, and, thanks to the energetic efforts of the District authorities, is now almost at an end. It is, however, with deep regret we record the death, etc."

Then the sickness really breaks out, and the less recording and reporting the better for the peace of the subscribers. But the Empires and the Kings continue to divert themselves as selfishly as before, and the Foreman thinks that a daily paper really ought to come out once in twenty-four hours, and all the people at the Hill-stations in the middle of their amusements say:—"Good gracious! Why can't the paper be sparkling? I'm sure there's plenty going on up here."

That is the dark half of the moon, and, as the advertisements say, "must be experienced to be appreciated."

It was in that season, and a remarkably evil season, that the paper began running the last issue of the week on Saturday night, which is to say Sunday morning, after the custom of a London paper. This was a great convenience, for immediately after the paper was put to bed, the dawn would lower the thermometer from 96 degrees to almost 84 degrees for half an hour, and in that chill—you have no idea how cold is 84 degrees on the grass until you begin to pray for it—a very tired man could set off to sleep ere the heat roused him.

One Saturday night it was my pleasant duty to put the paper to bed alone. A King or courtier or a courtesan or a community was going to die or get a new Constitution, or do something that was important on the other side of the world, and the paper was to be held open till the latest possible minute in order to catch the telegram. It was a pitchy black night, as stifling as a June night can be, and the *loo,* the red-hot wind from the westward, was booming among the tinder-dry trees and pretending that the rain was on its heels. Now and again a spot of almost boiling water would fall on the dust with the flop of a frog, but all our weary world knew that was only pretence. It was a shade cooler in the press-room than the office, so I sat there, while the type ticked and clicked, and the night-jars hooted at the windows, and the all but naked compositors wiped the sweat from their foreheads and called for water. The thing that was keeping us back, whatever it was, would not come off, though the *loo* dropped and the last type was set, and the whole round earth stood still in the choking heat, with its fingers on its lip, to wait the event. I drowsed, and wondered whether the telegraph was a blessing, and whether this dying man, or struggling people, was aware of the inconvenience the delay was causing. There was no special reason beyond the heat and worry to make tension, but, as the clock hands crept up to three o'clock and the machines spun their fly-wheels two and three times to see that all was in order, before I said the word that would set them off, I could have shrieked aloud.

Then the roar and rattle of the wheels shivered the quiet into little bits. I rose to go away, but two men in white clothes stood in front of me. The first one said:—"It's him!" The second said:—"So it is!" And they both laughed almost as loudly as the machinery roared, and mopped their foreheads. "We see there was a light burning across the road and we were sleeping in that ditch there for coolness, and I said to my friend here, The office is open. Let's come along and speak to him as turned us back from the Degumber State," said the smaller of the two. He was the man I had met in the Mhow train, and his fellow was the red-bearded man of Marwar Junction. There was no mistaking the eyebrows of the one or the beard of the other.

I was not pleased, because I wished to go to sleep, not to squabble with loafers. "What do you want?" I asked.

"Half an hour's talk with you cool and comfortable, in the office," said the red-bearded man. "We'd *like* some drink—the Contrack doesn't begin yet, Peachey, so you needn't look—but what we really want is advice. We don't want money. We ask you as a favor, because you did us a bad turn about Degumber."

I led from the press-room to the stifling office with the maps on the walls, and the red-haired man rubbed his hands. "That's something like," said he. "This was the proper shop to come to. Now, Sir, let me introduce to you Brother Peachey Carnehan, that's him, and Brother Daniel Dravot, that is *me*, and the less said about our professions the better, for we have been most things in our time. Soldier, sailor, compositor, photographer, proof-reader, street-preacher, and correspondents of the *Backwoodsman* when we thought the paper wanted one. Carnehan is sober, and so am I. Look at us first and see that's sure. It will save you cutting into my talk. We'll take one of your cigars apiece, and you shall see us light."

I watched the test. The men were absolutely sober, so I gave them each a tepid peg.

"Well *and* good," said Carnehan of the eyebrows, wiping the froth from his moustache. "Let me talk now, Dan. We have been all over India, mostly on foot. We have been boiler-fitters, engine-drivers, petty contractors, and all that, and we have decided that India isn't big enough for such as us."

They certainly were too big for the office. Dravot's beard seemed to fill half the room and Carnehan's shoulders the other half, as they sat on the big table. Carnehan continued:—"The country isn't half worked out because they that governs it won't let you touch it. They spend all their blessed time in governing it, and you can't lift a spade, nor chip a rock, nor look for oil, nor anything like that without all the Government saying—'Leave it alone and let us govern.' Therefore, such as it is, we will let it alone, and go away to some other place where a man isn't crowded and can come to his own. We are not little men, and there is nothing that we are afraid of except Drink, and we have signed a Contrack on that. *Therefore,* we are going away to be Kings."

"Kings in our own right," muttered Dravot.

"Yes, of course," I said. "You've been tramping in the sun, and it's a very warm night, and hadn't you better sleep over the notion? Come to-morrow."

"Neither drunk nor sunstruck," said Dravot. "We have slept over the notion half a year, and require to see Books and Atlases, and we have decided that there is only one place now in the world that two strong men can Sar-a-*whack*. They call it Kafiristan. But my reckoning it's the top right-hand corner of Afghanistan, not more than three hundred miles from Peshawur. They have two and thirty heathen idols there, and we'll be the thirty-third. It's a mountainous country, and the women of those parts are very beautiful."

"But that is provided against in the Contrack," said Carnehan. "Neither Women nor Liqu-or, Daniel."

"And that's all we know, except that no one has gone there, and they fight, and in any place where they fight a man who knows how to drill men can always be a King. We shall go to those parts and say to any King we find—'D' you want to vanquish your foes?'

and we will show him how to drill men; for that we know better than anything else. Then we will subvert that King and seize his Throne and establish a Dynasty."

"You'll be cut to pieces before you're fifty miles across the Border," I said. "You have to travel through Afghanistan to get to that country. It's one mass of mountains and peaks and glaciers, and no Englishman has been through it. The people are utter brutes, and even if you reached them you couldn't do anything."

"That's more like," said Carnehan. "If you could think us a little more mad we would be more pleased. We have come to you to know about this country, to read a book about it, and to be shown maps. We want you to tell us that we are fools and to show us your books." He turned to the bookcases.

"Are you at all in earnest?" I said.

"A little," said Dravot, sweetly. "As big a map as you have got, even if it's all blank where Kafiristan is, and any books you've got. We can read, though we aren't very educated."

I uncased the big thirty-two-miles-to-the-inch map of India, and two smaller Frontier maps, hauled down volume INF-KAN of the *Encyclopaedia Britannica,* and the men consulted them.

"See here!" said Dravot, his thumb on the map. "Up to Jagdallak, Peachey and me know the road. We was there with Roberts's Army. We'll have to turn off to the right at Jagdallak through Laghmann territory. Then we get among the hills—fourteen thousand feet— fifteen thousand—it will be cold work there, but it don't look very far on the map."

I handed him Wood on the *Sources of the Oxus.* Carnehan was deep in the *Encyclopaedia.*

"They're a mixed lot," said Dravot, reflectively; "and it won't help us to know the names of their tribes. The more tribes the more they'll fight, and the better for us. From Jagdallak to Ashang. H'mm!"

"But all the information about the country is as sketchy and inaccurate as can be," I protested. "No one knows anything about it really. Here's the file of the *United Services' Institute.* Read what Bellew says."

"Blow Bellew!" said Carnehan. "Dan, they're an all-fired lot of heathens, but this book here says they think they're related to us English."

I smoked while the men pored over *Raverty, Wood,* the maps, and the *Encyclopaedia.*

"There is no use your waiting," said Dravot, politely. "It's about four o'clock now. We'll go before six o'clock if you want to sleep, and we won't steal any of the papers. Don't you sit up. We're two harmless lunatics, and if you come, to-morrow evening, down to the Serai we'll say good-bye to you."

"You *are* two fools," I answered. "You'll be turned back at the Frontier or cut up the minute you set foot in Afghanistan. Do you want any money or a recommendation down-country? I can help you to the chance of work next week."

"Next week we shall be hard at work ourselves, thank you," said Dravot. "It isn't so easy being a King as it looks. When we've got our Kingdom in going order we'll let you know, and you can come up and help us to govern it."

"Would two lunatics make a Contrack like that?" said Carnehan, with subdued pride, showing me a greasy half-sheet of note-paper on which was written the following. I copied it then and there, as a curiosity:

> This Contract between me and you persuing witnesseth in the name of God—Amen and so forth.
>
> (One) That me and you will settle this matter together; *i.e.,* to be Kings of Kafiristan.
>
> (Two) That you and me will not, while this matter is being settled, look at any Liquor, nor any woman, black, white or brown, so as to get mixed up with one or the other harmful.
>
> (Three) That we conduct ourselves with dignity and discretion, and if one of us gets into trouble the other will stay by him.
>
> Signed by you and me this day.
>
> Peachey Taliaferro Carnehan.
>
> Daniel Dravot.
>
> Both Gentlemen at Large.

"There was no need for the last article," said Carnehan, blushing modestly; "but it looks regular. Now you know the sort of men that loafers are—we *are* loafers, Dan, until we get out of India—and *do* you think that we would sign a Contrack like that unless we was in earnest? We have kept away from the two things that make life worth having."

"You won't enjoy your lives much longer if you are going to try this idiotic adventure. Don't set the office on fire," I said, "and go away before nine o'clock."

I left them still poring over the maps and making notes on the back of the "Contrack." "Be sure to come down to the Serai tomorrow," were their parting words.

The Kumharsen Serai is the great four-square sink of humanity where the strings of camels and horses from the North load and unload. All the nationalities of Central Asia may be found there, and most of the folk of India proper. Balkh and Bokhara there meet Bengal and Bombay, and try to draw eye-teeth. You can buy ponies, turquoises, Persian pussy-cats, saddlebags, fat-tailed sheep and musk in the Kumharsen Serai, and get many strange things for nothing. In the afternoon I went down there to see whether my friends intended to keep their word or were lying about drunk.

A priest attired in fragments of ribbons and rags stalked up to me, gravely twisting a child's paper whirligig. Behind him was his servant bending under the load of a crate of mud toys. The two were loading up two camels, and the inhabitants of the Serai watched them with shrieks of laughter.

"The priest is mad," said a horse-dealer to me. "He is going up to Kabul to sell toys to the Amir. He will either be raised to honor or have his head cut off. He came in here this morning and has been behaving madly ever since."

"The witless are under the protection of God," stammered a flat-cheeked Usbeg in broken Hindi. "They foretell future events."

"Would they could have foretold that my caravan would have been cut up by the Shinwaris almost within shadow of the Pass!" grunted the Eusufzai agent of a Rajputana trading-house whose goods had been feloniously diverted into the hands of other robbers just across the Border, and whose misfortunes were the laughingstock of the bazaar. "Ohé, priest, whence come you and whither do you go?"

"From Roum have I come," shouted the priest, waving his whirligig; "from Roum, blown by the breath of a hundred devils across the sea! O thieves, robbers, liars, the blessing of Pir Khan on pigs, dogs, and perjurers! Who will take the Protected of God to the North to sell charms that are never still to the Amir? The camels shall not gall, the sons shall not fall sick, and the wives shall remain faithful while they are away, of the men who give me place in their caravan. Who will assist me to slipper the King of the Ross with a golden slipper with a silver heel? The protection of Pir Khan be upon his labors!" He spread out the skirts of his gaberdine and pirouetted between the lines of tethered horses.

"There starts a caravan from Peshawur to Kabul in twenty days, *Huzrut*," said the Eusufzai trader. "My camels go therewith. Do thou also go and bring us good-luck."

"I will go even now!" shouted the priest. "I will depart upon my winged camels, and be at Peshawur in a day! Ho! Hazar Mir Khan," he yelled to his servant, "drive out the camels, but let me first mount my own."

He leaped on the back of his beast as it knelt, and, turning round to me, cried:—"Come thou also, Sahib, a little along the road, and I will sell thee a charm—an amulet that shall make thee King of Kafiristan."

Then the light broke upon me, and I followed the two camels out of the Serai till we reached open road and the priest halted.

"What d' you think o' that?" said he in English. "Carnehan can't talk their patter, so I've made him my servant. He makes a handsome servant. 'Tisn't for nothing that I've been knocking about the country for fourteen years. Didn't I do that talk neat? We'll hitch on to a caravan at Peshawur till we get to Jagdallak, and then we'll see if we can get donkeys for our camels, and strike into Kafiristan. Whirligigs for the Amir, O Lor! Put your hand under the camel-bags and tell me what you feel."

I felt the butt of a Martini, and another and another.

"Twenty of 'em," said Dravot, placidly. "Twenty of 'em, and ammunition to correspond, under the whirligigs and the mud dolls."

"Heaven help you if you are caught with those things!" I said. "A Martini is worth her weight in silver among the Pathans."

"Fifteen hundred rupees of capital—every rupee we could beg, borrow, or steal—are invested on these two camels," said Dravot. "We won't get caught. We're going through the Khaiber with a regular caravan. Who'd touch a poor mad priest?"

"Have you got everything you want?" I asked, overcome with astonishment.

"Not yet, but we shall soon. Give us a memento of your kindness, *Brother*. You did me a service yesterday, and that time in Marwar.

Half my Kingdom shall you have, as the saying is." I slipped a small charm compass from my watch-chain and handed it up to the priest.

"Good-bye," said Dravot, giving me hand cautiously. "It's the last time we'll shake hands with an Englishman these days. Shake hands with him, Carnehan," he said, as the second camel passed me.

Carnehan leaned down and shook hands. Then the camels passed away along the dusty road, and I was left alone to wonder. My eye could detect no failure in the disguises. The scene in Serai attested that they were complete to the native mind. There was just the chance, therefore, that Carnehan and Dravot would be able to wander through Afghanistan without detection. But, beyond, they would find death, certain and awful death.

Ten days later a native friend of mine, giving me the news of the day from Peshawur, wound up his letter with:—"There has been much laughter here on account of a certain mad priest who is going in his estimation to sell petty gauds and insignificant trinkets which he ascribes as great charms to H. H. the Amir of Bokhara. He passed through Peshawur and associated himself to the Second Summer caravan that goes to Kabul. The merchants are pleased because through superstition they imagine that such mad fellows bring good-fortune."

The two, then, were beyond the Border. I would have prayed for them, but, that night, a real King died in Europe, and demanded an obituary notice.

•

The wheel of the world swings through the same phases again and again. Summer passed and winter thereafter, and came and passed again. The daily paper continued and I with it, and upon the third summer there fell a hot night, a night-issue, and a strained waiting for something to be telegraphed from the other side of the world, exactly as had happened before. A few great men had died in the past two years, the machines worked with more clatter, and some of the trees in the Office garden were a few feet taller. But that was all the difference.

I passed over to the press-room, and went through just a scene as I have already described. The nervous tension was stronger than it had been two years before, and I felt the heat more acutely. At three o'clock I cried, "Print off," and turned to go, when there crept to my chair what was left of a man. He was bent into a circle,

his head was sunk between his shoulders, and he moved his feet
one over the other like a bear. I could hardly see whether he walked
or crawled—this rag-wrapped, whining cripple who addressed me
by name, crying that he was come back. "Can you give me a drink?"
he whimpered. "For the Lord's sake, give me a drink!"

I went back to the office, the man following with groans of pain,
and I turned up the lamp.

"Don't you know me?" he gasped, dropping into a chair, and he
turned his drawn face, surmounted by a shock of grey hair, to the
light.

I looked at him intently. Once before had I seen eyebrows that
met over the nose in an inch-broad black band, but for the life of
me I could not tell where.

"I don't know you," I said, handing him the whiskey. "What can
I do for you?"

He took a gulp of the spirit raw, and shivered in spite of the
suffocating heat.

"I've come back," he repeated; "and I was the King of Kafiristan—me and Dravot—crowned Kings we was! In this office we
settled it—you setting there and giving us the books. I am Peachey—
Peachey Taliaferro Carnehan, and you've been setting here ever
since—O Lord!"

I was more than a little astonished, and expressed my feelings
accordingly.

"It's true," said Carnehan, with a dry cackle, nursing his feet,
which were wrapped in rags. "True as gospel. Kings we were, with
crowns upon our heads—me and Dravot—poor Dan—oh, poor,
poor Dan, that would never take advice, not though I begged of
him!"

"Take the whiskey," I said, "and take your own time. Tell me all
you can recollect of everything from beginning to end. You got
across the border on your camels, Dravot dressed as a mad priest
and you his servant. Do you remember that?"

"I ain't mad—yet, but I shall be that way soon. Of course I
remember. Keep looking at me, or maybe my words will go all to
pieces. Keep looking at me in my eyes and don't say anything."

I leaned forward and looked into his face as steadily as I could.
He dropped one hand upon the table and I grasped it by the wrist.
It was twisted like a bird's claw, and upon the back was a ragged,
red, diamond-shaped scar.

"No, don't look there. Look at *me*," said Carnehan.

"That comes afterward, but for the Lord's sake don't distrack me. We left with that caravan, me and Dravot playing all sorts of antics to amuse the people we were with. Dravot used to make us laugh in the evenings when all the people was cooking their dinners—cooking their dinners, and...what did they do then? They lit little fires with sparks that went into Dravot's beard, and we all laughed—fit to die. Little red fires they was, going into Dravot's big red beard—so funny." His eyes left mine and he smiled foolishly.

"You went as far as Jagdallak with that caravan," I said, at a venture "after you had lit those fires. To Jagdallak, where you turned off to try to get into Kafiristan."

"No, we didn't neither. What are you talking about? We turned off before Jagdallak, because we heard the roads was good. But they wasn't good enough for our two camels—mine and Dravot's. When we left the caravan, Dravot took off all his clothes and mine too, and said we would be heathen, because the Kafirs didn't allow Mohammedans to talk to them. So we dressed betwixt and between, and such a sight as Daniel Dravot I never saw yet nor expect to see again. He burned half his beard, and slung a sheep-skin over his shoulder, and shaved his head into patterns. He shaved mine, too, and made me wear outrageous things to look like a heathen. That was in a most mountainous country, and our camels couldn't go along any more because of the mountains. They were tall and black, and coming home I saw them fight like wild goats—there are lots of goats in Kafiristan. And these mountains, they never keep still, no more than the goats. Always fighting they are, and don't let you sleep at night."

"Take some more whiskey," I said, very slowly. "What did you and Daniel Dravot do when the camels could go no further because of the rough roads that led into Kafiristan?"

"What did which do? There was a party called Peachey Taliaferro Carnehan that was with Dravot. Shall I tell you about him? He died out there in the cold. Slap from the bridge fell old Peachey, turning and twisting in the air like a penny whirligig that you can sell to the Amir.—No; they was two for three ha' pence, those whirligigs, or I am much mistaken and woful sore. And then these camels were no use, and Peachey said to Dravot—'For the Lord's sake, let's get out of this before our heads are chopped off,' and with that they killed the camels all among the mountains, not having anything in particular to eat, but first they took off the boxes with the guns and the ammunition, till two men came along driving four mules. Dravot up and dances in front of them, singing,—'Sell me four mules.' Say the first man,—'If you are rich enough to buy, you are rich enough to rob;' but before ever he could put his hand to his knife, Dravot breaks his neck over his knee, and the other party runs away. So Carnehan loaded the mules with the rifles that was taken off the camels, and together we starts forward into those bitter cold mountainous parts, and never a road broader than the back of your hand."

He paused for a moment, while I asked him if he could remember the nature of the country through which he had journeyed.

"I am telling you as straight as I can, but my head isn't as good as it might be. They drove nails through it to make me hear better how Dravot died. The country was mountainous and the mules were most contrary, and the inhabitants was dispersed and solitary. They went up and up, and down and down, and that other party, Carnehan, was imploring of Dravot not to sing and whistle so loud, for fear of bringing down the tremenjus avalanches. But Dravot says that if a King couldn't sing it wasn't worth being King, and whacked the mules over the rump, and never took no heed for ten cold days. We came to a big level valley all among the mountains, and the mules were near dead, so we killed them, not having anything in special for them or us to eat. We sat upon the boxes, and played odd and even with the cartridges that was jolted out.

"Then ten men with bows and arrows ran down that valley, chasing twenty men with bows and arrows, and the row was tremenjus. They was fair men—fairer than you or me—with yellow hair and remarkable well built. Says Dravot, unpacking the guns— 'This is the beginning of the business. We'll fight for the ten men,' and with that he fires two rifles at the twenty men, and drops one of them at two hundred yards from the rock where we was sitting. The other men began to run, but Carnehan and Dravot sits on the boxes picking them off at all ranges, up and down the valley. Then we goes up to the ten men that had run across the snow too, and they fires a footy little arrow at us. Dravot he shoots above their heads and they all falls down flat. Then he walks over them and kicks them, and then he lifts them up and shakes hands all round to make them friendly like. He calls them and gives them the boxes

to carry, and waves his hand for all the world as though he was
King already. They takes the boxes and him across the valley and
up the hill into pine wood on the top, where there was half a dozen
big stone idols. Dravot he goes to the biggest—a fellow they call
Imbra—and lays a rifle and a cartridge at his feet, rubbing his
nose respectful with his own nose, patting him on the head, and
saluting in front of it. He turns round to the men and nods his
head, and says,—'That's all right. I'm in the know too, and all these
old jim-jams are my friends.' Then he opens his mouth and points
down it, and when the first man brings him food, he says—'No';
and when the second man brings him food, he says—'No'; but
when one of the old priests and the boss of the village brings him
food, he says—'Yes'; very haughty, and eats it slow. That was how
we came to our first village, without any trouble, just as though we
had tumbled from the skies. But we tumbled from one of those
damned rope-bridges, you see, and you couldn't expect a man to
laugh much after that."

"Take some more whiskey and go on," I said. "That was the first
village you came into. How did you get to be King?"

"I wasn't King," said Carnehan. "Dravot he was the King, and a
handsome man he looked with the gold crown on his head and all.
Him and the other party stayed in that village, and every morning
Dravot sat by the side of old Imbra, and the people came and
worshipped. That was Dravot's order. Then a lot of men came into
the valley, and Carnehan and Dravot picks them off with the rifles
before they knew where they was, and runs down into the valley
and up again the other side, and finds another village, same as the
first one, and the people all falls down flat on their faces, and
Dravot says,—'Now what is the trouble between you two villages?'
and the people points to a woman, as fair as you or me, that was
carried off, and Dravot takes her back to the first village and counts
up the dead—eight there was. For each dead man Dravot pours
a little milk on the ground and waves his arms like a whirligig and
'That's all right,' says he. Then he and Carnehan takes the big boss
of each village by the arm and walks them down the valley, and
shows them how to scratch a line with a spear right down the valley,
and gives each a sod of turf from both sides o' the line. Then all
the people comes down and shouts like the devil and all, and Dravot
says,—'Go and dig the land, and be fruitful and multiply,' which
they did, though they didn't understand. Then we asks the names

of things in their lingo—bread and water and fire and idols and such, and Dravot leads the priest of each village up to the idol, and says he must sit there and judge the people, and if anything goes wrong he is to be shot.

"Next week they was all turning up the land in the valley as quiet as bees and much prettier, and the priests heard all the complaints and told Dravot in dumb show what it was about. 'That's just the beginning,' says Dravot. 'They think we're Gods.' He and Carnehan picks out twenty good men and shows them how to click off a rifle, and form fours, and advance in line, and they was very pleased to do so, and clever to see the hang of it. Then he takes out his pipe and his baccy-pouch and leaves one at one village and one at the other, and off we two goes to see what was to be done in the next valley. That was all rock, and there was a little village there, and Carnehan says,—'Send 'em to the old valley to plant,' and takes 'em there and gives 'em some land that wasn't took before. They were a poor lot, and we blooded 'em with a kid before letting 'em into the new Kingdom. That was to impress the people, and then they settled down quiet, and Carnehan went back to Dravot who had got into another valley, all snow and ice and most mountainous. There was no people there and the Army got afraid, so Dravot shoots one of them, and goes on till he finds some people in a village, and the Army explains that unless the people wants to be killed they had better not shoot their little matchlock; for they had matchlocks. We makes friends with the priest and I stays there alone with two of the Army, teaching the men how to drill, and a thundering big Chief comes across the snow with kettle-drums and horns twanging, because he heard there was a new God kicking about. Carnehan sights for the brown of the men half a mile across the snow and wings one of them. Then he sends a message to the Chief that, unless he wished to be killed, he must come and shake hands with me and leave his arms behind. The Chief comes alone first, and Carnehan shakes hands with him and whirls his arms about, same as Dravot used, and very much surprised that Chief was, and strokes my eyebrows. Then Carnehan goes alone to the Chief, and asks him in dumb show if he had an enemy he hated. 'I have,' says the Chief. So Carnehan weeds out the pick of his men, and sets the two of the Army to show them drill and at the end of two weeks the men can manoeuvre about as well as Volunteers. So he marches with the Chief to a great big plain on the top of a mountain, and the Chief's men rushes into a village and takes it; we three Martinis firing into the brown of the enemy. So we took that village too, and I gives the Chief a rag from my coat and says, 'Occupy till I come:' which was scriptural. By way of a reminder, when me and the Army was eighteen hundred yards away, I drops a bullet near him standing on the snow, and all the people falls flat on their faces. Then I sends a letter to Dravot, wherever he be by land or by sea."

At the risk of throwing the creature out of train I interrupted,— "How could you write a letter up yonder?"

"The letter?—Oh!—The Letter! Keep looking at me between the eyes, please. It was a string-talk letter, that we'd learned the way of it from a blind beggar in the Punjab."

I remember that there had once come to the office a blind man with a knotted twig and a piece of string which he wound round the twig according to some cypher of his own. He could, after the lapse of days or hours, repeat the sentence which he had reeled up. He had reduced the alphabet to eleven primitive sounds; and tried to teach me his method, but failed.

"I sent that letter to Dravot," said Carnehan; "and told him to come back because this Kingdom was growing too big for me to handle, and then I struck for the first valley, to see how the priests were working. They called the village we took along with the Chief, Bashkai, and the first village we took, Er-Heb. The priests at Er-Heb was doing all right, but they had a lot of pending cases about land to show me, and some men from another village had been firing arrows at night. I went out and looked for that village and fired four rounds at it from a thousand yards. That used all the cartridges I cared to spend, and I waited for Dravot, who had been away two or three months, and I kept my people quiet.

"One morning I heard the devil's own noise of drums and horns, and Dan Dravot marches down the hill with his Army and a tail of hundreds of men, and, which was the most amazing—a great gold crown on his head. 'My Gord, Carnehan,' said Daniel, 'this is a tremenjus business, and we've got the whole country as far as it's worth having. I am the son of Alexander by Queen Semiramis, and you're my younger brother and a God too! It's the biggest thing we've ever seen. I've been marching and fighting for six weeks with the Army, and every footy little village for fifty miles has come in rejoiceful; and more than that, I've got the key of the whole show,

as you'll see, and I've got a crown for you! I told 'em to make two
of 'em at a place called Shu, where the gold lies in the rock like
suet in mutton. Gold I've seen, and turquoise I've kicked out of
the cliffs, and there's garnets in the sands of the river, and here's
a chunk of amber that a man brought me. Call up all the priests
and, here, take your crown.'

"One of the men opens a black hair bag and I slips the crown
on. It was too small and too heavy, but I wore it for the glory.
Hammered gold it was—five pound weight, like a hoop of a barrel.

"'Peachey,' says Dravot, 'we don't want to fight no more. The
Craft's the trick so help me!' and he brings forward that same Chief
that I left at Bashkai—Billy Fish we called him afterward, because
he was so like Billy Fish that drove the big tank-engine at Mach on
the Bolan in the old days. 'Shake hands with him,' says Dravot, and
I shook hands and nearly dropped, for Billy Fish gave me the Grip.
I said nothing, but tried him with the Fellow Craft Grip. He answers, all right, and I tried the Master's Grip, but that was a slip.
'A Fellow Craft he is!' I says to Dan. 'Does he know the word?' 'He
does,' says Dan, 'and all the priests know. It's a miracle! The Chiefs
and the priests can work a Fellow Craft Lodge in a way that's very
like ours, and they've cut the marks on the rocks, but they don't
know the Third Degree, and they've come to find out. It's Gord's
Truth. I've known these long years that the Afghans knew up to
the Fellow Craft Degree, but this is a miracle. A God and a Grand-
Master of the Craft am I, and a Lodge in the Third Degree I will
open, and we'll raise the head priests and the Chiefs of the villages.'

"'It's against all the law,' I says, 'holding a Lodge without warrant
from any one; and we never held office in any Lodge.'

"'It's a master-stroke of policy,' says Dravot. 'It means running
the country as easy as a four-wheeled bogy on a down grade. We
can't stop to inquire now, or they'll turn against us. I've forty Chiefs
at my heel, and passed and raised according to their merit they
shall be. Billet these men on the villages and see that we run up a
Lodge of some kind. The temple of Imbra will do for the Lodge-
room. The women must make aprons as you show them. I'll hold
a levee of Chiefs to-night and Lodge to-morrow.'

"I was fair run off my legs, but I wasn't such a fool as not to see
what a pull this Craft business gave us. I showed the priests' families
how to make aprons of the degrees, but for Dravot's apron the
blue border and marks was made of turquoise lumps on the white

hide, not cloth. We took a great square stone in the temple for the Master's chair, and little stones for the officers' chairs, and painted the black pavement with white squares, and did what we could to make things regular.

"At the levee which was held that night on the hillside with big bonfires, Dravot gives out that him and me were Gods and sons of Alexander, and Past Grand-Masters in the Craft, and was come to make Kafiristan a country where every man should eat in peace and drink in quiet, and specially obey us. Then the Chiefs come around to shake hands, and they was so hairy and white and fair it was just shaking hands with old friends. We gave them names according as they was like men we had known in India—Billy Fish, Holly Dilworth, Pikky Kergan that was Bazar-master when I was at Mhow, and so on and so on.

"*The* most amazing miracle was at Lodge next night. One of the old priests was watching us continuous, and I felt uneasy, for I knew we'd have to fudge the Ritual, and I didn't know what the men knew. The old priest was a stranger come in from beyond the village of Bashkai. The minute Dravot puts on the Master's apron that the girls had made for him, the priest fetches a whoop and a howl, and tries to overturn the stone that Dravot was sitting on. 'It's all up now,' I says. 'That comes of meddling with the Craft without warrant!' Dravot never winked an eye, not when ten priests took and tilted over the Grand-Master's chair—which was to say the stone of Imbra. The priest begins rubbing the bottom end of it to clear away the black dirt, and presently he shows all the other priests the Master's Mark, same as was on Dravot's apron, cut into the stone. Not even the priests of the temple of Imbra knew it was there. The old chap falls flat on his face at Dravot's feet and kisses 'em. 'Luck again,' says Dravot, across the Lodge to me, 'they say it's the missing Mark that no one could understand the why of. We're more than safe now.' Then he bangs the butt of his gun for a gavel and says:—'By virtue of the authority vested in me by my own right hand and the help of Peachey, I declare myself Grand-Master of all Freemasonry in Kafiristan in this the Mother Lodge o' the country, and King of Kafiristan equally with Peachey!' At that he puts on his crown and I puts on mine—I was doing Senior Warden—and we opens the Lodge in most ample form. It was a amazing miracle! The priests moved in Lodge through the first two degrees almost without telling, as if the memory was coming back to them. After that, Peachey and Dravot raised such as was worthy—high priests and Chiefs of far-off villages. Billy Fish was the first, and I can tell you we scared the soul out of him. It was not in any way according to Ritual, but it served our turn. We didn't raise more than ten of the biggest men because we didn't want to make the Degree common. And they was clamoring to be raised.

"'In another six months,' says Dravot, 'we'll hold another Communication and see how you are working.' Then he asks them about their villages, and learns that they was fighting one against the other and were fair sick and tired of it. And when they wasn't doing that they was fighting with the Mohammedans. 'You can fight those when they come into our country,' says Dravot. 'Tell off every tenth man of your tribes for a Frontier guard, and send two hundred at a time to this valley to be drilled. Nobody is going to be shot or speared any more so long as he does well, and I know that you won't cheat me because you're white people—sons of Alexander—and not like common, black Mohammedans. You are *my* people and by God,' says he, running off into English at the end—'I'll make a damned fine Nation of you, or I'll die in the making!'

"I can't tell all we did for the next six months because Dravot did a lot I couldn't see the hang of, and he learned their lingo in a way I never could. My work was to help the people plough, and now and again go out with some of the Army and see what the other villages were doing, and make 'em throw rope-bridges across the ravines which cut up the country horrid. Dravot was very kind to me, but when he walked up and down in the pine wood pulling that bloody red beard of his with both fists I knew he was thinking plans I could not advise him about, and I just waited for orders.

"But Dravot never showed me disrespect before the people. They were afraid of me and the Army, but they loved Dan. He was the best of friends with the priests and the Chiefs; but any one could come across the hills with a complaint and Dravot would hear him out fair, and call four priests together and say what was to be done. He used to call in Billy Fish from Bashkai, and Pikky Kergan from Shu, and an old Chief we called Kafuzelum—it was like enough to his real name—and hold councils with 'em when there was any fighting to be done in small villages. That was his Council of War, and the four priests of Bashkai, Shu, Khawak, and Madora was his Privy Council. Between the lot of 'em they sent me, with forty men and twenty rifles, and sixty men carrying turquoises, into the Ghor-

band country to buy those hand-made Martini rifles, that come out
of the Amir's workshops at Kabul, from one of the Amir's Herati
regiments that would have sold the very teeth out of their mouths
for turquoises.

"I stayed in Ghorband a month, and gave the Governor there
the pick of my baskets for hush-money, and bribed the Colonel of
the regiment some more, and, between the two and the tribes-
people, we got more than a hundred hand-made Martinis, a hundred
good Kohat Jezails that'll throw to six hundred yards, and forty
man-loads of very bad ammunition for the rifles. I came back with
what I had, and distributed 'em among the men that the Chiefs
sent to me to drill. Dravot was too busy to attend to those things,
but the old Army that we first made helped me, and we turned
out five hundred men that could drill, and two hundred that knew
how to hold arms pretty straight. Even those cork-screwed, hand-
made guns was a miracle to them. Dravot talked big about powder-
shops and factories, walking up and down in the pine wood when
the winter was coming on.

"'I won't make a Nation,' says he. 'I'll make an Empire! These
men aren't niggers; they're English! Look at their eyes—look at
their mouths. Look at the way they stand up. They sit on chairs in
their own houses. They're the Lost Tribes, or something like it,
and they've grown to be English. I'll take a census in the spring if
the priests don't get frightened. There must be a fair two million
of 'em in these hills. The villages are full o' little children. Two
million people—two hundred and fifty thousand fighting men—
and all English! They only want the rifles and a little drilling. Two
hundred and fifty thousand men, ready to cut in on Russia's right
flank when she tries for India! Peachey, man,' he says, chewing his
beard in great hunks, 'we shall be Emperors—Emperors of the
Earth! Rajah Brooke will be a suckling to us. I'll treat with the
Viceroy on equal terms. I'll ask him to send me twelve picked
English—twelve that I know of—to help us govern a bit. There's
Mackray, Sergeant-pensioner at Segowli—many's the good dinner
he's given me, and his wife a pair of trousers. There's Donkin, the
Warder of Tounghoo Jail; there's hundreds that I could lay my
hand on if I was in India. The Viceroy shall do it for me. I'll send
a man through in the spring for those men, and I'll write for a
dispensation from the Grand Lodge for what I've done as Grand-
Master. That—and all the Sniders that'll be thrown out when the

native troops in India take up the Martini. They'll be worn smooth, but they'll do for fighting in these hills. Twelve English, a hundred thousand Sniders run through the Amir's country in driblets—I'd be content with twenty thousand in one year—and we'd be an Empire. When everything was shipshape, I'd hand over the crown— this crown I'm wearing now—to Queen Victoria on my knees, and she'd say: "Rise up, Sir Daniel Dravot." Oh, it's big! It's big, I tell you! But there's so much to be done in every place—Bashkai, Khawak, Shu, and everywhere else.'

"'What is it?' I says. 'There are no more men coming in to be drilled this autumn. Look at those fat, black clouds. They're bringing the snow.'

"'It isn't that,' says Daniel, putting his hand very hard on my shoulder; 'and I don't wish to say anything that's against you, for no other living man would have followed me and made me what I am as you have done. You're a first-class Commander-in-Chief, and the people know you; but—it's a big country, and somehow you can't help me, Peachey, in the way I want to be helped.'

"'Go to your blasted priests, then!' I said, and I was sorry when I made that remark, but it did hurt me sore to find Daniel talking so superior when I'd drilled all the men, and done all he told me.

"'Don't let's quarrel, Peachey,' says Daniel, without cursing. 'You're a King too, and the half of this Kingdom is yours; but can't you see, Peachey, we want cleverer men than us now—three or four of 'em, that we can scatter about for our Deputies. It's a hugeous great State, and I can't always tell the right thing to do, and I haven't time for all I want to do, and here's the winter coming on and all.' He put half his beard into his mouth, and it was as red as the gold of his crown.

"'I'm sorry, Daniel,' says I. 'I've done all I could. I've drilled the men and shown the people how to stack their oats better; and I've brought in those tinware rifles from Ghorband—but I know what you're driving at. I take it Kings always feel oppressed that way.'

"'There's another thing, too,' says Dravot, walking up and down. 'The winter's coming and these people won't be giving much trouble, and if they do we can't move about. I want a wife.'

"'For Gord's sake leave the women alone!' I says. 'We've both got all the work we can, though I *am* a fool. Remember the Contrack, and keep clear o' women.'

"'The Contrack only lasted till such time as we was Kings; and

Kings we have been these months past,' says Dravot, weighing his crown in his hand. 'You go get a wife too, Peachey—a nice, strappin', plump girl that'll keep you warm in the winter. They're prettier than English girls, and we can take the pick of 'em. Boil 'em once or twice in hot water, and they'll come as fair as chicken and ham.'

"'Don't tempt me!' I says. 'I will not have any dealings with a woman not till we are a dam' side more settled than we are now. I've been doing the work o' two men, and you've been doing the work o' three. Let's lie off a bit, and see if we can get some better tobacco from Afghan country and run in some good liquor; but no women.'

"'Who's talking o' *women?*' says Dravot. 'I said *wife*—a Queen to breed a King's son for the King. A Queen out of the strongest tribe, that'll make them your blood-brothers, and that'll lie by your side and tell you all the people thinks about you and their own affairs. That's what I want.'

"'Do you remember that Bengali woman I kept at Mogul Serai when I was a plate-layer?' says I. 'A fat lot o' good she was to me. She taught me the lingo and one or two other things; but what happened? She ran away with the Station Master's servant and half my month's pay. Then she turned up at Dadur Junction in tow of a half-caste, and had the impidence to say I was her husband—all among the drivers in the running-shed!'

"'We've done with that,' says Dravot. 'These women are whiter than you or me, and a Queen I will have for the winter months.'

"'For the last time o' asking, Dan, do *not*,' I says. 'It'll only bring us harm. The Bible says that Kings ain't to waste their strength on women, 'specially when they've got a new raw Kingdom to work over.'

"'For the last time of answering I will,' said Dravot, and he went away through the pine-trees looking like a big red devil. The low sun hit his crown and beard on one side and the two blazed like hot coals.

"But getting a wife was not as easy as Dan thought. He put it before the Council, and there was no answer till Billy Fish said that he'd better ask the girls. Dravot damned them all round. 'What's wrong with me?' he shouts, standing by the idol Imbra. 'Am I a dog or am I not enough of a man for your wenches? Haven't I put the shadow of my hand over this country? Who stopped the last

Afghan raid?' It was me really, but Dravot was too angry to remember. 'Who brought your guns? Who repaired the bridges?
Who's the Grand-Master of the sign cut in the stone?' and he
thumped his hand on the block that he used to sit on the Lodge,
and at Council, which opened like Lodge always. Billy Fish said
nothing and no more did the others. 'Keep your hair on, Dan,' said
I; 'and ask the girls. That's how it's done at Home, and these people
are quite English.'

"'The marriage of the King is a matter of State,' says Dan, in a
white-hot rage, for he could feel, I hope, that he was going against
his better mind. He walked out of the Council-room, and the others
sat still, looking at the ground.

"'Billy Fish,' says I to the Chief of Bashkai, 'what's the difficulty
here? A straight answer to a true friend.' 'You know,' says Billy
Fish. 'How should a man tell you who know everything? How can
daughters of men marry Gods or Devils? It's not proper.'

"I remembered something like that in the Bible; but if, after
seeing us as long as they had, they still believed we were Gods, it
wasn't for me to undeceive them.

"'A God can do anything,' says I. 'If the King is fond of a girl
he'll not let her die.' 'She'll have to,' said Billy Fish. 'There are all
sorts of Gods and Devils in these mountains, and now and again a
girl marries one of them and isn't seen any more. Besides, you two
know the Mark cut in the stone. Only the Gods know that. We
thought you were men till you showed the sign of the Master.'

"I wished then that we had explained about the loss of the genuine secrets of a Master-Mason at the first go-off; but I said nothing.
All that night there was a blowing of horns in a little dark temple
half-way down the hill, and I heard a girl crying fit to die. One of
the priests told us that she was being prepared to marry the King.

"'I'll have no nonsense of that kind,' says Dan. 'I don't want to
interfere with your customs, but I'll take my own wife.' 'The girl's
a little bit afraid,' says the priest. 'She thinks she's going to die, and
they are a-heartening of her up down in the temple.'

"'Hearten her very tender, then,' says Dravot, 'or I'll hearten
you with the butt of a gun so that you'll never want to be heartened
again.' He licked his lips, did Dan, and stayed up walking about
more than half the night, thinking of the wife that he was going
to get in the morning. I wasn't any means comfortable, for I knew
that dealings with a woman in foreign parts, though you was a

crowned King twenty times over, could not but be risky. I got up very early in the morning while Dravot was asleep, and I saw the priests talking together in whispers, and the Chiefs talking together too, and they looked at me out of the corners of their eyes.

"'What is up, Fish?' I says to the Bashkai man, who was wrapped up in his furs and looking splendid to behold.

"'I can't rightly say,' says he; 'but if you can induce the King to drop all this nonsense about marriage, you'll be doing him and me and yourself a great service.'

"'That I do believe,' says I. 'But sure, you know, Billy, as well as me, having fought against and for us, that the King and me are nothing more than two of the finest men that God Almighty ever made. Nothing more, I do assure you.'

"'That may be,' says Billy Fish, 'and yet I should be sorry if it was.' He sinks his head upon his great fur cloak for a minute and thinks. 'King,' says he, 'be you man or God or Devil, I'll stick by you to-day. I have twenty of my men with me, and they will follow me. We'll go to Bashkai until the storm blows over.'

"A little snow had fallen in the night, and everything was white except the greasy fat clouds that blew down and down from the north. Dravot came out with his crown on his head, swinging his arms and stamping his feet, and looking more pleased than Punch.

"'For the last time, drop it, Dan,' says I, in a whisper. 'Billy Fish here says that there will be a row.'

"'A row among my people!' says Dravot. 'Not much. Peachey, you're a fool not to get a wife too. Where's the girl?' says he, with a voice as loud as the braying of a jackass. 'Call up all the Chiefs and priests, and let the Emperor see if his wife suits him.'

"There was no need to call any one. They were all there leaning on their guns and spears round the clearing in the centre of the pine wood. A deputation of priests went down to the little temple to bring up the girl, and the horns blew up fit to wake the dead. Billy Fish saunters round and gets as close to Daniel as he could, and behind him stood his twenty men with matchlocks. Not a man of them under six feet. I was next to Dravot, and behind me was twenty men of the regular Army. Up comes the girl, and a strapping wench she was, covered with silver and turquoises but white as death, and looking back every minute at the priests.

"'She'll do,' said Dan, looking her over. 'What's to be afraid of, lass? Come and kiss me.' He puts his arm round her. She shuts her eyes, gives a bit of a squeak, and down goes her face in the side of Dan's flaming red beard.

"'The slut's bitten me!' says he, clapping his hand to his neck, and, sure enough, his hand was red with blood. Billy Fish and two of his matchlock-men catches hold of Dan by the shoulders and drags him into the Bashkai lot, while the priests howl in their lingo,—'Neither God nor Devil but a man!' I was all taken aback, for a priest cut at me in front, and the Army behind began firing into the Bashkai men.

"'God A-mighty!' says Dan. 'What is the meaning o' this?'

"'Come back! Come away!' says Billy Fish. 'Ruin and Mutiny is the matter. We'll break for Bashkai if we can.'

"I tried to give some sort of orders to my men—the men o' the regular Army—but it was no use, so I fired into the brown of 'em with an English Martini and drilled three beggars in a line. The valley was full of shouting, howling creatures, and every soul was shrieking, 'Not a God nor a Devil but only a man!' The Bashkai troops stuck to Billy Fish all they were worth, but their matchlocks wasn't half as good as the Kabul breech-loaders, and four of them dropped. Dan was bellowing like a bull, for he was very wrathy; and Billy Fish had a hard job to prevent him running out at the crowd.

"'We can't stand,' says Billy Fish. 'Make a run for it down the valley! The whole place is against us.' The matchlock-men ran, and we went down the valley in spite of Dravot's protestations. He was swearing horribly and crying out that he was a King. The priests rolled great stones on us, and the regular Army fired hard, and there wasn't more than six men, not counting Dan, Billy Fish, and Me, that came down to the bottom of the valley alive.

"Then they stopped firing and the horns in the temple blew again. 'Come away—for Gord's sake come away!' says Billy Fish. 'They'll send runners out to all the villages before ever we get to Bashkai. I can protect you there, but I can't do anything now.'

"My own notion is that Dan began to go mad in his head from that hour. He stared up and down like a stuck pig. Then he was all for walking back alone and killing the priests with his bare hands; which he could have done. 'An Emperor am I,' says Daniel, 'and next year I shall be a Knight of the Queen.'

"'All right, Dan,' says I; 'but come along now while there's time.'

"'It's your fault,' says he, 'for not looking after your Army better.

There was mutiny in the midst, and you didn't know—you damned engine-driving, plate-laying, missionary's-pass hunting hound!' He sat upon a rock and called me every foul name he could lay tongue to. I was too heart-sick to care, though it was all his foolishness that brought the smash.

"'I'm sorry, Dan,' says I, 'but there's no accounting for natives. This business is our Fifty-Seven. Maybe we'll make something out of it yet, when we've got to Bashkai.'

"'Let's get to Bashkai,' says Dan, 'and, by God, when I come back here again I'll sweep the valley so there isn't a bug in a blanket left!'

"We walked all that day, and all that night Dan was stumping up and down on the snow, chewing his beard and muttering to himself.

"'There's no hope o' getting clear,' said Billy Fish. 'The priests will have sent runners to the villages to say that you are only men. Why didn't you stick on as Gods till things was more settled? I'm a dead man,' says Billy Fish, and he throws himself down on the snow and begins to pray to his Gods.

"Next morning we was in a cruel bad country—all up and down, no level ground at all, and no food either. The six Bashkai men looked at Billy Fish hungry-wise as if they wanted to ask something, but they said never a word. At noon we came to the top of a flat mountain all covered with snow, and when he climbed up into it, behold, there was an Army in position waiting in the middle!

"'The runners have been very quick,' says Billy Fish, with a little bit of a laugh. 'They are waiting for us.'

"Three or four men began to fire from the enemy's side, and a chance shot took Daniel in the calf of the leg. That brought him to his senses. He looks across the snow at the Army, and sees the rifles that we had brought into the country.

"'We're done for,' says he. 'They are Englishmen, these people,— and it's my blasted nonsense that has brought you to this. Get back, Billy Fish, and take your men away; you've done what you could, and now cut for it. Carnehan,' says he, 'shake hands with me and go along with Billy. Maybe they won't kill you. I'll go and meet 'em alone. It's me that did it. Me, the King!'

"'Go!' says I. 'Go to Hell, Dan. I'm with you here. Billy Fish, you clear out, and we two will meet those folk.'

"'I'm a Chief,' says Billy Fish, quite quiet. 'I stay with you. My men can go.'

"The Bashkai fellows didn't wait for a second word but ran off, and Dan and me and Billy Fish walked across to where the drums were drumming and the horns were horning. It was cold—awful cold. I've got that cold in the back of my head now. There's a lump of it there."

The punkah-coolies had gone to sleep. Two kerosene lamps were blazing in the office, and the perspiration poured down my face and splashed on the blotter as I leaned forward. Carnehan was shivering, and I feared that his mind might go. I wiped my face, took a fresh grip of the piteously mangled hands, and said:—"What happened after that?"

The momentary shift of my eyes had broken the clear current.

"What was you pleased to say?" whined Carnehan. "They took them without any sound. Not a little whisper all along the snow, not though the King knocked down the first man that set hand on him—not though old Peachey fired his last cartridge into the brown of 'em. Not a single solitary sound did those swines make. They just closed up tight, and I tell you their furs stunk. There was a man called Billy Fish, a good friend of us all, and they cut his throat, Sir, then and there, like a pig; and the King kicks up the bloody snow and says:—'We've had a dashed fine run for our money. What's coming next?' But Peachey, Peachey Taliaferro, I tell you, Sir, in confidence as betwixt two friends, he lost his head, Sir. No, he didn't neither. The King lost his head, so he did, all along o' one of those cunning rope-bridges. Kindly let me have the paper-cutter, Sir. It tilted this way. They marched him a mile across that snow to a rope-bridge over a ravine with a river at the bottom. You may have seen such. They prodded him behind like an ox. 'Damn your eyes!' says the King. 'D'you suppose I can't die like a gentleman?' He turns to Peachey—Peachey that was crying like a child. 'I've brought you to this, Peachey,' says he. 'Brought you out of your happy life to be killed in Kafiristan, where you was late Commander-in-Chief of the Emperor's forces. Say you forgive me, Peachey.' 'I do,' says Peachey. 'Fully and freely do I forgive you, Dan.' 'Shake hands, Peachey,' says he. 'I'm going now.' Out he goes, looking neither right nor left, and when he was plumb in the middle of those dizzy dancing ropes, 'Cut, you beggars,' he shouts; and they cut, and old Dan fell, turning round and round and round twenty thousand miles, for he took half an hour to fall till he struck the water, and I could see his body caught on a rock with the gold crown close beside.

"But do you know what they did to Peachey between two pines trees? They crucified him, Sir, as Peachey's hand will show. They used wooden pegs for his hands and his feet; and he didn't die. He hung there and screamed, and they took him down next day, and said it was a miracle that he wasn't dead. They took him down— poor old Peachey that hadn't done them any harm—that hadn't done them any..."

He rocked to and fro and wept bitterly, wiping his eyes with the back of his scarred hands and moaning like a child for some ten minutes.

"They was cruel enough to feed him up in the temple, because they said he was more of a God than old Daniel that was a man. Then they turned him out on the snow, and told him to go home, and Peachey came home in about a year, begging along the roads quite safe; for Daniel Dravot he walked before and said:—'Come along, Peachey. It's a big thing we're doing.' The mountains they danced at night, and the mountains they tried to fall on Peachey's head, but Dan he held up his hand, and Peachey came along bent double. He never let go of Dan's hand, and he never let go of Dan's head. They gave it to him as a present in the temple, to remind him not to come again, and though the crown was pure gold, and Peachey was starving, never would Peachey sell the same. You knew Dravot, Sir! You knew Right Worshipful Brother Dravot! Look at him now!"

He fumbled in the mass of rags round his bent waist; brought out a black horsehair bag embroidered with silver thread; and shook therefrom on to my table—the dried, withered head of Daniel Dravot! The morning sun that had long been paling the lamps struck the red beard and blind sunken eyes; struck, too, a heavy circlet of gold studded with raw turquoises, that Carnehan placed tenderly on the battered temples.

"You behold now," said Carnehan, "the Emperor in his habit as he lived—the King of Kafiristan with his crown upon his head. Poor old Daniel that was a monarch once!"

I shuddered, for, in spite of defacements manifold, I recognized the head of the man of Marwar Junction. Carnehan rose to go. I attempted to stop him. He was not fit to walk abroad. "Let me take away the whiskey, and give me a little money," he gasped. "I was a King once. I'll go to the Deputy Commissioner and ask to set in the Poorhouse till I get my health. No, thank you, I can't wait till you get a carriage for me. I've urgent private affairs—in the south— at Marwar."

He shambled out of the office and departed in the direction of the Deputy Commissioner's house. That day at noon I had occasion to go down the blinding hot Mall, and I saw a crooked man crawling along the white dust of the roadside, his hat in his hand, quavering dolorously after the fashion of street-singers at Home. There was not a soul in sight, and he was out of all possible earshot of the houses. And he sang through his nose, turning his head from right to left:

> "The Son of Man goes forth to war,
>   A golden crown to gain;
> His blood-red banner streams afar—
>   Who follows in his train?"

I waited to hear no more, but put the poor wretch into my carriage and drove him off to the nearest missionary for eventual transfer to the Asylum. He repeated the hymn twice while he was with me whom he did not in the least recognize, and I left him singing it to the missionary.

Two days later I inquired after his welfare of the Superintendent of the Asylum.

"He was admitted suffering from sunstroke. He died early yesterday morning," said the Superintendent. "Is it true that he was half an hour bareheaded in the sun at midday?"

"Yes," said I, "but do you happen to know if he had anything upon him by any chance when he died?"

"Not to my knowledge," said the Superintendent.

And there the matter rests.

William Butler Yeats

THE CRUCIFIXION OF THE OUTCAST

NOBEL PRIZE 1923

William Butler Yeats (1865–1939), the greatest Irish poet in the English language, was born in what is now part of Dublin. His literary career falls into three phases. First, he decided to concentrate on poetry after the publication of Mosada: A Dramatic Poem *in 1886. He moved to London and dabbled in several metaphysical systems including theology, theosophy, and Indian philosophy. Then, in 1896 he returned to Ireland and helped start the Irish Literary Theatre, serving as a director and playwright. During this time, his works of prose (The Celtic Twilight, 1893), poetry (The Green Helmet and Other Poems, 1910), and drama (Deirdre, 1907) helped promote an Irish literary revival and a feeling of nationalism. Finally, he served as an Irish senator from 1922 to 1928, during which period he began writing plays modeled on Japanese theater, and reached his zenith as a poet.*

A MAN, WITH THIN brown hair and a pale face, half ran, half walked, along the road that wound from the south to the town of Sligo. Many called him Cumhal, the son of Cormac, and many

called him the Swift, Wild Horse; and he was a gleeman, and he
wore a short parti-colored doublet, and had pointed shoes, and a
bulging wallet. Also he was of the blood of the Ernaans, and his
birth-place was the Field of Gold; but his eating and sleeping places
were the four provinces of Eri, and his abiding place was not upon
the ridge of the earth. His eyes strayed from the Abbey tower of
the White Friars and the town battlements to a row of crosses which
stood out against the sky upon a hill a little to the eastward of the
town, and he clenched his fist, and shook it at the crosses. He knew
they were not empty, for the birds were fluttering about them; and
he thought how, as like as not, just such another vagabond as
himself was hanged on one of them; and he muttered: "If it were
hanging or bowstringing, or stoning or beheading, it would be bad
enough. But to have the birds pecking your eyes and the wolves
eating your feet! I would that the red wind of the Druids had
withered in his cradle the soldier of Dathi, who brought the trees
of death out of barbarous lands, or that the lightning, when it smote
Dathi at the foot of the mountain, had smitten him also, or that
his grave had been dug by the green-haired and green-toothed
merrows deep at the roots of the deep sea."

While he spoke, he shivered from head to foot, and the sweat
came out upon his face, and he knew not why, for he had looked
upon many crosses. He passed over two hills and under the bat-
tlemented gate, and then round by a left-hand way to the door of
the Abbey. It was studded with great nails, and when he knocked
at it, he roused the lay brother who was the porter, and of him he
asked a place in the guest-house. Then the lay brother took a
glowing turf on a shovel, and led the way to a big and naked
outhouse strewn with very dirty rushes; and lighted a rush-candle
fixed between two of the stones of the wall, and set the glowing
turf upon the hearth and gave him two unlighted sods and a wisp
of straw, and showed him a blanket hanging from a nail, and a
shelf with a loaf of bread and a jug of water, and a tub in a far
corner. Then the lay brother left him and went back to his place
by the door. And Cumhal the son of Cormac began to blow upon
the glowing turf that he might light the two sods and the wisp of
straw; but the sods and the straw would not light, for they were
damp. So he took off his pointed shoes, and drew the tub out of
the corner with the thought of washing the dust of the highway

from his feet; but the water was so dirty that he could not see the bottom. He was very hungry, for he had not eaten all that day; so he did not waste much anger upon the tub, but took up the black loaf, and bit into it, and then spat out the bite, for the bread was hard and mouldy. Still he did not give way to his anger, for he had not drunken these many hours; having a hope of heath beer or wine at his day's end, he had left the brooks untasted, to make his supper more delightful. Now he put the jug to his lips, but he flung it from him straightway, for the water was bitter and ill-smelling. Then he gave the jug a kick, so that it broke against the opposite wall, and he took down the blanket to wrap it about him for the night. But no sooner did he touch it than it was alive with skipping fleas. At this, beside himself with anger, he rushed to the door of the guest-house, but the lay brother, being well accustomed to such outcries, had locked it on the outside; so he emptied the tub and began to beat the door with it, till the lay brother came to the door and asked what ailed him, and why he woke him out of sleep. "What ails me!" shouted Cumhal, "are not the sods as wet as the sands of the Three Rosses? and are not the fleas in the blanket as many as the waves of the sea and as lively? and is not the bread as hard as the heart of a lay brother who has forgotten God? and is not the water in the jug as bitter and as ill-smelling as his soul? and is not the foot-water the color that shall be upon him when he has been charred in the Undying Fires?" The lay brother saw that the lock was fast, and went back to his niche, for he was too sleepy to talk with comfort. And Cumhal went on beating at the door, and presently he heard the lay brother's foot once more, and cried out to him, "O cowardly and tyrannous race of friars, persecutors of the bard and the gleeman, haters of life and joy! O race that does not draw the sword and tell the truth! O race that melts the bones of the people with cowardice and with deceit!"

"Gleeman," said the lay brother, "I also make rhymes; I make many while I sit in my niche by the door, and I sorrow to hear the bards railing upon the friars. Brother, I would sleep, and therefore I make known to you that it is the head of the monastery, our gracious abbot, who orders all things concerning the lodging of travelers."

"You may sleep," said Cumhal, "I will sing a bard's curse on the abbot." And he set the tub upside down under the window, and stood upon it, and began to sing in a very loud voice. The singing awoke the abbot, so that he sat up in bed and blew a silver whistle until the lay brother came to him. "I cannot get a wink of sleep with that noise," said the abbot. "What is happening?"

"It is a gleeman," said the lay brother, "who complains of the sods, of the bread, of the water in the jug, of the foot-water, and of the blanket. And now he is singing a bard's curse upon you, O brother abbot, and upon your father and your mother, and your grandfather and your grandmother, and upon all your relations."

"Is he cursing in rhyme?"

"He is cursing in rhyme, and with two assonances in every line of his curse."

The abbot pulled his night-cap off and crumpled it in his hands, and the circular brown patch of hair in the middle of his bald head looked like an island in the midst of a pond, for in Connaught they had not yet abandoned the ancient tonsure for the style then coming into use. "If we do not somewhat," he said, "he will teach his curses to the children in the street, and the girls spinning at the doors, and to the robbers upon Ben Bulben."

"Shall I go, then," said the other, "and give him dry sods, a fresh loaf, clean water in a jug, clean foot-water, and a new blanket, and make him swear by the blessed Saint Benignus, and by the sun and moon, that no bond be lacking, not to tell his rhymes to the children in the street, and the girls spinning at the doors, and the robbers upon Ben Bulben?"

"Neither our blessed Patron nor the sun and moon would avail at all," said the abbot; "for tomorrow or the next day the mood to curse would come upon him, or a pride in those rhymes would move him, and he would teach his lines to the children, and the girls, and the robbers. Or else he would tell another of his craft how he fared in the guest-house and he in his turn would begin to curse, and my name would wither. For learn there is no steadfastness of purpose upon the roads, but only under roofs, and between four walls. Therefore I bid you go and awaken Brother Kevin, Brother Dove, Brother Little Wolf, Brother Bald Patrick, Brother Bald Brandon, Brother James and Brother Peter. And they shall take the man, and bind him with ropes, and dip him into the river that he may cease to sing. And in the morning, lest this but make him curse the louder, we will crucify him."

"The crosses are all full," said the lay brother.

"Then we must make another cross. If we do not make an end of him another will, for who can eat and sleep in peace while men like him are going about the world? Ill should we stand before Blessed Saint Benignus, and sour would be his face when he comes to judge us at the Last Day, were we to spare an enemy of his when we had him under our thumb! Brother, the bards and the gleemen are an evil race, ever cursing and ever stirring up the people, and immoral and immoderate in all things, and heathen in their hearts, always longing after the Son of Lir, and Aengus, and Bridget, and the Dagda, and Dana the Mother, and all the false gods of the old days; always making poems in praise of those kings and queens of the demons, Finvaragh, whose home is under Cruachmaa, and Red Aodh of Cnoc-na-Sidhe, and Cleena of the Wave, and Aoibhell of the Grey Rock, and him they call Donn of the Vats of the Sea; and railing against God and Christ and the blessed Saints." While he was speaking he crossed himself, and when he had finished he drew the nightcap over his ears, to shut out the noise, and closed his eyes, and composed himself to sleep.

The lay brother found Brother Kevin, Brother Dove, Brother Little Wolf, Brother Bald Patrick, Brother Bald Brandon, Brother James and Brother Peter sitting up in bed, and he made them get up. Then they bound Cumhal, and they dragged him to the river, and they dipped him in it at the place which was afterwards called Buckley's Ford.

"Gleeman," said the lay brother, as they led him back to the guesthouse, "why do you ever use the wit which God has given you to make blasphemous and immoral tales and verses? For such is the way of your craft. I have, indeed, many such tales and verses well nigh by rote, and so I know that I speak true! And why do you praise with rhyme those demons, Finvaragh, Red Aodh, Cleena, Aoibhell and Donn? I, too, am a man of great wit and learning, but I ever glorify our gracious abbot, and Benignus our Patron, and the princes of the province. My soul is decent and orderly, but yours is like the wind among the salley gardens. I said what I could for you, being also a man of many thoughts, but who could help such a one as you?"

"Friend," answered the gleeman, "my soul is indeed like the wind, and it blows me to and fro, and up and down, and puts many things into my mind and out of my mind, and therefore am I called the Swift, Wild Horse." And he spoke no more that night, for his teeth were chattering with the cold.

The abbot and the friars came to him in the morning, and bade him get ready to be crucified, and led him out of the guest-house. And while he still stood upon the step a flock of great grass-barnacles passed high above him with clanking cries. He lifted his arms to them and said, "O great grass-barnacles, tarry a little, and mayhap my soul will travel with you to the waste places of the shore and to the ungovernable sea!" At the gate a crowd of beggars gathered about them, being come there to beg from any traveler or pilgrim who might have spent the night in the guest-house. The abbot and the friars led the gleeman to a place in the woods at some distance, where many straight young trees were growing, and they made him cut one down and fashion it to the right length, while the beggars stood round them in a ring, talking and gesticulating. The abbot then bade him cut off another and shorter piece of wood, and nail it upon the first. So there was his cross for him; and they put it upon his shoulder, for his crucifixion was to be on the top of the hill where the others were. A half-mile on the way he asked them to stop and see him juggle for them; for he knew, he said, all the tricks of Aengus the Subtle-hearted. The old friars were for pressing on, but the young friars would see him: so he did many wonders for them, even to the drawing of live frogs out of his ears. But after a while they turned on him, and said his tricks were dull and a shade unholy, and set the cross on his shoulders again. Another half-mile on the way, and he asked them to stop and hear him jest for them, for he knew, he said, all the jests of Conan the Bald, upon whose back a sheep's wool grew. And the young friars, when they had heard his merry tales, again bade him take up his cross, for it ill became them to listen to such follies. Another half-mile on the way, he asked them to stop and hear him sing the story of White-breasted Deirdre, and how she endured many sorrows, and how the sons of Usna died to serve her. And the young friars were mad to hear him, but when he had ended they grew angry, and beat him for waking forgotten longings in their hearts. So they set the cross upon his back, and hurried him to the hill.

When he was come to the top, they took the cross from him, and began to dig a hole to stand it in, while the beggars gathered round, and talked among themselves. "I ask a favor before I die," says Cumhal.

"We will grant you no more delays," says the abbot.

"I ask no more delays, for I have drawn the sword, and told the truth, and lived my vision, and am content."

"Would you, then, confess?"

"By sun and moon, not I; I ask but to be let eat the food I carry in my wallet. I carry food in my wallet whenever I go upon a journey, but I do not taste of it unless I am well-nigh starved. I have not eaten now these two days."

"You may eat, then," says the abbot, and he turned to help the friars dig the hole.

The gleeman took a loaf and some strips of cold fried bacon out of his wallet and laid them upon the ground. "I will give a tithe to the poor," says he, and he cut a tenth part from the loaf and the bacon. "Who among you is the poorest?" And thereupon was a great clamor, for the beggars began the history of their sorrows and their poverty, and their yellow faces swayed like Gara Lough when the floods have filled it with water from the bogs.

He listened for a little, and, says he, "I am myself the poorest, for I have traveled the bare road, and by the edges of the sea; and the tattered doublet of parti-colored cloth upon my back and the torn pointed shoes upon my feet have ever irked me, because of the towered city full of noble raiment which was in my heart. And I have been the more alone upon the roads and by the sea because I heard in my heart the rustling of the rose-bordered dress of her who is more subtle than Aengus, the Subtle-hearted, and more full of the beauty of laughter than Conan the Bald, and more full of the wisdom of tears than White-breasted Deirdre, and more lovely than a bursting dawn to them that are lost in the darkness. Therefore, I award the tithe to myself; but yet, because I am done with all things, I give it unto you."

So he flung the bread and the strips of bacon among the beggars, and they fought with many cries until the last scrap was eaten. But meanwhile the friars nailed the gleeman to his cross, and set it upright in the hole, and shovelled the earth in at the foot, and trampled it level and hard. So then they went away, but the beggars stared on, sitting round the cross. But when the sun was sinking, they also got up to go, for the air was getting chilly. And as soon as they had gone a little way, the wolves, who had been showing themselves on the edge of a neighboring coppice, came nearer, and the birds wheeled closer and closer. "Stay, outcasts, yet a little while," the crucified one called in a weak voice to the beggars, "and keep the beasts and the birds from me." But the beggars were angry because he had called them outcasts, so they threw stones and mud at him, and went their way. Then the wolves gathered at the foot of the cross, and the birds flew lower and lower. And presently the birds lighted all at once upon his head and arms and shoulders, and began to peck at him, and the wolves began to eat his feet. "Outcasts," he moaned, "have you also turned against the outcast?"

George Bernard Shaw

DON GIOVANNI
EXPLAINS

NOBEL PRIZE 1925

George Bernard Shaw (1856–1950) was born in Dublin, Ireland. An indifferent student, he acquired much knowledge about literature, music, and painting by reading, attending concerts, and visiting art galleries. In 1876 he moved to London to further his literary career. Unsuccessful as a novelist, he honed his wit as a member of the Zetetical and Fabian Societies, and gained fame as a music and drama critic. In the early 1890s the plays he began writing were too unpleasant for his contemporary audiences, but after switching to lighter fare, Arms and the Man *(1894) brought him wealth and international fame. His more than forty subsequent works include such classics as* Caesar and Cleopatra *(1899);* Man and Superman *(1901 – 1903);* Pygmalion *(1912), which later formed the basis of Lerner and Loewe's musical,* My Fair Lady; Androcles and the Lion *(1913); and* Saint Joan *(1923).*

THAT YOU MAY CATCH the full flavor of my little story I must tell you to begin with that I am a very pretty woman. If you think there is any impropriety in my saying so, then you can turn over to some of the other stories by people whose notions of womanly modesty are the same as your own. The proof of my prettiness is that men waste a good deal of time and money in making themselves ridiculous about me. And so, though I am only a provincial beauty, I know as much about courtships and flirtations as any woman of my age in the world, and can tell you beforehand, if you are a man of the sort I attract, exactly what you will say to me and how you will say it at our first, second, third, or what interview you please. I have been engaged rather often, and broke it off sometimes because I thought he wanted me to, and sometimes made him break it off by shewing him that I wanted him to. In the former case *I* was sorry: in the latter, *he* was; though, in spite of our feelings, the sense of relief at getting loose was generally equal on both sides.

I suppose you—whoever you are—now quite understand my character, or at least think you do. Well, you are welcome to flatter yourself. But let me tell you that flirtation is the one amusement I never went out of my way to seek, and never took any trouble to learn. I am fond of dress, dancing and lawn tennis, just as you thought. I am also fond of good music, good books, botany, farming, and teaching children, just as you didn't think. And if I am better known about our place as a beauty and a flirt than as a botanist or a teacher, it is because nobody will admit that I have any other business in the world than to make a good marriage. The men, even the nicest of them, seek my society to gloat over my face and figure, and not to exercise their minds. I used to like the sense of power being able to torture them gave me; but at last I saw that as they liked the torture just as children liked to be tickled, wielding my sceptre meant simply working pretty hard for their amusement. If it were not for the foolish boys, who dont gloat, but really worship me, poor fellows! and for a few thoroughgoing prigs who are always ready to botanize and to play the bass in pianoforte duet arrangements of Haydn's symphonies, I should count the hours I spend in male society the weariest of my life.

One evening in October, I heard by telegram from some friends in our provincial capital, twenty-five miles off by rail, that they had a box for the opera, with a place to spare for me. (In case you are a cockney, I may tell you that opera companies make tours through the provinces like other theatrical people, and are often a good deal better appreciated there than in London.) There was only just time to rush upstairs, make myself radiant, snatch a cup of tea, and catch the ten to seven train. I went by myself: if I were not able to go about alone, I should simply have to stay always in the house. My brothers have something else to do than to be my footmen; my father and mother are too old and quiet in their tastes to be dragged about to a girl's amusements or kept up to her late hours; and as to a maid, I have enough to do to take care of myself without having to take care of another grown-up woman as well. Besides, being in the train at our place is like being at home: all the guards on the line know us as well as they know their own families. So you need not hold up your hands at my fastness because I habitually go up to town by rail; drive to the theatre; find my friend's box there; drive back to the station; and—culminating impropriety!—come back at night by the half-past eleven train: all without chaperone or escort.

The opera was Don Giovanni; and of course the performance was a wretched sell. Most operatic performances are—to those who know enough about music to read operas for themselves, as other people read Shakespear. The Don was a conceited Frenchman, with a toneless, dark, nasal voice, and such a tremolo that he never held a note steady long enough to let us hear whether it was in tune or not. Leporello was a podgy, vulgar Italian buffo, who quacked instead of singing. The tenor, a reedy creature, left out Dall sua pace because he couldn't trust himself to get through it. The parts of Masetto and the Commendatore were doubled: I think by the call-boy. As to the women, Donna Anna was fat and fifty; Elvira was a tearing, gasping, "dramatic" soprano, whose voice I expected to hear break across every time she went higher than F sharp; and Zerlina, a beginner on her trial trip, who finished Batti, batti and Vedrai carino with cadenzas out of the mad scene in Lucia, was encored for both in consequence. The orchestra was reinforced by local amateurs, the brass parts being played on things from the band of the 10th Hussars. Everybody was delighted; and when I said I wasnt, they said, "Oh! youre so critical and so hard to please. Dont you think youd enjoy yourself far more if you were not so very particular." The idea of throwing away music like Mozart's on such idiots!

When the call-boy and the Frenchman sank into a pit of red fire to the blaring of the 10th Hussars and the quacking of the podgy creature under the table, I got up to go, disgusted and disappointed, and wondering why people will pay extra prices to hear operas mutilated and maltreated in a way that nobody would stand with a modern comedy or Box and Cox. It was raining like anything when we got out; and we had to wait nearly ten minutes before a cab could be got for me. The delay worried me because I was afraid of losing the last train; and though I was a little soothed when I caught it with three minutes to spare, I was in no very high spirits when the guard locked me into a first class compartment by myself.

At first, I leant back in the corner and tried to sleep. But the train had gone only a little way out of the station when a fog signal went bang bang; and we stopped. Whilst I was waiting, broad awake and very cross, for us to go on again, a dreary rush of rain against the glass made me turn to the window, where, the night being pitchy dark, I saw nothing but the reflection of the inside of the carriage, including, of course, myself. And I never looked prettier in my life. I was positively beautiful. My first sensation was the pleasurable one of gratified vanity. Then came aggravation that it was all thrown away, as there was nobody in the carriage to look at me. In case you, superior reader, should be so plain that it has never been worth your while to study the subject of good looks, let me mention that even handsome people only look really lovely and interesting now and then. There are disappointing days when you are comparatively not worth looking at, and red-letter days when you are irresistible—when you cant look into your own eyes and face without emotion. But you are not like that every day: no quantity of soap and water, paint, powder, bothering about your hair, or dressing, will bring it. When it comes then life is worth living, except that it may happen, as it did with me just then, that you lose all the kudos through being in some out-of-the-way place, or alone, or with your family, who naturally dont concern them-selves about your appearance. However, it made me happy enough to prevent my catching cold, as I generally do when I come home late out of humor.

At last there was a great clanking of coupling chains and clashing of buffers: meaning that a goods train was getting out of the way. We started with a jerk; and I settled myself in my corner with my face turned to the window, and had a good look as we went along. Mind: I did not close my eyes for a moment: I was as wide awake as I am now. I thought about a lot of things, the opera running through my head a good deal; and I remember it occurred to me that if Don Giovanni had met me, I might have understood him better than the other women did, and we two have hit it off together. Whether or no, I felt sure he could not have fooled me so easily as he did them, particularly if he had been like the Frenchman with the tremolo. Still, the real Don Giovanni might have been something very different; for experience has taught me that people who are much admired often get wheedled or persecuted into love affairs with persons whom they would have let alone if they themselves had been let alone.

I had got about thus far in my thoughts when I looked round— I dont know why; for I certainly had not the least idea that there was anybody or anything to see; and there, seated right opposite me, was a gentleman, wrapped in a cloak of some exquisitely fine fabric in an "art shade" of Indian red, that draped perfectly, and would, I could see, wear a whole lifetime and look as nice as new at the end. He had on a superbly shaped cartwheel hat of beautiful black felt. His boots, which came to his knees, were of soft kid, the color of a ripening sloe: I never saw anything like them except a pair of shoes I once bought in Paris for forty francs, which were more like a baby's skin than leather. And to complete him, he had a sword with a guard of plain gold, but shaped so that it was a treasure and a delight to look at.

Why I should have taken all this in before it occurred to me to wonder how he came there, I cant tell; but it was so. Possibly, of course, he was coming from a fancy ball, and had got in while the train was at a standstill outside the station. But when I ventured to glance casually at his face—for I need hardly say that an experienced young woman does not begin by staring right into a man's eyes when she finds herself alone with him in a railway carriage—away went all notion of anything so silly as a fancy ball in connexion with *him*. It was a steadfast, tranquil, refined face, looking over and beyond me into space. It made me feel unutterably small, though I remembered with humble thankfulness that I was looking my most spiritual. Then it struck me what nonsense it was: he was only a man. I had no sooner stirred up my baser nature, as it were, by thinking thus, than sudden horror seized me; and I believe I was on the point of making a frantic plunge at the communicator when a slight frown, as if I had disturbed him, shewed for the first time that he was aware of me.

"Pray be quiet," he said, in a calm, fine voice, that suited his face exactly; and speaking—I noticed even then—with no more sense of my attractiveness than if I had been a naughty little girl of ten or twelve. "You are alone. I am only what you call a ghost, and have not the slightest interest in meddling with you."

"A ghost!" I stammered, trying to keep up my courage and pretend I didnt believe in ghosts.

"You had better convince yourself by passing your fan through my arm," he said coldly, presenting his elbow to me, and fixing me with his eye.

My tongue clove to the roof of my mouth. It came into my head that if I did not do something to get over that moment of terror, my hair would turn grey; and nothing worse could well happen to me than that. I put my shut fan on his sleeve. It went right through as if his arm did not exist; and I screamed as if the fan were a knife going through my own flesh. He was deeply displeased, and said crushingly,

"Since I incommode you, I had better get into another carriage." And I have no doubt he would have vanished there and then if I, actually trying to catch at his insubstantial cloak, had not said, almost crying,

"Oh no, no: please dont. I *darent* stay here by myself after seeing you."

He did not exactly smile; but he became a little more human in his manner, looking at me with something between pity and interest. "I shall stay with you if it will save you any anxiety," he said. "But you must really conduct yourself like an educated lady, and not scream at me."

The microscope has not yet been invented that can make visible any living creature smaller than I felt then. "I beg your pardon, sir," I said, abjectly: "I am not used to it." Then, to change the subject—for he had not taken the least notice of my apology—I added, "It seems so strange that you should travel by rail."

"Why?"

"No doubt it is not stranger, when one comes to think of it, than many things that are taken as a matter of course every day," I said, trying feebly to shew him that I was really an educated lady. "But couldnt you fly quicker—more quickly, I mean?"

"Fly!" he repeated gravely. "Am I a bird?"

"No, sir; but I thought a ghost could—not exactly fly, but project itself—himself—yourself, I mean—through space somehow; and—that is, if you are conditioned by time and space." No sooner were the words out than I felt frightfully priggish.

But priggishness seemed to suit him. He replied quite amiably, "I am so conditioned. I can move from place to place—project myself, as you call it. But the train saves me the trouble."

"Yes; but isnt it slower?"

"Having eternity at my disposal, I am not in a hurry."

I felt that I was a fool not to have seen this. "Of course," I said. "Excuse my stupidity."

He frowned again, and shook out his cloak a little. Then he said, severely, "I am willing to answer your questions, and help you to the fullest extent of my opportunities and information. But I must tell you that apologies, excuses, regrets, and needless explanations are tedious to me. Be good enough to remember that nothing that you can do can possibly injure, offend, or disappoint me. If you are stupid or insincere it will be useless for me to converse with you: that is all."

When I had recovered a little from this snubbing, I ventured to say, "Must I keep on asking you questions? There is a tradition that that is necessary with gho—with people from—with ladies and gentlemen from the other world."

"The other world!" he said, surprised. "What other world?"

I felt myself blushing, but did not dare to apologize.

"It is generally necessary to ask ghosts questions for this reason," he said. "They have no desire to converse with you; and even were it otherwise, they are not sufficiently in sympathy with you to be able to guess what would interest you. At the same time, as knowledge is the common right of all, no ghost who is not naturally a thief or a miser would refuse information to an inquirer. But you must not expect us to volunteer random conversation."

"Why?" I said, growing a little restive under his cold superiority.

"Because I have not the slightest interest in making myself agreeable to you."

"I am very sorry," I said; "but I cant think of anything to ask you. There are lots of things, if I could only recollect them. At least, the ones that come into my head seem so personal and unfeeling."

"If they seem so to you after due consideration of my disem-
bodiment, you are probably a fool," he replied quietly and gently,
like a doctor telling me something the matter with me.

"No doubt I am," I said, my temper beginning to rise. "However,
if you dont choose to speak civilly, you can keep your information
to yourself."

"Mention when I offend you; and I shall endeavor to avoid doing
so," he said, not a bit put out. "You had better ask your questions,
bearing in mind that between a ghost of some centuries and a girl
of twenty years there can be no question of manners."

He was so adorably patient in his contempt for me that I caved
in. Besides, I was four years older than he thought. "I should like
to know, please," I said, "who you are: that is, who you were; and
whether it hurts much to die. I hope the subject is not a painful
one. If so—"

He did not wait for the rest of my ridiculous apologetics. "My
experience of death was so peculiar," he said, "that I am really not
an authority on the subject. I was a Spanish nobleman, much more
highly evolved than most of my contemporaries, who were re-
vengeful, superstitious, ferocious, gluttonous, intensely prejudiced
by the traditions of their caste, brutal and incredibly foolish when
affected by love, and intellectually dishonest and cowardly. They
considered me eccentric, wanting in earnestness, and destitute of
moral sense."

I gasped, overpowered by his surprising flow of language.

"Though I was the last of the Tenario family, members of which
had held official positions at court for many generations, I refused
to waste my time as a titled lackey; and as my refusal was, according
to the ideas of my time and class, extremely indecent, I was held
to have disgraced myself. This troubled me very little. I had money,
health, and was my own master in every sense. Reading, travelling,
and adventure were my favorite pursuits. In my youth and early
manhood, my indifference to conventional opinions, and a hu-
morously cynical touch in conversation, gained me from censorious
people the names atheist and libertine; but I was in fact no worse
than a studious and rather romantic freethinker. On rare occasions,
some woman would strike my young fancy; and I would worship
her at a distance for a long time, never venturing to seek her
acquaintance. If by accident I was thrown into her company, I was

too timid, too credulous, too chivalrously respectful, to presume on what bystanders could plainly perceive to be the strongest encouragement; and in the end some more experienced cavalier would bear off the prize without a word of protest from me. At last a widow lady at whose house I sometimes visited, and of whose sentiments towards me I had not the least suspicion, grew desperate at my stupidity, and one evening threw herself into my arms and confessed her passion for me. The surprise, the flattery, my inexperience, and her pretty distress, overwhelmed me. I was incapable of the brutality of repulsing her; and indeed for nearly a month I enjoyed without scruple the pleasure she gave me, and sought her company whenever I could find nothing better to do. It was my first consummated love affair; and though for nearly two years the lady had no reason to complain of my fidelity, I found the romantic side of our intercourse, which seemed never to pall on her, tedious, unreasonable, and even forced and insincere except at rare moments, when the power of love made her beautiful, body and soul. Unfortunately, I had no sooner lost my illusions, my timidity, and my boyish curiosity about women, than I began to attract them irresistibly. My amusement at this soon changed to dismay. I became the subject of fierce jealousies: in spite of my utmost tact there was not a married friend of mine with whom I did not find myself sooner or later within an ace of a groundless duel. My servant amused himself by making a list of these conquests of mine, not dreaming that I never took advantage of them, much less that my preference for young and unmarried admirers, on which he rallied me as far as he dared, was due to the fact that their innocence and shyness protected me from advances which many matrons of my acquaintance made without the least scruple as soon as they found that none were to be expected from me. I had repeatedly to extricate myself from disagreeable positions by leaving the neighborhood, a method of escape which my wandering habits made easy to me, but which, also, I fear, brought me into disrepute as a vagabond. In the course of time, my servant's foolish opinion of me began to spread; and I at last became reputed an incorrigible rake, in which character I was only additionally fascinating to the women I most dreaded. Such a reputation grows, as it travels, like a snowball. Absurd stories about me became part of the gossip of the day. My family disowned me; and I had enough Spanish egotism left to disdain all advances towards reconciliation.

Shortly afterwards I came actually under the ban of the law. A severely pious young lady, daughter of the Commandant at Seville, was engaged to a friend of mine. Full of what she had heard against me, she held me in the utmost horror; but this my friend, desiring to spare my feelings, concealed from me. One day, I unluckily conceived the idea of making the acquaintance of his future wife. Accordingly, presuming on a tie of blood between the Commandant's family and my own, I ventured on a visit. It was late in the evening when I was shewn into her presence; and in the twilight she mistook me for my friend and greeted me with an embrace. My remonstrances undeceived her; but instead of apologizing for her mistake, which I did not myself understand until afterwards, she raised an alarm, and, when her father arrived sword in hand, accused me of insulting her. The Commandant, without waiting for an explanation, made a determined attempt to murder me, and would assuredly have succeeded if I had not, in self defence, run him through the body. He has since confessed that he was in the wrong; and we are now very good friends; especially as I have never set up any claim to superiority as a swordsman on the strength of our encounter, but have admitted freely that I made a mere lucky thrust in the dark. However, not to anticipate, he died in less than five minutes after I hit him; and my servant and I had to take to our heels to avoid being killed by his household.

"Now, unluckily for me, his daughter was, even for a female Spanish Catholic, extraordinarily virtuous and vindictive. When the town councillors of Seville erected a fine equestrian statue to her father's memory, she, by a few well-placed presents, secured a majority on the council in support of a motion that one of the panels of the pedestal should bear an inscription to the effect that the Commandant was awaiting the vengeance of Heaven upon his murderer. She also raised such a hue and cry, and so hunted me from place to place, that the officers of justice repeatedly begged me to fly from their jurisdiction lest they should be compelled by her exertions and by public opinion to do their duty and arrest me, in spite of my social position. She also refused to marry my friend until I had expiated my crime, as she called it. Poor Ottavio, whose disposition was mild and reasonable, and who was by no means sorry to be rid of a short-tempered and arbitrary father-in-law, knew as well as possible that she was as much to blame as I. So, whilst in her presence, he swore by all the saints never to sheathe his sword until it was red with my heart's blood, he privately kept me well informed of her proceedings, and, though he followed her about like a dog—for he was deeply in love—took care that our paths should not cross.

"At last my absurd reputation, my female admirers, and my Sevillian persecutors became so wearisome that I resolved to shake them all off at a blow by settling down as a respectable married man. In the hope that the women of Old Castile might prove less inconveniently susceptible than those of Andalusia, I went to Burgos, and there made the acquaintance of a young lady who was finishing her education at a convent. When I felt satisfied that she was a well-conducted girl with no special attachment to me or to anyone else, I married her. Tranquillity and leisure for study, not happiness, were my objects. But she no sooner discovered—by instinct, I believe—that I had not married her for love, and that I had no very high opinion of her intellect, than she became insanely jealous. Only those who have been watched by a jealous spouse can imagine how intolerable such espionage is. I endured it without word or sign; and she of course discovered nothing. Then she began to torture herself by making inquiries among friends who had correspondents in Seville; and their reports wrought her jealousy to a point at which it became apparent to me that, as she said, I was killing her. One day she so far broke through a certain restraint which my presence put upon her as to say that if I did not either confess my infidelities or prove to her that I loved her, she should die. Now I had nothing to confess; and, as to my loving her, nothing short of my extreme reluctance to mortify any person could have enabled me to conceal the extent to which by this time she wearied me. Clearly there was nothing to be done but to decamp. I had sent away my servant some time before to please her, because she had suspected him of carrying messages between me and my imaginary mistresses; but he was still in my pay, and quite ready to resume our wanderings, since he had himself been brought to the verge of marriage by some foolish intrigue. On receiving a message from me, he came to our house; continued to make my wife suspect that I had an assignation in the cathedral that afternoon; and, whilst she was watching for me there, packed up my pistols with a change of linen, and joined me before sundown on the road to Seville. From Burgos to Seville is a hundred Spanish leagues as the crow flies; and, as there were no railways in those days, I did not believe that my wife could follow me so far, even if she guessed my destination.

"When I turned my horse's head south, Burgos seemed—as indeed it was—a gloomy, iron-barred den of bigots: Seville, fairyland. We arrived safely; but I soon found that my old luck had deserted me. Some time after our journey, I saw a lady in the street apparently in distress. On going to her assistance, I discovered that she was my wife. When she demanded an explanation of my flight, I was at my wit's end, seeing how brutal and how incomprehensible to her must be the naked truth. In desperation, I referred her to my servant, and slipped away the moment he had engaged her attention. Now no sooner was my back turned than, fearful lest a reconciliation between us might lead to his being compelled to return with me to Burgos, the rascal shewed her his old list of my conquests, including 1003 in Spain alone, and many others in countries which I had never visited. Elvira, who would never believe any true statement concerning me, accepted the obviously impossible thousand and three conquests with eager credulity. The list contained the names of six women who had undoubtedly been violently in love with me, and some fifteen to whom I had paid a compliment or two. The rest was a fabrication, many of the names having been copied from the account books of my servant's father, a wine shop keeper.

"When Leporello had made as much mischief as possible between me and my wife, he got rid of her simply by running away. Meanwhile, I had retreated to a house of mine in the country, where I tried to amuse myself by mixing with the peasantry. Their simplicity at first interested, but soon saddened me. My ill luck, too, pursued me. One day, walking upon the village common, I came upon the Commandant's daughter, still in deep mourning, which became her very ill, with poor Ottavio at her heels. Fortunately she did not recognize me in the open daylight; and I might have got away with a polite speech or two and a private exchange of signals with Ottavio, had not my wife appeared—from the clouds, as it seemed—and began to abuse me quite frantically. Had she exercised a little self-control she might have betrayed me at the first word to Ottavio's betrothed, Doña Aña. But she was quite out of her senses; and I simply said so, whereupon she rushed away raving, and I after her. Once away from Aña, and knowing that I could do no good to Elvira, I went home as fast as I could. I had invited my peasant acquaintances to a dance that evening, the occasion being a wedding between a couple of my tenants, who were having a very pleasant party at the expense of my carpets, my furniture, and my cellar. But for this I should have left the place forthwith. As it was I resolved to leave early next morning. Meanwhile, there was nothing for it but to change my dress and receive my guests as pleasantly as possible. They were noisy and clumsy enough after their first strangeness wore off; but my attention was very soon taken from them by the entrance of three masked strangers, in whom I instantly recognized my wife, Aña, and Ottavio. Of course I, pretending that I did not know them, made them welcome, and kept up the dancing. Ottavio presently managed to send me a note to say that Aña had suddenly recollected my voice and had sought out and talked over her grievances with Elvira. They had become fast friends, and had insisted on coming to my party in masks in order to denounce me to my guests. He had not been able to dissuade them; and all he could suggest was that if I saw my way to making a rush to get clear, he would put himself forward as my opponent and play into my hands as far as he dared with Aña's eye on him.

"I was by this time at the end of my patience. I bade Leporello get my pistols and keep them in his pocket. I then joined the dancers, taking for my partner the peasant bride, whom I had before rather avoided, as the bridegroom was inclined to be jealous, and she had shewn some signs of succumbing to the infernal fascination which I still, in spite of myself, exercised. I tried to dance a minuet with her; but that was a failure. Then we went into another circle and tried to waltz. This was also beyond her rustic skill; but when we joined in a country dance, she acquitted herself so vigorously that I soon had to find her a seat in one of the smaller rooms. I noticed that my two fair maskers watched our retirement in great excitement. Turning then to the girl, and speaking to her for the first time *en grand seigneur,* I bade her do instantly whatever she was told. Then I went to the door; closed it; and waited. Presently Leporello hurried in, and begged me, for Heaven's sake, to take care what I did, as my proceedings were being commented on outside. I told him sternly to give the girl a piece of money as a reward for obeying my orders. When he had done so, I said to her peremptorily: 'Scream, Scream like the devil.' She hesitated; but Leporello, seeing that I was not to be trifled with, pinched her arm; and she screamed like not one but a thousand devils. Next moment the door was broken in by the bridegroom and his friends; and we all struggled out with a great hubbub into the saloon. But for Ottavio, who, assuming the leadership, flourished his sword and lectured me, they might have plucked up courage to attack me. I told him that if the girl was hurt it was Leporello's doing. At this the storm of menace and denunciation rose to such a pitch that for a moment I nearly lost my head. When I recovered I wholly lost my temper; drew on them; and would certainly have done mischief but for the persistence with which Ottavio kept in front of me. Finally Leporello produced the pistols; and we got to the door, when he ran for his life. After a moment's consideration I followed his example, and we both took horse at the nearest post-house, and reached Seville in safety.

"For some time after that, I lived in peace. One evening my wife descried me from a window; but, after a soft word or two, I got rid of her by wrapping Leporello in my cloak and palming him off on her as myself. As she was, like most jealous women, far too egotistical to suspect that I avoided her simply because she was disagreeable, she spread a report that I had sent her off with Leporello so that I might court her maid in her absence: a statement for which there was no foundation whatever, but which was very generally believed.

"I now come to the curious incident which led to my death. That very evening, Leporello, having escaped from my wife, rejoined me in the square close by the statue of the Commandant, of which I have spoken in connexion with the inscription and the Town Council. In the course of our conversation, I happened to laugh. Immediately, to my astonishment, the Commandant, or rather his statue, complained that I was making an unbecoming disturbance. Leporello, who heard him distinctly, was terrified beyond measure; so that I at last, disgusted by his cowardice, forced him to approach the statue and read the inscription, much as I have often forced a shying horse to go up to the object of his apprehension. But the inscription did not reassure the poor fellow; and when, to give the affair a whimsical aspect, I pretended to insist on his inviting the statue home to supper with us, he tried to persuade me that the stone man had actually bowed his head in assent. My curiosity was now greatly excited. I watched the statue carefully, and deliberately asked whether it would come to supper. It said 'Yes' in a strange stone-throated voice, but did not thank me, which was the more surprising as the Commandant had been of the old school, punctilious in etiquette. I grew alarmed as to the state of my health; for it seemed to me that I must be going mad, or else, since Leporello had heard the voice also, that I was dreaming. I could think of only two possible explanations. We had both fasted since the middle of the day, and were hungry enough, perhaps, to have illusions and infect one another with them. Or someone might have played a trick on us. I determined to satisfy myself on that point by returning next day and examining the place closely. In the meantime, however, we hurried home and fell to supper with a will. Presently, to my utter dismay, my wife rushed in, and, instead of the usual reproaches, made a rambling appeal to me to change my way of life. I first spoke kindly to her, and then tried to laugh her out of her hysterical anxiety. This only made her indignant; and in the end she ran out, but presently came back screaming and fled in the direction of the kitchen. Leporello, who had gone to see whether anything outside had alarmed her, returned panic stricken. He gasped out something about the statue, as I understood him; and tried to lock the door. Then came a loud stolid knocking. It occurred to me that the house was on fire, and the watchman come to give the alarm; for indeed no one on earth but a watchman could have given such a knock. I opened the door, and found the statue standing on the mat. At this my nerves gave way: I recoiled speechless. It followed me a pace or two into the room. Its walk was a little bandy, from the length of time it had been seated on horseback; and its tread shook the house so that at every step I expected the floor to give way and land it in the basement—and indeed I should not have been sorry to get it out of my sight even at the cost of a heavy bill for repairs. There was no use in asking it to sit down: not a chair in the place could have borne its weight. Without any loss of time, it began talking in a voice that vibrated through and through me. I had invited it to supper, it said; and there it was. I could say no less than that I was delighted; and so, with an apology for having sat down without waiting, I told Leporello to lay the table afresh, rather wondering at the same time what a solid stone thing could eat. It then said it would not trouble us, but would entertain me at supper if I had the courage to come with it. Had I not been frightened, I should have politely declined. As it was, I defiantly declared that I was ready to do anything and go anywhere. Leporello had disappeared; but I could hear his teeth chattering under the table. The thing then asked for my hand, which I gave, still affecting to bear myself like a hero. As its stone hand grasped mine, I was seized with severe headache, with pain in the back, giddiness, and extreme weakness. I perspired profusely, and, losing my power of co-ordinating my movements, saw double, and reeled like a man with locomotor ataxy. I was conscious of fearful sights and sounds. The statue seemed to me to be shouting 'Aye, aye' in an absurd manner; and I, equally absurdly, shouted 'No, no' with all my might, deliriously fancying that we were in the English house of Parliament, which I had visited once in my travels. Suddenly the statue stepped on a weak plank; and the floor gave way at last. I had sunk about twenty-five feet when my body seemed to plunge away from me into the centre of the universe. I gave a terrible gasp as it went, and then found myself dead, and in hell."

Here he paused for the first time. My hair had been trying to stand on end for the last five minutes. I would have given anything for courage to scream or throw myself out of the carriage. But I only stammered an inquiry as to what the place he had mentioned was like.

"If I speak of it as a place at all," he replied, "I only do so in order to make my narrative comprehensible, just as I express myself to you phenomenally as a gentleman in hat, cloak, and boots, although such things are no part of the category to which I belong. Perhaps you do not follow me."

"Oh, perfectly," I said. "I am fond of reading metaphysics."

"Then I must leave you to reach the answer to your own question by a series of abstractions, the residue of which you will have an opportunity of verifying by experience. Suffice it to say that I found society there composed chiefly of vulgar, hysterical, brutish, weak, good-for-nothing people, all well intentioned, who kept up the reputation of the place by making themselves and each other as unhappy as they were capable of being. They wearied and disgusted me; and I disconcerted them beyond measure. The Prince of Darkness is not a gentleman. His knowledge and insight are very remarkable as far as they go; but they do not go above the level of his crew. He kept up a certain pretence of liking my company and conversation; and I was polite to him, and did what I could to prevent him from feeling his inferiority. Still I felt that the cordiality of our relations was a strain on us both. One day a companion of his came to me, and, professing that he respected me too much to connive at my being ill spoken of behind my back, told me that the Prince had publicly said that my coming to the place was all a mistake, and that he wished I would go to heaven and be blest. This was very strong language; and I went at once to the Prince, and told him what I had heard. He first said, in a coarse conversational style which always grated on me, that my informant was a liar; but on my refusing to accept that explanation he sulkily apologized, and assured me, first, that he had only wished me to go to heaven because he honestly thought—though he confessed he could not sympathize with my taste—that I should be more comfortable there; and, second, that my coming into his set really was a mistake, as the Commandant, whom he described as a silly old Portland-stone son of a gun, had misled them concerning my character; and so, he said, they had let me through at the wrong end. I asked him by what right then did he detain me. He answered that he did not detain me at all, and demanded whether anybody or anything did or could prevent me from going where I pleased. I was surprised, and asked him further why, if hell was indeed Liberty Hall, all the devils did not go to heaven. I can only make his reply intelligible to you by saying that the devils do not go for exactly the same reason that your English betting men do not frequent the Monday Popular Concerts, though they are as free to go to them as you are. But the Devil was good enough to say that perhaps heaven would suit me. He warned me that the heavenly people were unfeeling, uppish, precise, and frightfully dry in their conversation and amusements. However, I could try them; and if I did not like them, I could come back. He should always be glad to see me, though I was not exactly the sort of person the Commandant had led him to expect. He added that he had been against the statue business from the first, as people were growing out of that sort of tomfoolery; and to go on with it in the world at this time of day was simply to make hell ridiculous. I agreed with him, and bade him adieu. He was relieved at the prospect of my departure; but still he had sufficient hankering after my good opinion to ask me not to be too hard on them down there. They had their faults, he said; but, after all, if I wanted real heart and feeling and sentiment, honest, wholesome robust humor, and harmless love of sport, I should have to come to them for it. I told him frankly that I did not intend to come back, and that he was far too clever not to know that I was right. He seemed flattered; and we parted on friendly terms. His vulgarity jarred every fibre in me; but he was quite honest in it, and his popularity was not wholly undeserved.

"Since then, I have travelled more than is usual with persons in my condition. Among us, the temptation to settle down once the congenial circle is found, is almost irresistible. A few, however, still find that a circle perfectly congenial to them has yet to be established. Some of these—myself for example—retain sufficient interest in the earth to visit it occasionally. We are regarded as rather eccentric on that account: in fact, ghosts are the lunatics of what you just now called the other world. With me it is a mere hobby, and one that I do not often indulge. I have now answered your question as to who I was, and whether it hurt me to die. Are you satisfied?"

"It is kind of you, I'm sure, to take so much trouble," I said, suddenly realizing that he had told me all this from a sense of duty, because I asked for it. "I should like to know what became of Doña Aña and the others."

"She nursed Ottavio through a slight illness with such merciless assiduity that he died of it, a circumstance he did not afterwards regret. She put on fresh mourning, and made a feature of her bereavements until she was past forty, when she married a Scotch presbyterian and left Spain. Elvira, finding it impossible to get into society after her connexion with me, went back to her convent for a while. Later on she tried hard to get married again; but somehow she did not succeed: I do not know why; for she was a pretty woman. Eventually she had to support herself by giving lessons in singing. The peasant girl, whose name I forget, became famous in a small way for her skill as a laundress."

"Her name was Zerlina, was it not?"

"Very likely it was; but pray how do you know that?"

"By tradition. Don Giovanni di Tenario is quite well remembered still. There is a very great play, and a very great opera, all about you."

"You surprise me. I should like to witness a performance of these works. May I ask do they give a fair representation of my character?"

"They represent that women used to fall in love with you."

"Doubtless; but are they particular in pointing out that I never fell in love with them—that I earnestly endeavored to recall them to a sense of their duty, and inflexibly resisted their advances? Is that made quite clear?"

"No, sir, I am afraid not. Rather the opposite, I think."

"Strange! how slander clings to a man's reputation. And so I, of all men, am known and execrated as a libertine."

"Oh, not execrated, I assure you. You are very popular. People would be greatly disappointed if they knew the truth."

"It may be so. The wives of my friends, when I refused to elope with them, and even threatened to tell their husbands if they did not cease to persecute me, used to call me a fish and a vegetable. Perhaps you sympathize with them."

"No," I said. Then—I dont know what possessed me; but of course it was not the same with him as with ordinary men—I put out my hand, and said, "You were right: they were not true women. If they had known what was due to themselves, they would never have made advances to a man; but I—I—I love—" I stopped, paralysed by the spreading light in his astonished eyes.

"Even to my ghost!" he exclaimed. "Do you not know, señorita, that young English ladies are not usually supposed to make uninvited declarations to strange gentlemen in railway carriages at night?"

"I know all about it; and I dont care. Of course I should not say it if you were not a ghost. I cant help it. If you were real, I would walk twenty miles to get a glimpse of you; and I would *make* you love me in spite of your coldness."

"Exactly what they used to say to me! Word for word, except that they said it in Spanish! Stay: you are going to put your arms timidly about my neck; ask me whether I do not love you a very little; and have a quiet little cry on my chest. It is useless: my neck and chest are part of the dust of Seville. Should you ever do it to one of your contemporaries, remember that your weight, concentrated on the nape of a tall man's neck, will fatigue him more than he will admit."

"Thank you: I had no such intention. One question more before the train stops. Were you as sure of your fascination when you were alive as you are now?"

"Conceited, they used to call it. Not naturally: I was born a shy man. But repeated assurances confirmed me in a favorable opinion of my attractions, which, I beg you to recollect, only embittered my existence."

The train stopped; and he rose and walked through the wood and glass of the door. I had to wait for the guard to unlock it. I let down the window, and made a bid for a last word and look from him.

"Adieu, Don Giovanni!" I said.

"Lively young English lady, adieu. We shall meet again, within eternity."

I wonder whether we shall, some day. I hope so.

Sinclair Lewis

YOU KNOW HOW WOMEN ARE

NOBEL PRIZE 1930

America's first Nobel laureate in literature, Sinclair Lewis (1885–1951) was born in the small town of Sauk Center, Minnesota. He received a degree from Yale University, where he served as editor of the Yale Literary Magazine. *During this period he lived part of each year at Helicon Hall, Upton Sinclair's socialistic community in Englewood, New Jersey, an experience that contributed to his strong commitment to social justice. He became a full-time writer at the age of thirty-one after holding a variety of jobs, including work in journalism and book publishing. He refused to accept a Pulitzer Prize awarded to him in 1926.*

One of America's great realistic novelists, he is best known for his often savage attacks on professions and occupations, attacks which took place in novels like Babbitt *(1922; middle-class business practices),* Arrowsmith *(1925; the medical profession),* Elmer Gantry *(1927; the clergy), and* Dodsworth *(1929; American business overseas). He was certainly one of the premier writers of the 1920s, and although his work declined in later years he will always be remembered for his exposure of the conformity that characterized American life.*

—AND I TELL YOU, Walt, now we have a chance to sit down here by ourselves in your den and have a real chat—and say, from what I've seen, I don't believe there's a more elegant house for its size in Troy, and then of course you always were my favorite cousin, and one of the few people whose business judgment I'd trust and—

If you can see your way clear to making this loan, you'll never regret it. Business hasn't gone quite so good the last six months, as I admitted, but now I've got the exclusive Zenith agency for Zenith for these new cash registers—and say, what the cash register means, what it *means* to the modern and efficient conduct of business; it's almost, you might say, the symbol of modern industry, like the sword is of war—now I've got that, I can guarantee a big increase in turnover, taking one thing with another, and I want you to examine the analysis of my business with the greatest care.

And I certainly do admit all your criticisms, and I'm going to ponder on 'em and try to profit by 'em.

I'm afraid I do get too kind of talkee-talkee during business hours, and maybe waste time and money. And I admit what you said about my college course. It's perfectly true: I didn't quit Amherst because my Dad died—fact, he didn't die till nine months after I was fired, and it's true I was dropped for flunking all my college courses, as you said—though I thought you threw that up to me a little unnecessarily; almost hurt my feelings, in fact; don't know that I'd 've stood it from anybody but you, but of course you always were my favorite cousin—

You see, I don't go around telling everybody that version of the story, because what I figure is, what they don't know won't hurt 'em none, and it's none of their business.

But it's not true, as you kind of hinted and suggested, that I didn't know President Coolidge in college. It's a fact that for some years I did have him mixed up with another fellow in our class that looked something like him, but here some time ago I happened to run into this other fellow, and now I've got the two of 'em perfectly straight.

Why, I can remember just as if it was yesterday, Cal—as we used to call him—Cal and I were going into class together, and I says to him, "Cal, old boy," I said, "what's the Latin for 'battle'?" And he said—he said—well, he gave the word right out, without any hemming and hawing and beating around the bush.

But you're right, I do kind of get to talking too much. Henceforth I'm going to cut it short, and you'll never regret it if you put in that loan.

And I don't think that even you, with all the insight that you show into human nature, quite understand how and why it is that in certain moods I do run on a good deal. There's reasons for it. In the first place, I'm called on so constantly for speeches and oratory in Zenith—you've never been there and you couldn't understand, but—

Well, you take like this, for instance. I was attending a meeting of the Americanization Committee of the Zenith Chamber of Commerce, and we were discussing birth control. Well, the chairman insisted I make 'em a long speech on the subject.

"Shucks, boys," I said, "you know just as much about it as I do," but they talked and they insisted, and they wouldn't let me go until I'd made a long spiel for 'em, summing up the arguments on both sides and, you might say, kind of clarifying it for 'em. See how I mean? But you, Walt, you just think of business night and day, and prob'ly that's a more practical way to think of it. But I get dragged into all these public and influential occasions and get kind of into a habit of oratory and philosophy, see how I mean?

And then—

I hate to say it, and there isn't another human being living, Walt, that I'd tell this to, and I want you to treat it as strictly confidential, but—

The fact is, what really cramps my style is my wife.

•

That girl—

And in many ways I've got nothing but praise for Mamie. She means well, and as far as her lights lead her, she does everything she can for me, but the fact is she don't quite understand me, and say, the way she drives me and makes demands on me and everything, why say, it just about drives me crazy.

And Delmerine same way. Thinking the Old Man's *made* of money!

And what I've done for Mamie—yes, and what modern American science has done! Think of the advantage of canned goods, of delicatessen shops with every delicacy from salads to cold turkey, all ready to serve without any preparation; of baker's bread without having to bake bread at home. Think of the electric dish-washing machine, reducing the work of dish-washing to, you might say, practically a minimum, and the vacuum cleaner, and what an invention *that* is!—no more sweeping, no more beating rugs—why say, the preachers can talk about these mysteries and all like that, but I guess in the vacuum cleaner America has added to the world *its* own mystery, that'll last when the columns of the Acropolis have crumbled to mere dust!

And then think of the modern laundries with their marvelous machinery.

It's true that they don't wash the clothes quite as good as my old mother used to—fact, they simply tear hell out of my handkerchiefs, and I always was a man to appreciate a high grade of fine linen handkerchief. But still, think of the labor-saving.

And so I've provided Mame with every device to save her labor, so whether it's a question of her telling the maid what to do, or during those comparatively rare intervals when we haven't got a hired girl and she has to do some of the work herself, she can get it all done in a jiffy, you might say, and be free for all the pleasures and self-improvement of leisure. She's free to play bridge nearly every afternoon, and also to give a lot of attention to her literary club, the William Lyon Phelps Ladies' Book and Literary Society, and get a lot of culture.

Now myself, I've always given a lot of attention to intellectual matters. Of course I'm right up on history—I've read clear through both Wells' "Outline of History," or practically clear through it, and also Van Lear's "Story of Mankind," especially studying the illustrations. And of course—maybe I'm a little rusty on it now, but as a boy I used to be able to chatter German like a native, you might say, as my father often talked it to us at home. And now I'm kind of specializing on philosophy. I've read a lot of this "Story of Philosophy" by—I can't at the moment exactly remember the professor's name, but it gives you the whole contents of all philosophy in one book; and while these business cares have for the moment interrupted my reading the book, I expect to go right on and finish it.

But Mame, she has the opportunity to go ahead and knock all *my* culture into a cocked hat. Here recently her club had a very fine lecture about the excavation of King Tut's tomb, from a gentleman that had been right there on the ground—of course he couldn't go *into* the tomb, because nobody's allowed inside it except the excavating staff, but he saw the place at first hand, and my wife learned a lot about Egyptology from him.

And they've had a whole course in dietetics. She learned, for example, that the ordinary housewife uses more butter in cooking than is at all necessary—that while maybe butter may make grub *taste* a little better, it doesn't add proportionately to the calories or whatever they are, and so she learned one way in which to economize. And my God, these days, what with the cost of gasoline and golf balls, a fellow has to economize on something.

So as I say, she has a chance to lead a free life and have a lot of dandy times, because I've provided her with all the household conveniences. But who paid for 'em? Where did the money to pay for 'em come from? From my toil and efforts, that's where it came from, and do you think I can get her to appreciate that? Not for one moment!

All day long I slave and work to keep her in luxury, and then when I come home at night all tired out, do I find her ready to comfort me? I do not!

I might as well not have a wife at all. And then when I try to make her understand what I've been doing—like telling her how hard I've worked to sell a new adding-machine to some fellow that didn't want it and maybe didn't need it, do you think she appreciates it? She does not!

Why, she always makes out like she wishes I was a doctor, or one of these he-lecturers that goes around spieling to women's clubs, or some darn' arty thing like that, and sometimes she practically up and says she wishes I could make love like one of these Wop counts, or a movie actor!

She says I just think of business and not of her. But I notice she's good and plenty glad to grab all the money I bring home from that business, all right!

It was—

Now I wouldn't say this to anybody else on God's green earth, and for heaven's sake don't you ever breathe a syllable of it, even to your wife, but I've been beginning to think here lately that it was all wrong with Mame and me right from the beginning.

Not that I'd ever do anything about it, you understand—even though I *have* got a lady friend in New York, simply a little darling and at least twelve years younger than Mame, too—but I don't believe in divorce, and then there's the children to think of. But it was all wrong—

I've learned a lot here lately. I've been studying and delving into psychoanalysis. Know anything about psychoanalysis?

Well, I do, and say, it certainly is a revelation. I've read almost clear through a manual on it—a very authoritative book written by a lady, Miss Alexandrine Applebaugh, that's a great authority on the subject, because she studied with a man that was a pupil of one of the biggest pupils of old Freud, and it was Freud that invented psychoanalysis.

Well, now I'll explain what psychoanalysis is. It's like this:

Everybody ought to have a rich, full sex-life, and all human activities are directed toward that. Whenever a guy is doing something, it's directed toward making himself attractive sexually, especially if it's something big and important—no matter whether it's painting a picture or putting over a big deal in Florida town-lots or discovering a new eclipse or pitching in a World Series game or preaching a funeral sermon or writing a big advertisement or any of them things. On the other hand, when fellows like us *do* put over something, we want to be appreciated, and we got a right to expect it, and if we don't get appreciated at home, we ought to find new mates, see how I mean?

Only you get into so doggone many complications and trouble and all that maybe it ain't practical, even with a cute girl like this one in New York I was speaking about—Ain't really worth it.

And then there's a lot in psychoanalysis about dreams. All dreams mean you ought to have a different kind of a wife—oh, they're *mighty* important!

And so now you'll understand psychoanalysis—as well as anybody does, anyway.

•

Well, as I say, now that I've mastered psychoanalysis, I can see things was all wrong with Mame and me from the beginning.

I was a young fellow, just come to Zenith, then, working in a wholesale paper house and living in a boarding-house out in the Benner Park district, and in those days that district was just like a small town. I met a dandy crowd of young people at the church and so on, and we used to have dances and picnics and sleigh-rides and everything—rube stuff, but lots of fun.

Well, Mame—her father was in the roofing business, did a pretty good business, too, for them days—she was one of the jolliest girls in the bunch, but she was awful on the level. There was some of the girls in our crowd that you could get pretty fresh with—nothing wrong, you understand, or not hardly ever, but still when you was all cuddled down together in the hay on a sleigh-ride, you could hold their hands and maybe even pat their knees a little.

But Mame—never! No sir! Why say, she was so pure and religious that one time at a dance when I tried to kiss her, she slapped hell out of me!

So of course that just led me on. Made me think she was the living wonder.

Maybe if I'd known then as much as I know now, I'd 've known that it isn't so bad for a girl that you're going to spend your life with, intimate, you might say, to have a little of the Old Nick in her and not be so doggone adverse to a little scientific cuddling—within reason I mean, of course, you see how I mean?

Well, so we got married and she never did get so she liked—

I mean, she hints around sometimes and kind of hints that it's because I'm just a poor plain plug American business man that she's never warmed up. But my God, I've never had any encouragement! I don't expect I'd ever be any Valentino, anyway, but how can I even begin to learn to show her a good time when she's always acted like she was afraid I *would* try to kiss her?

I tell you, Walt, I'm kind of puzzled. Sometimes I almost kind of wonder (though I wouldn't want to be quoted) whether with all the great things we got in this greatest nation in the world, with more autos and radios and furnaces and suits of clothes and miles of cement pavements and skyscrapers than the rest of the world put together, and with more deep learning—hundreds of thousands of students studying Latin and bookkeeping and doctoring and domestic science and literature and banking and window-dressing—even with all of this, I wonder if we don't lack something in American life when you consider that you almost never see an American married couple that really like each other and like to be with each other?

I wonder. But I guess it's too much for me. I just don't understand—

•

But I'm getting away from my subject. To return to Mame:

Aside from her apparently not wanting me to be anything what-soever around the house except the guy that pays the bills and carves the duck and fixes the furnace and drives her car out of the garage so she can go off to a hen bridge-party, here lately we've got into kind of a bad way of quarreling.

Well, here's an example:

We used to have dogs for quite a while after we were married, and I always did like to have a good dog around the house. Kind of gives you somebody to talk to when you come home and there ain't anybody around—just sits and listens while you explain things to him, and looks like he *understood!* But here about six years ago, just at a moment when we didn't happen to have a dog, somebody gave Mrs. Schmaltz—gave Mamie, I mean—a very fine expensive cat by the name Minnie—not exactly a full-bred Persian, I guess, but pretty full-bred at that.

But at the same time, even appreciating how much money she was worth, I never did *like* that damn' cat!

You see, we also had a canary, a very valuable little canary named Dicky, a real genuwine Hertz Mountains canary, and intelligent—say, there's those that say a canary isn't intelligent, but I want to tell you that that canary *knew* me, and when I'd stand near the cage he'd chirp just like he was talking to me.

He was a lot of comfort to me, not having a dog at that time—I was looking for a high-class English setter, and hadn't been able to find one at the price I felt justified in paying.

Well sir, here was a surprising thing. We fed that cat and fed her—I'd hate to tot up all the money we've paid out for milk and meat for that cat—but even so, she was bound and determined she was going to get at that poor little canary. She'd hang around underneath the cage and look up at Dicky, absolutely bloodthirsty, and one time when somebody (and I always thought it was Mame did it herself, too, and not the hired girl)—when somebody left a chair right practically under the cage, Minnie lep' up on the chair and absolutely did her best to leap up and get at the cage.

Of course Mame and I had words about that—

And then that damn' cat never *would* be friendly, at least not to me.

I used to say to Mame, "Well, what does the fool cat do for its living, anyway? Think we're sent into the world just to loaf around and enjoy ourselves and sponge on other people?" I says.

Wouldn't sit in my lap—no sir, not for a minute. I used to get so sore at that cat that I'd kick it good and plenty hard, when nobody was looking—I showed it its place, by God—and *still* I couldn't get it to be friendly.

And we talked a lot about it, about the cat and the canary, and one thing often led to another—

You know how it is.

And when I talked about getting another dog, no *sir*, Mame wouldn't hear to it—said a dog would frighten her ittly, bittly, sweetsy, bitsy, high-hatting, canary-murdering damn' *cat*, by God!

Well, I made up my mind that I was going to be master in my own household, but—Oh well, things just kind of floated along for several months, and I didn't do anything special about buying a dog, and then one day—

I remember just like it was yesterday. I'd been out to the country club for a few holes of golf—I remember I was playing with Joe Minchin, the machinery king, Willis Ijams, our leading—or certainly one of the leading hardware dealers, and fellow named George Babbitt, the great real-estate dealer. But I was driving home alone, and I remember there was something wrong—car kept kind of bucking—couldn't exactly figure out what it was, so I stops the car right by the side of the road—it was late autumn—and I lifts the hood and I'm trying to figure out what's wrong when I hears a kind of a whining and a whimpering, and I looks down, and by golly there's a nice water spaniel—not very old, not more'n say two or maybe nearer two and a half years old, sitting there and looking up at me so pathetic—say, it was absolutely pathetic. And he held up his paw like it'd been hurt.

"Well, what's the trouble, old man?" I says to him.

And he looks up, so intelligent—By golly, I just loved that damn' tyke. Well, make a long story short, I looks at his paw, and way I figured it out, he'd cut it on some broken glass—but not bad. Fortunately I had some old but clean rags there in the door-pocket of the car, and so I sat down on the running-board and kind of bound up his paw, and meantime I noticed—and a good, high-

grade dog he was, too—I noticed he didn't have any collar or license
or anything. And when I'd finished, doggoned if he didn't jump
up into my sedan like he belonged there.

"Well, who d'you think you are?" I says to him. "What are you
trying to do, you old hijacker," I says to him. "Steal my car? Poor
old Pop Schmaltz with his car stolen," I says.

And he just curls up on the back seat and wags his tail, much as
to say, "You're a great little kidder, but I know which side my meat
is buttered on."

Well, I looks up and down the road and there wasn't anybody
in sight that looked like they were looking for a dog, and there was
only a couple of houses in sight, and when I got the car to acting
Christian again—seems the carburetor needed a little adjusting—
I drives to both these houses, and *they* didn't know nothing about
no lost dog, so I says, "Well, don't like to leave old Jackie here—"

That's what I named the pup, and that's what I call him to this
very day.

"I'd better not leave him here to get run over," thinks I, "and
when we get back home, I'll advertise and see if I can find his
owner."

Well, when I got home, Robby—you remember my boy, Walt—
Robby was just as crazy about having a dog as I was, but Mame
gets sniffy about how the dog'd scare that damn' cat Minnie of
hers. But she let me keep Jackie, that's the dog, out in the garage
till I'd advertised.

Well, I advertised and I advertised—

No, come to think of it, I guess it was just one ad I put in, because
I thinks to myself, "Jackie looks to me like a regular man's dog,
and if his owner ain't keeping a look-out, can't expect *me* to do all
the work!"

Anyway, never got an answer, and in 'long about a week, Mame
wakes up and begins to realize, here I am with a dog that ain't
going to be buddies with her cat—and say, was she right? Say, the
first time Minnie comes pee-rading out on the lawn to see if she
can't murder a few sparrows, Jackie, his paw was well enough for
that, he takes one look at her, and say, honest, you'd 've laughed
fit to bust; he chases her 'way clean up our elm tree, and keeps
her there, too, by golly.

Well, after that, there was a hell of a powwow with Big Chief
Wife, and no peace-pipe in sight. She gets me in the house, away

from Robby, who'd 've backed me up, and she rides the wild mustango up and down the living-room, and throws her tomahawk into the tortured victims, meaning me, and she says:

"Lowell Schmaltz, I've told you, and if I've told you once, I've told you a hundred times, that Minnie is a *very* sensitive and high-bred cat, and I will not have her nerves all shattered by being annoyed by a lot of horrid dogs. I want you to find the rightful owner of this horrid dog and give him back."

"Give who back? The owner?" I says, just sitting down and lighting a cigar and trying to look like I was amused and there was nothing she could do or say that would get my goat. And of course I had her there: "Give who back? The owner?" I says.

"You know perfectly well and good what I mean," she says. "And I want you to find the horrid thing's owner at once!"

"Fine!" I says. "Sure! Of course all I've done is to advertise extensively in the *Advocate-Times,* which only has more circulation than any other two papers in this territory put together—or so they claim, and I've looked into it and I'm disposed to accept their figures," I says. "But of course that isn't enough. All right, I'll just tuck Jackie under my arm, and start right out—Let's see," I says, "there's only about six hundred thousand people in Zenith and the neighboring towns, within perhaps a twenty-eight or thirty mile radius of City Hall, and all I'll have to do will be to run around to *each* of 'em and say, 'Hey, mister, lost a dog?' That's all I'll have to do."

"Well, then, you can take the horrid beast out where you found him and leave him there," she says.

"I can, and I ain't going to," I says—flat. "I'm not going to have him run over by some damn' fool careless motorist," I says. "He's a valuable dog," I says.

"He's horrid—and he's terribly dirty. I never did see such a terribly dirty dog," she says.

"Oh, sure," I says. "Of course aside from the notorious fact that he's a water spaniel—and water spaniels' being, even if they ain't at present as fashionable as cocker spaniels or wire-haired terriers or Airedales, merely notoriously the cleanest dogs that exist," I says, "aside from that, you're dead right."

"But we don't need a dog anyway," she says.

Well say, that kind of got my goat.

"No," I says, "sure we don't. I don't, anyway. Think what I've got here to be chummy with in the evening. Elegant! This nice, fluffy, expensive feline cat, that hates me like hell, that won't sit in my lap, that cottons to you because you got nothing to do all day but stay home and pet it, while I have to be in my store, working my head off—to support a damn' cat! Fine!" I says.

But then I got serious, and after some remarks back and forth about how she *did* have things to do, like running the house and looking after my clothes and Robby and Delmerine—*you* know how any woman can make out like she works like a slave—after that I got serious, and I says:

"But seriously," I says, "when you come to look at it in a serious manner, what is a dog? What is a dog? What is he but man's greatest friend! Who so unselfish as a dog! Who so welcomes the weary man—yes, or woman, for that matter, if she treats 'em right!—when they come home weary from the day's labor? To say nothing of their being in many lands also useful in a practical way in helping to haul carts, also as watchmen.

"You forget," I told her, "all the wonderful things we've seen Rin Tin Tin do in the movies. Why say, I'll bet that dog's salary is higher than that of any film-author or even camera-man. But aside from that, think of some of the dogs of history. Think of those brave Saint Bernard dogs, going out with little barrels of brandy under their chins to rescue belated travelers in that pass in Germany, or wherever it was—though I never could understand," I admits, "why there were so many travelers that kept taking a chance and getting belated in the snow that they had to keep a whole corps of dogs running to rescue them all the time. But still, that was in old historic times, and maybe things were different from now, and of course no railroads—

"But in modern times," I told her, "I've heard an anecdote, and I got it mighty straight, from a fellow who knew the fellow who was in the story, and it seems this fellow was a trapper or a miner or a prospector or something like that, anyway he had a cabin 'way off in the Sierras or some place like that—high mountains, anyway—and seems it was the depth of winter, and this fellow's cabin was all snowed in, also the tracks and trails and all were deep buried in the snow.

"Well, seems this fellow had an accident, slipped down a crevasse or something like that, and busted his leg, seriously, but he managed to make his way with great difficulty back to his cabin where his faithful dog, I never did learn the name of the dog, was waiting for him, and then as a result of the accident, he fell into a kind of fever, I suppose it was, and he lay there simply shot to pieces, and in great suffering, and attended only by this faithful dog, who couldn't, of course, do much to help him, but he did his best, and he was a mighty smart, clever dog, and the trapper, or whatever this fellow was, he trained this dog so's he'd bring a match or a drink of water or whatever it was the poor devil needed.

"But there wasn't any way of cooking any food—it goes without saying that that was something the dog couldn't help him with—and the trapper got worse and worse, and he was in great pain, and you could see the dog was worried about what to do, and then all of a sudden, one day by golly the dog gives a kind of a short quick yelp, and he dives right through the cabin window, head on, and he's gone—not one sound from him.

"Well, of course, the poor devil of a trapper, he thought his only friend had deserted him, and he gave himself up to die, and it was almost as bitter as the pain itself to think that he'd been deserted by the only friend he had.

"But all this time, the dog was not idle. He goes lickety-split, following the snow-obliterated trails as if by instinct, 'way down and down and down to the far-distant nearest village, and comes up to the doctor's house, where he'd been once several years before with his master.

"Well, the door is slightly ajar, and the dog busts in and whines at the feet of the doc, who was at dinner.

"'You get to hell out of here—how'd you ever get in here anyway?' the doctor says, naturally not understanding the situation, and he chases the dog out and closes the door, but the dog stands there on the door-step, whining and otherwise trying to draw the attention of the doctor, till the doctor's wife begins to think something is wrong, and they cautiously let the dog in again and try to feed it, but it keeps tugging at the doc's pants-legs and refuses to eat a single morsel, till at last the doc says, 'Maybe I'm needed somewhere, and come to think of it, this dog looks like the dog that that trapper had back in the mountains when he came here one time.'

"So anyway, he takes a chance on it—of course he hasn't got any more idea than the man in the moon where this fellow lives, but he hitches up his cutter, and the dog runs along in front of them, picking out the best road, and they come to this cabin, hours and hours from anywhere, and the doc goes in, and here's this fellow with the fever and busted leg in dire need. Well, he tends to him and gets him some chow and is all ready to move him to civilization when he thinks of this poor dog that's saved him, and he turns to find him, and the poor little tyke has crawled into a corner and fallen dead, exhausted by his terrible race for life!

"That's what dogs can do," I tell her, and then I tells her some other absolutely authentic anecdotes about dogs and we pass a lot of remarks back and forth, and final result is, she says all right; she'll stand my keeping the dog, but he's got to stay out of the house, and I can build him a dog-kennel out beside the garage.

•

But you know how things go. One morning I gets up early and has breakfast by myself, and there's Jackie whining outside, and I takes a chance and lets him in and feeds him, and that cat comes marching into the room like a Episcopalopian rector leading a procession, and Jackie gets one squint at her and chases her up on the buffet, and just then Mamie comes in and—

Say, I didn't stop with no buffet; I didn't stop till I'd reached the top of the Second National Bank Tower. But seriously, though, she certainly give Jackie and me such an earful that—

Well, Joe Minchin had planned a poker party for that evening and I hadn't kind of intended to go, but Mame bawled hell out of me so at breakfast that later in the day I said I'd go, and I went, and I got lit to the eyebrows, if the truth be known—say, I was simply ossified.

So I comes home late, thinking I was both the King and Queen of Sheba, and then I got dizzy and just about the time Mame'd thought up her adjectives and was ready to describe me for the catalogue of domestic sons of guns, I couldn't tarry, oh, no longer— I had to be wending my way into the bathroom P.D.Q., and there, say, I lost everything but my tonsils. Wow!

Well, Mame was awful' nice to me. She helped me back into bed, and she bathed my forehead, and she got some black coffee for me—only what I wanted was a good cyanide of potassium cock- tail—and when I woke up in the morning she just kind of laughed, and I thought I was going to get by without the matrimonial cat- o'-nine-tails—I actually thought that, and me married over twenty years to her!

So when my head gets itself reduced to not more'n six or seven normal times its ordinary or wearing size, and I gets up for breakfast, not more'n twenty or twenty-two hours late, and she's still bright and—oh God, what a blessing!—still keeping her trap shut and not telling me about salvation, why, I thinks I'm safe, and then just when I stagger up from breakfast and thinks I'll go down to my store, if I can remember where I left my garage last night, why, she smiles brighter'n ever, and says in a nice, sweet, cool, Frigidaire voice:

"Sit down a moment, will you please, Low. There's something I want to say to you."

Well—

Oh, I died with my face to the foemen. I tried to take the barricades in one gallant dash, like Douglas Fairbanks. I says briefly, "I know what you want to say," I says. "You want to say I was lit, last night. Say, that isn't any news. By this time it's so old and well known that you can find it among the problems in the sixth-grade arithmetic book," I says. "Look here," I says, "it wasn't entirely my fault. It was that God-awful bootleg hootch I got at Joe's. It'd been all right if it'd been honest liquor."

"You were *disgusting*," she says. "If my poor father and mother hadn't passed away, and if my sister Edna wasn't such a crank about theosophy that nobody could live with her, I'd 've left you before dawn, let me tell you that."

Well, I got sore. I'm not a bad-tempered cuss, as you know, but after along about twenty years, this threatening-to-leave-you business gets a little tiresome.

"Fine," I says. "You're always blowing about how much you know about clothes. I'll be glad to give you a knock-down to some of the big guys at Benson, Hanley and Koch's," I says, "and probably they'll make you buyer in the ladies' garments department," I says, "and you won't have to go on standing for a gorilla of a husband like me."

And she says all right, by God she'll do it!

And we seesaw back and forth, and I kind of apologizes, and she says she didn't mean it, and then we really gets down to business.

"But just the same," she says, "I'm not going to have that dog in the house again! You've not got the least consideration for my feelings. You talk so much about your dear old friends, like this horrible Joe Minchin, but you never give one moment's thought to what I need or like. You don't know what the word 'thought-fulness' means."

"All right, I'll look it up in the dictionary," I says. "And speaking of *thoughtfulness,*" I says, "when I was going out last night, I found you'd been using my safety razor and hadn't cleaned it, and I was in a hurry and you'd neglected—By God," I says, "when I was a boy, a man had his sweaters to himself, without his wife or sister calmly up and using 'em, and he had his razor to himself, and he had his barber-shop to himself—"

"Yes, and he had his saloons to himself, and still has," she comes back at me. "And you talk about neglect! It isn't only me you neglect," she says, "when you go and get full of liquor, and it isn't simply the example you set the children, but it's the way you neglect the church and religion," she says.

"And of course I'm only a deacon in the church," I says. You know—sarcastic.

"Yes, and you know mighty good and well you only took the job because it'd give you a stand-in with the religious folks, and every Sunday you can, you sneak off and play golf instead of going to church. And that morning when Dr. Hickenlooper came in from Central Methodist and preached for us—that time when poor Dr. Edwards was sick and couldn't preach himself—"

"Sick? He was sick like a fox," I told her. "He just had a sore throat because he'd been off on a lecture trip, shooting his mouth off before a lot of women's clubs to rake in some extra dough, when he ought to stayed home here and tended to his job."

"That's entirely aside from the question," she says, "and anyway, instead of listening to Dr. Hickenlooper like you ought to, you and a couple other deacons stayed out in the lobby of the church."

"Yuh, there's something to what you say," I told her. "Hicken-looper is a fine man. He's all for charity—providing some rich man provides the money for the charity. I don't believe he's ever smoked a cigar or had a nip of liquor in his life. He's a credit to the Methodist clergy. It's true he does bawl out his wife and his kids all the time, and it's true he nags his secretary all day long, but you can't blame a man that's busy with the Lord's work for being maybe a little irritable. In fact there's only one trouble with the holy man—he's the worst and most consistent liar in seven counties!

"I've heard him tell as his own experience things I know he read in books, because I've seen the books. And here's a story that our

own pastor, Edwards, told us. Seems Hickenlooper met him in front
of our church one Monday morning, and Hickenlooper says, 'Well,
Dr. Edwards, my brother-in-law heard you preach yesterday, and
he said it was the best sermon he ever heard in his life.'

"'Well, that's nice,' Dr. Edwards says, 'but it just happens that I
didn't preach yesterday.'

"I guess I'm a kind of a blowhard," I says to Mamie, "and in
general I'm just a plug business man, while Hickenlooper addresses
Chautauquas and addresses colleges and addresses Methodist con-
ferences and writes articles for the magazines and writes lovely
books about how chummy he and God and the sunsets are, but
say, if that holy liar knew what even poor, ordinary business men
like me really thought about him and what they said privately, he'd
sneak off to a desert and never open his mouth again!"

•

Well say, that had Mamie wild—and don't you think for one
moment, Walt, that she let me get by without a few interruptions
that I haven't put into the story. And what I've just told you about
this Hickenlooper bird—he looks like a prizefighter and talks like
a glad-hand circus ballyhooer, and he lies like a politician—was all
straight, and she knew it. I've done a little lying myself, but I've
never made a three-ring circus of it like him. But Mamie had a
sneaking kind of admiration for him, I guess because he's big and
strong and a great baby-kisser and girl-jollier. And she let loose on
me, and what she said—Whee!

She said I encouraged Robby to smoke. She said I never used
an ashtray—always scattered my ashes around the house—and I'm
afraid she had me there. And she said she was sick of having my
friends around the house all the time, and I bawled her out for
high-hattin' 'em, and she said something about my driving too fast,
and I come back with a few short sweet words about back-seat
driving—she's the best single-handed non-participating Major Sea-
grove of the entire inhabited world. And—

And so on.

And that's just typical of a few home Board of Directors con-
ferences we been having, and I'm pretty sick of it.

Not but what I'm just as mean as she is, at that, I suppose.

But I did by God keep old Jackie!

But I'm getting sick of the whole business—

Not, you understand, but what Mame is just as nice a pal as you'd want to find, in between tantrums. That time we were here and saw you and then went on and had our long talk with Coolidge in Washington, she was jolly the whole time. But more and more—

•

Say, I don't know as I ought to tell you about this, hardly, but this girl I was speaking of in New York—well, she isn't exactly a girl any more, but she's only thirty-eight and that's seventeen years younger'n I am—Erica, her name is, and say, she's one of the most talented little women I ever met.

By rights, she ought to be a world-renowned portrait-painter, but she's always run into the damnedest hard luck, and just now for a few years she's been working for the Pillstein and Lipshutz Christmas and Easter Greeting Card Company, where I always get my greeting cards. Of course by rights I'm not a stationer but stick right to office supplies, but same time, along at these holiday times, I feel it does kind of brighten up the business to stock a few handsome cards, and pay—say, it brings me in hundreds a year.

Well, Erica designs a lot of cards—*darn'* smart intelligent girl— does the drawings and the poems and the whole thing. Say, you've probably seen some of her cards. It was her that wrote that famous one that had such a big sale—the one with the two kids shaking hands in front of an old schoolhouse, and then a lot of holly and so on, and the poem:

> Dear friend, this season of ice and snow
> Does not make love the colder grow,
> But on contrary pries apart
> Wider the cockles of the heart.
>
> 'Tis years since we were boys together
> In jolly winter and summer weather,
> 'Tis years indeed since we have met,
> But our old friendship I'll ne'er forget.

Say, it'd surprise you how many of those cards a lot of hard-boiled old business men buy to send to fellows they haven't seen for years. I tell you, that fellow Manny Pillstein is a genius. Of course there've been greeting cards for years, but he was the first one to put the business on a scientific, nationally advertised basis, and really standardize and Fordize all this Holiday Good Will so it'd amount to something. They say he's increased the business 10,000 percent.—made it as practical as chain grocery stores or even Mother's Day.

Well, I met Erica there at his place, and I was alone in New York, and I invited her to dinner, and I blew her to a nice little feed with a bottle of real domestic Chianti. Well, we got to talking and telling our ideas and so on, and come to find out, poor kid, she was pretty near as lonely in New York as I was.

And then every time I blew into the Big Burg—alone—I'd see her, and—

Now say, her relations and mine was just as pure as the driven snow. Maybe I'd kiss her in a taxicab, or something like that, and tell the truth I don't know how far I'd 've gone if I'd got her off to Atlantic City or something like that, but my God, with my position and my responsibilities, both financial and social, I didn't want to get into no complications. To tell the truth (and I'd never tell another living soul but you), one evening I did go up to her flat— But only that once! And I got scared, and just used to see her at restaurants.

But be the cause what it may, our relations were entirely and absolutely friendly and intellectual, and know what she told me?

When I told her what I thought of her work—and to me, and I told her so, she's the best greeting-card artist in the country— she told me my appreciation was the greatest encouragement and the greatest incentive to go onward and upward to finer and better art that she'd ever received! And let me tell you, I've never had anything buck *me* up, in turn, like her appreciation of my appreciation. Whereas at home—

If I try to tell Mame that she plays a good mitt of bridge, or that I think she's got on an elegant new dress, or she sang some song at some church affair real pretty, or like that, she just looks like she was saying, "Who the hell ever told you *you* was a connooser?"

Oh God, I suppose we'll always go on, just about the same, but if I was younger—

Well, I ain't!

•

Well, Walt, I guess it's getting late and about time for us to turn in—you'll have to be in your office tomorrow, and I think I'll take that 12:18 for home, if I can get a Pullman.

It's been a mighty great privilege to have this frank talk with you. I certainly will take your advice. I'll try to keep from talking and running on so much—you noticed this evening at supper I hardly said a word, but just listened to your good wife. You bet. I've learned my lesson. I'm going to concentrate on selling the goods, and not discuss subjects and topics all the time.

And I hope you'll give my schedule a mighty close once-over and see your way to advance me the loan.

You remember how I've always turned to you. Remember that month I spent with you boys on your granddad's farm when we were 'long about twelve?

God, what fun that was! Regular idyl, you might say, like a fellow can't touch again in these later care-ridden and less poetic years. Remember how we stole those mushmelons from that old farmer, and when he got sassy about it we went back and smashed all the rest of 'em? Remember how we hid the alarm-clock in the church so it went off during the sermon? Remember how we greased the springboard so's that Irish kid slipped on it and almost busted his back? Gosh, I had to laugh!

Oh, those were great days, and you and me always did understand each other, Walt, and don't forget that there's no firm in the world could give you better security for the loan.

John Galsworthy

SALVATION OF A FORSYTE

NOBEL PRIZE 1932

John Galsworthy (1867–1933) was born in Kingston Hills, Surrey, England. After attending Oxford, he studied law and was admitted to the bar in 1890. Soon, however, he switched careers, eventually becoming one of his country's most famous novelists and playwrights. His magnum opus (part of which was recently filmed by the BBC) is his multivolumed study of the upper-middle-class Forsyte family. It includes The Man of Property *(1906),* Indian Summer of a Forsyte *(1918),* In Chancery *(1920),* Awakening *(1920), and* To Let *(1921), which were collected as* The Forsyte Saga *(1922);* The White Monkey *(1924),* The Silver Spoon *(1926), and* Swan Song *(1928), which were collected as* A Modern Comedy *(1929); and* Maid in Waiting *(1931),* Flowering Wilderness *(1932), and* Over the River *(1933), which were posthumously collected as* End of the Chapter *(1934).*

I

SWITHIN FORSYTE LAY IN bed. The corners of his mouth under his white moustache drooped towards his double chin. He panted: "My doctor says I'm in a bad way, James."

92

His twin-brother placed his hand behind his ear. "I can't hear you. They tell me I ought to take a cure. There's always a cure wanted for something. Emily had a cure."

Swithin replied: "You mumble so. I hear my man, Adolph. I trained him.... You ought to have an ear-trumpet. You're getting very shaky, James."

There was silence; then James Forsyte, as if galvanized, remarked: "I s'pose you've made your will. I s'pose you've left your money to the family; you've nobody else to leave it to. There was Danson died the other day, and left his money to a hospital."

The hairs of Swithin's white moustache bristled. "My fool of a doctor told me to make my will," he said; "I hate a fellow who tells you to make your will. My appetite's good; I ate a partridge last night. I'm all the better for eating. He told me to leave off champagne! I eat a good breakfast. I'm not eighty. You're the same age, James. You look very shaky."

James Forsyte said: "You ought to have another opinion. Have Blank; he's the first man now. I had him for Emily; cost me two hundred guineas. He sent her to Homburg; that's the first place now. The prince was there—everybody goes there."

Swithin Forsyte answered: "I don't get any sleep at night, now I can't get out; and I've bought a new carriage—gave a pot of money for it. D'you ever have bronchitis? They tell me champagne's dangerous; it's my belief I couldn't take a better thing."

James Forsyte rose.

"You ought to have another opinion. Emily sent her love; she would have come in, but she had to go to Niagara. Everybody goes there; it's *the* place now. Rachael goes every morning; she overdoes it—she'll be laid up one of these days. There's a fancy ball there to-night; the Duke gives the prizes."

Swithin Forsyte said angrily: "I can't get things properly cooked here; at the club I get spinach decently done." The bed-clothes jerked at the tremor of his legs.

James Forsyte replied: "You must have done well with Tintos; you must have made a lot of money by them. Your ground-rents must be falling in, too. You must have any amount you don't know what to do with." He mouthed at the words, as if his lips were watering.

Swithin Forsyte glared. "Money!" he said; "my doctor's bill's enormous."

James Forsyte stretched out a cold, damp hand. "Good-bye! You ought to have another opinion. I can't keep the horses waiting: they're a new pair—stood me in three hundred. You ought to take care of yourself. I shall speak to Blank about you. You ought to have him—everybody says he's the first man. Good-bye!"

Swithin Forsyte continued to stare at the ceiling. He thought: "A poor thing, James! a selfish beggar! Must be worth a couple of hundred thousand!" He wheezed, meditating on life....

He was ill and lonely. For many years he had been lonely, and for two years ill; but as he had smoked his first cigar, so he would live his life—stoutly, to its predestined end. Every day he was driven to the club; sitting forward on the spring cushions of a single brougham, his hands on his knees, swaying a little, strangely solemn. He ascended the steps into that marble hall—the folds of his chin wedged into the aperture of his collar—walking squarely with a stick. Later he would dine, eating majestically, and savouring his food, behind a bottle of champagne set in an ice-pail—his waistcoat defended by a napkin, his eyes rolling a little or glued in a stare on the waiter. Never did he suffer his head or back to droop, for it was not distinguished so to do.

Because he was old and deaf, he spoke to no one; and no one spoke to him. The club gossip, an Irishman, said to each newcomer: "Old Forsyte! Look at 'um! Must ha' had something in his life to sour 'um!" But Swithin had had nothing in his life to sour him.

For many days now he had lain in bed in a room exuding silver, crimson, and electric light, and smelling of opopanax and of cigars. The curtains were drawn, the firelight gleamed: on a table by his bed were a jug of barley-water and *The Times*. He had made an attempt to read, failed, and fell again to thinking. His face with its square chin looked like a block of pale leather bedded in the pillow. It was lonely! A woman in the room would have made all the difference! Why had he never married? He breathed hard, staring frog-like at the ceiling; a memory had come into his mind. It was a long time ago—forty odd years—but it seemed like yesterday....

•

It happened when he was thirty-eight, for the first and only time in his life travelling on the Continent, with his twin-brother James and a man named Traquair. On the way from Germany to Venice, he had found himself at the Hôtel Goldene Alp at Salzburg. It was

late August, and weather for the gods: sunshine on the walls and
the shadows of the vine-leaves, and at night, the moonlight, and
again on the walls the shadows of the vine-leaves. Averse to the
suggestions of other people, Swithin had refused to visit the Citadel;
he had spent the day alone in the window of his bedroom, smoking
a succession of cigars, and disparaging the appearance of the passers-by. After dinner he was driven by boredom into the streets.
His chest puffed out like a pigeon's, and with something of a pigeon's cold and inquiring eye, he strutted, annoyed at the frequency
of uniforms, which seemed to him both needless and offensive. His
spleen rose at this crowd of foreigners who spoke an unintelligible
language, wore hair on their faces, and smoked bad tobacco. "A
queer lot!" he thought. The sound of music from a *café* attracted
him, he walked in, vaguely moved by a wish for the distinction of
adventure, without the trouble which adventure usually brought
with it; spurred too, perhaps, by an after-dinner demon. The *café*
was the *bier-halle* of the 'Fifties, with a door at either end, and lighted
by a large wooden lantern. On a small dais three musicians were
fiddling. Solitary men, or groups, sat at some dozen tables, and the
waiters hurried about replenishing glasses; the air was thick with
smoke. Swithin sat down. "Wine!" he said sternly. The astonished
waiter brought him wine. Swithin pointed to a beer-glass on the
table. "Here!" he said, with the same ferocity. The waiter poured
out the wine. "Ah!" thought Swithin, "they can understand if they
like." A group of officers close by were laughing; Swithin stared
at them uneasily. A hollow cough sounded almost in his ear. To
his left a man sat reading, with his elbows on the corners of a
journal, and his gaunt shoulders raised almost to his eyes. He had
a thin, long nose, broadening suddenly at the nostrils; a black-
brown beard, spread in a savage fan over his chest; what was visible
of the face was the colour of old parchment. A strange, wild,
haughty-looking creature! Swithin observed his clothes with some
displeasure—they were the clothes of a journalist or strolling actor.
And yet he was impressed. This was singular. How could he be
impressed by a fellow in such clothes! The man reached out a hand,
covered with black hairs, and took up a tumbler that contained a
dark-coloured fluid: "Brandy!" thought Swithin. The crash of a
falling chair startled him—his neighbour had risen. He was of
immense height, and very thin; his great beard seemed to splash
away from his mouth; he was glaring at the group of officers, and

speaking. Swithin made out two words: "*Hunde! Deutsche Hunde!*"
"Hounds! Dutch hounds!" he thought: "Rather strong!" One of
the officers had jumped up, and now drew his sword. The tall man
swung his chair up, and brought it down with a thud. Everybody
round started up and closed on him. The tall man cried out: "To
me, Magyars!"

Swithin grinned. The tall man fighting such odds excited his
unwilling admiration; he had a momentary impulse to go to his
assistance. "Only get a broken nose!" he thought, and looked for
a safe corner. But at that moment a thrown lemon struck him on
the jaw. He jumped out of his chair and rushed at the officers.
The Hungarian, swinging his chair, threw him a look of gratitude—
Swithin glowed with momentary admiration of himself. A sword
blade grazed his arm: he felt a sudden dislike of the Hungarian.
"This is too much," he thought, and, catching up a chair, flung it
at the wooden lantern. There was a crash—faces and swords vanished. He struck a match, and by the light of it bolted for the door.
A second later he was in the street.

II

A voice said in English, "God bless you, brother!"

Swithin looked round, and saw the tall Hungarian holding out
his hand. He took it, thinking, "What a fool I've been!" There was
something in the Hungarian's gesture which said, "You are worthy
of me!" It was annoying, but rather impressive. The man seemed
even taller than before; there was a cut on his cheek, the blood
from which was trickling down his beard. "You English!" he said.
"I saw you stone Haynau—I saw you cheer Kossuth. The free blood
of your people cries out to us." He looked at Swithin. "You are a
big man, you have a big soul—and strong, how you flung them
down! Ha!" Swithin had an impulse to take to his heels. "My name,"
said the Hungarian, "is Boleskey. You are my friend." His English
was good.

"Bulsh-kai-ee, Burlsh-kai-ee," thought Swithin; "what a devil of
a name!" "Mine," he said sulkily, "is Forsyte."

The Hungarian repeated it.

"You've had a nasty jab on the cheek," said Swithin; the sight of
the matted beard was making him feel sick. The Hungarian put
his fingers to his cheek, brought them away wet, stared at them,

then with an indifferent air gathered a wisp of his beard and crammed it against the cut.

"Ugh!" said Swithin. "Here! Take my handkerchief!"

The Hungarian bowed. "Thank you!" he said; "I couldn't think of it! Thank you a thousand times!"

"Take it!" growled Swithin; it seemed to him suddenly of the first importance. He thrust the handkerchief into the Hungarian's hand, and felt a pain in his arm. "There!" he thought, "I've strained a muscle."

The Hungarian kept muttering, regardless of passers-by, "Swine! How you threw them over! Two or three cracked heads, anyway— the cowardly swine!"

"Look here!" said Swithin suddenly; "which is my way to the Goldene Alp?"

The Hungarian replied, "But you are coming with me, for a glass of wine?"

Swithin looked at the ground. "Not if I know it!" he thought.

"Ah!" said the Hungarian with dignity, "you do not wish for my friendship!"

"Touchy beggar!" thought Swithin. "Of course," he stammered, "if you put it in that way——"

The Hungarian bowed, murmuring, "Forgive me!"

They had not gone a dozen steps before a youth, with a beardless face and hollow cheeks, accosted them. "For the love of Christ, gentlemen," he said, "help me!"

"Are you a German?" asked Boleskey.

"Yes," said the youth.

"Then you may rot!"

"Master, look here!" Tearing open his coat, the youth displayed his skin, and a leather belt drawn tight round it. Again Swithin felt that desire to take to his heels. He was filled with horrid forebodings—a sense of perpending intimacy with things such as no gentleman had dealings with.

The Hungarian crossed himself. "Brother," he said to the youth, "come you in!"

Swithin looked at them askance, and followed. By a dim light they groped their way up some stairs into a large room, into which the moon was shining through a window bulging over the street. A lamp burned low; there was a smell of spirits and tobacco, with a faint, peculiar scent, as of rose leaves. In one corner stood a czymbal, in another a great pile of newspapers. On the wall hung some old-fashioned pistols, and a rosary of yellow beads. Everything was tidily arranged, but dusty. Near an open fireplace was a table with the remains of a meal. The ceiling, floor, and walls were all of dark wood. In spite of the strange disharmony, the room had a sort of refinement.

The Hungarian took a bottle out of a cupboard and, filling some glasses, handed one to Swithin. Swithin put it gingerly to his nose. "You never know your luck! Come!" he thought, tilting it slowly into his mouth. It was thick, too sweet, but of a fine flavour.

"Brothers!" said the Hungarian, refilling, "your healths!"

The youth tossed off his wine. And Swithin this time did the same; he pitied this poor devil of a youth now. "Come round to-morrow!" he said, "I'll give you a shirt or two." When the youth was gone, however, he remembered with relief that he had not given his address.

"Better so," he reflected. "A humbug, no doubt."

"What was that you said to him?" he asked of the Hungarian.

"I said," answered Boleskey, "'You have eaten and drunk; and now you are my enemy!'"

"Quite right!" said Swithin, "quite right! A beggar is every man's enemy."

"You do not understand," the Hungarian replied politely. "While he was a beggar—I, too, have had to beg" (Swithin thought, "Good God! this is awful!"), "but now that he is no longer hungry, what is he but a German? No Austrian dog soils my floors!"

His nostrils, as it seemed to Swithin, had distended in an unpleasant fashion; and a wholly unnecessary raucousness invaded his voice. "I am an exile—all of my blood are exiles. Those Godless dogs!" Swithin hurriedly assented.

As he spoke, a face peeped in at the door.

"Rozsi!" said the Hungarian. A young girl came in. She was rather short, with a deliciously round figure and a thick plait of hair. She smiled, and showed her even teeth; her little, bright, wide-set grey eyes glanced from one man to the other. Her face was round, too, high in the cheek-bones, the colour of wild roses, with brows that had a twist-up at the corners. With a gesture of alarm, she put her hand to her cheek, and called, "Margit!" An older girl appeared, taller, with fine shoulders, large eyes, a pretty mouth, and what Swithin described to himself afterwards as a "pudding" nose. Both girls, with little cooing sounds, began attending to their father's face. Swithin turned his back to them. His arm pained him.

"This is what comes of interfering," he thought sulkily; "I might have had my neck broken!" Suddenly a soft palm was placed in his, two eyes, half-fascinated, half-shy, looked at him; then a voice called, "Rozsi!" the door was slammed, he was alone again with the Hungarian, harassed by a sense of soft disturbance.

"Your daughter's name is Rosy?" he said; "we have it in England—from rose, a flower."

"Rozsi (Rozgi)," the Hungarian replied; "your English is a hard tongue, harder than French, German, or Czechish, harder than Russian, or Roumanian—I know no more."

"What?" said Swithin, "six languages?" Privately he thought, "He knows how to lie, anyway."

"If you lived in a country like mine," muttered the Hungarian, "with all men's hands against you! A free people—dying—but not dead!"

Swithin could not imagine what he was talking of. This man's face, with its linen bandage, gloomy eyes, and great black wisps of beard, his fierce mutterings, and hollow cough, were all most unpleasant. He seemed to be suffering from some kind of mental dog-bite. His emotion indeed appeared so indecent, so uncontrolled and open, that its obvious sincerity produced a sort of awe in Swithin. It was like being forced to look into a furnace. Boleskey stopped roaming up and down. "You think it's over?" he said; "I tell you, in the breast of each one of us Magyars there is a hell. What is sweeter than life? What is more sacred than each breath we draw? Ah! my country!" These words were uttered so slowly, with such intense mournfulness, that Swithin's jaw relaxed; he converted the movement to a yawn.

"Tell me," said Boleskey, "what would you do if the French conquered you?"

Swithin smiled. Then suddenly, as though something had hurt him, he grunted, "The 'Froggies'? Let 'em try!"

"Drink!" said Boleskey—"there is nothing like it"; he filled Swithin's glass. "I will tell you my story."

Swithin rose hurriedly. "It's late," he said. "This is good stuff, though; have you much of it?"

"It is the last bottle."

"What?" said Swithin; "and you gave it to a beggar?"

"My name is Boleskey-Stefan," the Hungarian said, raising his head; "of the Komorn Boleskeys." The simplicity of this phrase— as who shall say: What need of further description?—made an impression on Swithin; he stopped to listen. Boleskey's story went on and on. "There were many abuses," boomed his deep voice, "much wrong done—much cowardice. I could see clouds gathering—rolling over our plains. The Austrian wished to strangle the breath of our mouths—to take from us the shadow of our liberty—the shadow—all we had. Two years ago—the year of '48, when every man and boy answered the great voice—brother, a dog's life!—to use a pen when all of your blood are fighting, but it was decreed for me! My son was killed; my brothers taken—and myself was thrown out like a dog—I had written out of my heart, I had written out all the blood that was in my body!" He seemed to tower, a gaunt shadow of a man, with gloomy, flickering eyes staring at the wall.

Swithin rose, and stammered, "Much obliged—very interesting." Boleskey made no effort to detain him, but continued staring at the wall. "Good-night!" said Swithin, and stamped heavily downstairs.

III

When at last Swithin reached the Goldene Alp, he found his brother and friend standing uneasily at the door. Traquair, a prematurely dried-up man, with whiskers and a Scotch accent, remarked, "Ye're airly, man!" Swithin growled something unintelligible, and swung up to bed. He discovered a slight cut on his arm. He was in a savage temper—the elements had conspired to show him things he did not want to see; yet now and then a memory of Rozsi, of her soft palm in his, a sense of having been stroked and flattered, came over him. During breakfast next morning his brother and Traquair announced their intention of moving on. James Forsyte, indeed, remarked that it was no place for a "collector," since all the "old" shops were in the hands of Jews or very grasping persons—he had discovered this at once. Swithin pushed his cup aside. *"You* may do what you like," he said, *"I'm* staying here."

James Forsyte replied, tumbling over his own words: "Why! what do you want to stay here for? There's nothing for you to do here—

there's nothing to see here, unless you go up the Citadel, an' you won't do that."

Swithin growled, "Who says so?" Having gratified his perversity, he felt in a better temper. He had slung his arm in a silk sash, and accounted for it by saying he had slipped. Later he went out and walked on to the bridge. In the brilliant sunshine spires were glistening against the pearly background of the hills; the town had a clean, joyous air. Swithin glanced at the Citadel and thought, "Looks a strong place! Shouldn't wonder if it were impregnable!" And this for some occult reason gave him pleasure. It occurred to him suddenly to go and look for the Hungarian's house.

About noon, after a hunt of two hours, he was gazing about him blankly, pale with heat, but more obstinate than ever, when a voice above him called "Mister!" He looked up and saw Rozsi. She was leaning her round chin on her round hand, gazing down at him with her deep-set, clever eyes. When Swithin removed his hat, she clapped her hands. Again he had the sense of being admired, caressed. With a careless air, that sat grotesquely on his tall square person, he walked up to the door; both girls stood in the passage. Swithin felt a confused desire to speak in some foreign tongue. "Maam'selles," he began, "er—*bong jour*—er your father—*père, comment?*"

"We also speak English," said the elder girl; "will you come in, please?"

Swithin swallowed a misgiving and entered. The room had a worn appearance by daylight, as if it had always been the nest of tragic or vivid lives. He sat down, and his eyes said: "I am a stranger, but don't try to get the better of me, please—that is impossible." The girls looked at him in silence. Rozsi wore a rather short skirt of black stuff, a white shirt, and across her shoulders an embroidered yoke; her sister was dressed in dark green, with a coral necklace; both girls had their hair in plaits. After a minute Rozsi touched the sleeve of his hurt arm.

"It's nothing!" muttered Swithin.

"Father fought with a chair, but you had no chair," she said in a wondering voice.

He doubled the fist of his sound arm and struck a blow at space. To his amazement she began to laugh. Nettled at this, he put his hand beneath the heavy table and lifted it. Rozsi clapped her hands. "Ah! now I see—how strong you are!" She made him a curtsey and whisked round to the window. He found the quick intelligence of her eyes confusing; sometimes they seemed to look beyond him at something invisible—this, too, confused him. From Margit he learned that they had been two years in England, where their father had made his living by teaching languages; they had now been a year in Salzburg.

"We wait," suddenly with Rozsi; and Margit, with a solemn face, repeated, "We wait."

Swithin's eyes swelled a little with his desire to see what they were waiting for. How queer they were, with their eyes that gazed beyond him! He looked at their figures. "She would pay for dressing," he thought, and he tried to imagine Rozsi in a skirt with proper flounces, a thin waist, and hair drawn back over her ears. She would pay for dressing, with that supple figure, fluffy hair, and little hands! And instantly his own hands, face, and clothes disturbed him. He got up, examined the pistols on the wall, and felt resentment at the faded, dusty room. "Smells like a pot-house!" he thought. He sat down again close to Rozsi.

"Do you love to dance?" she asked: "to dance is to live. First you hear the music—how your feet itch! It is wonderful! You begin slow, quick—quicker; you fly—you know nothing—your feet are in the air. It is wonderful!"

A slow flush had mounted into Swithin's face.

"Ah!" continued Rozsi, her eyes fixed on him, "when I am dancing—out there I see the plains—your feet go one—two—three—quick, quick, quick, quicker—you fly."

She stretched herself, a shiver seemed to pass all down her. "Margit! dance!" and, to Swithin's consternation, the two girls—their hands on each other's shoulders—began shuffling their feet and swaying to and fro. Their heads were thrown back, their eyes half-closed; suddenly the step quickened, they swung to one side, then to the other, and began whirling round in front of him. The sudden fragrance of rose leaves enveloped him. Round they flew again. While they were still dancing, Boleskey came into the room. He caught Swithin by both hands.

"Brother, welcome! Ah! your arm is hurt! I do not forget." His yellow face and deep-set eyes expressed a dignified gratitude. "Let me introduce to you my friend Baron Kasteliz."

Swithin bowed to a man with a small forehead, who had appeared softly, and stood with his gloved hands touching his waist. Swithin conceived a sudden aversion for this cat-like man. About Boleskey there was that which made contempt impossible—the sense of comradeship begotten in the fight; the man's height; something lofty and savage in his face; and an obscure instinct that it would not pay to show distaste; but this Kasteliz, with his neat jaw, low brow, and velvety, volcanic look, excited his proper English animosity. "Your friends are mine," murmured Kasteliz. He spoke with suavity, and hissed his s's. A long, vibrating twang quavered through the room. Swithin turned and saw Rozsi sitting at the czymbal; the notes rang under the little hammers in her hands, incessant, metallic, rising and falling with that strange melody. Kasteliz had fixed his glowing eyes on her; Boleskey, nodding his head, was staring at the floor; Margit, with a pale face, stood like a statue.

"What can they see in it?" thought Swithin; "it's not a tune." He took up his hat. Rozsi saw him and stopped; her lips had parted with a faintly dismayed expression. His sense of personal injury diminished; he even felt a little sorry for her. She jumped up from her seat and twirled round with a pout. An inspiration seized on Swithin. "Come and dine with me," he said to Boleskey, "tomorrow—the Goldene Alp—bring your friend." He felt the eyes of the whole room on him—the Hungarian's fine eyes; Margit's wide glance; the narrow, hot gaze of Kasteliz; and lastly—Rozsi's. A glow of satisfaction ran down his spine. When he emerged into the street he thought gloomily, "Now I've done it!" And not for some paces did he look round; then, with a forced smile, turned and removed his hat to the faces at the window.

Notwithstanding this moment of gloom, however, he was in an exalted state all day, and at dinner kept looking at his brother and Traquair enigmatically. "What do they know of life?" he thought; "they might be here a year and get no farther." He made jokes, and pinned the menu to the waiter's coat-tails. "I like this place," he said, "I shall spend three weeks here." James, whose lips were on the point of taking in a plum, looked at him uneasily.

IV

On the day of the dinner Swithin suffered a good deal. He reflected gloomily on Boleskey's clothes. He had fixed an early hour—there would be fewer people to see them. When the time approached he attired himself with a certain neat splendour, and though his arm was still sore, left off the sling....

Nearly three hours afterwards he left the Goldene Alp between his guests. It was sunset, and along the river-bank the houses stood out, unsoftened by the dusk; the streets were full of people hurrying home. Swithin had a hazy vision of empty bottles, of the ground before his feet, and the accessibility of all the world. Dim recollections of the good things he had said, of his brother and Traquair seated in the background eating ordinary meals with inquiring, acid visages, caused perpetual smiles to break out on his face, and he steered himself stubbornly, to prove that he was a better man than either of his guests. He knew, vaguely, that he was going somewhere with an object; Rozsi's face kept dancing before him, like a promise. Once or twice he gave Kasteliz a glassy stare. Towards Boleskey, on the other hand, he felt quite warm, and recalled with admiration the way he had set his glass down empty, time after time. "I like to see him take his liquor," he thought; "the fellow's a gentleman, after all."

Boleskey strode on, savagely inattentive to everything; and Kasteliz had become more like a cat than ever. It was nearly dark when they reached a narrow street close to the cathedral. They stopped at a door held open by an old woman. The change from the fresh air to a heated corridor, the noise of the door closed behind him, the old woman's anxious glances, sobered Swithin.

"I tell her," said Boleskey, "that I reply for you as for my son."

Swithin was angry. What business had this man to reply for him!

They passed into a large room, crowded with men and women; Swithin noticed that they all looked at him. He stared at them in turn—they seemed of all classes, some in black coats or silk dresses, others in the clothes of work-people; one man, a cobbler, still wore his leather apron, as if he had rushed there straight from his work. Laying his land on Swithin's arm, Boleskey evidently began explaining who he was; hands were extended, people beyond reach bowed to him. Swithin acknowledged the greetings with a stiff motion of his head; then seeing other people dropping into seats, he, too, sat down. Some one whispered his name—Margit and Rozsi were just behind him.

"Welcome!" said Margit; but Swithin was looking at Rozsi. Her face was so alive and quivering! "What's the excitement all about?" he thought. "How pretty she looks!" She blushed, drew in her hands with a quick tense movement, and gazed again beyond him in the room. "What is it?" thought Swithin; he had a longing to lean back and kiss her lips. He tried angrily to see what she was seeing in those faces turned all one way.

Boleskey rose to speak. No one moved; not a sound could be heard but the tone of his deep voice. On and on he went, fierce and solemn, and with the rise of his voice, all those faces—fair or swarthy—seemed to be glowing with one and the same feeling. Swithin felt the white heat in those faces—it was not decent! In that whole speech he only understood the one word—"Magyar"— which came again and again. He almost dozed off at last. The twang of a czymbal woke him. "What?" he thought, "more of that infernal music!" Margit, leaning over him, whispered: "Listen! Racoczy! it is forbidden!" Swithin saw that Rozsi was no longer in her seat; it was she who was striking those forbidden notes. He looked round— everywhere the same unmoving faces, the same entrancement, and fierce stillness. The music sounded muffled, as if it, too, were bursting its heart in silence. Swithin felt within him a touch of panic. Was this a den of tigers? The way these people listened, the ferocity of their stillness, was frightful!...He gripped his chair and broke into a perspiration; was there no chance to get away? "When it stops," he thought, "there'll be a rush!" But there was only a greater silence. It flashed across him that any hostile person coming in then would be torn to pieces. A woman sobbed. The whole thing was beyond words unpleasant. He rose, and edged his way furtively towards the doorway. There was a cry of "Police!" The whole crowd came pressing after him. Swithin would soon have been out, but a little behind he caught sight of Rozsi swept off her feet. Her frightened eyes angered him. "She doesn't deserve it," he thought sulkily; "letting all this loose!" and forced his way back to her. She clung to him, and a fever went stealing through his veins; he butted forward at the crowd, holding her tight. When they were outside he let her go.

"I was afraid," she said.

"Afraid!" muttered Swithin; "I should think so." No longer touching her, he felt his grievance revive.

"But you are so strong," she murmured.

"This is no place for you," growled Swithin. "I'm going to see you home."

"Oh!" cried Rozsi; "but papa and—Margit!"

"That's their lookout!" and he hurried her away.

She slid her hand under his arm; the soft curves of her form brushed him gently, each touch only augmented his ill-humour. He burned with a perverse rage, as if all the passions in him were simmering and ready to boil over; it was as if a poison were trying to work its way out of him through the layers of his stolid flesh. He maintained a dogged silence; Rozsi, too, said nothing, but when they reached the door, she drew her hand away.

"You are angry!" she said.

"Angry," muttered Swithin; "no! How d'you make that out?" He had a torturing desire to kiss her.

"Yes, you are angry," she repeated; "I wait here for papa and Margit."

Swithin also waited, wedged against the wall. Once or twice, for his sight was sharp, he saw her steal a look at him, a beseeching look, and hardened his heart with a kind of pleasure. After five minutes Boleskey, Margit, and Kasteliz appeared. Seeing Rozsi they broke into exclamations of relief, and Kasteliz, with a glance at Swithin, put his lips to her hand. Rozsi's look said, "Wouldn't you like to do that?" Swithin turned short on his heel, and walked away.

V

All night he hardly slept, suffering from fever, for the first time in his life. Once he jumped out of bed, lighted a candle, and going to the glass, scrutinised himself long and anxiously. After this he fell asleep, but had frightful dreams. His first thought when he woke was, "My liver's out of order!" and, thrusting his head into cold water, he dressed hastily and went out. He soon left the house behind. Dew covered everything; blackbirds whistled in the bushes, the air was fresh and sweet. He had not been up so early since he was a boy. Why was he walking through a damp wood at this hour of the morning? Something intolerable and unfamiliar must have sent him out. No fellow in his senses would do such a thing! He came to a dead stop, and began unsteadily to walk back. Regaining the hotel, he went to bed again, and dreamed that in some wild country he was living in a room full of insects, where a housemaid— Rozsi—holding a broom, looked at him with mournful eyes. There seemed an unexplained need for immediate departure; he begged her to forward his things, and shake them out carefully before she put them into the trunk. He understood that the charge for sending

would be twenty-two shillings, thought it a great deal, and had the
horrors of indecision. "No," he muttered, "pack, and take them
myself." The housemaid turned suddenly into a lean creature; and
he awoke with a sore feeling in his heart.

His eye fell on his wet boots. The whole thing was scaring, and
jumping up, he began to throw his clothes into his trunks. It was
twelve o'clock before he went down, and found his brother and
Traquair still at the table arranging an itinerary; he surprised them
by saying that he too was coming; and without further explanation
set to work to eat. James had heard that there were salt-mines in
the neighbourhood—his proposal was to start, and halt an hour
or so on the road for their inspection: he said: "Everybody'll ask
you if you've seen the salt-mines: I shouldn't like to say I hadn't
seen the salt-mines. What's the good, they'd say, of your going
there if you haven't seen the salt-mines?" He wondered, too, if they
need fee the second waiter—an idle chap!

A discussion followed; but Swithin ate on glumly, conscious that
his mind was set on larger affairs. Suddenly on the far side of the
street Rozsi and her sister passed, with little baskets on their arms.
He started up, and at that moment Rozsi looked round—her face
was the incarnation of enticement, the chin tilted, the lower lip
thrust a little forward, her round neck curving back over her shoulder. Swithin muttered, "Make your own arrangements—leave me
out!" and hurried from the room, leaving James beside himself
with interest and alarm.

When he reached the street, however, the girls had disappeared.
He hailed a carriage. "Drive!" he called to the man, with a flourish
of his stick, and as soon as the wheels had begun to clatter on the
stones he leaned back, looking sharply to right and left. He soon
had to give up thought of finding them, but made the coachman
turn round and round again. All day he drove about, far into the
country, and kept urging the driver to use greater speed. He was
in a strange state of hurry and elation. Finally, he dined at a little
country inn; and this gave the measure of his disturbance—the
dinner was atrocious.

Returning late in the evening he found a note written by Traquair. "Are you in your senses, man?" it asked; "we have no more
time to waste idling about here. If you want to rejoin us, come on
to Danielli's Hotel, Venice." Swithin chuckled when he read it, and
feeling frightfully tired, went to bed and slept like a log.

VI

Three weeks later he was still in Salzburg, no longer at the Gold-ene Alp, but in rooms over a shop near the Boleskeys'. He had spent a small fortune in the purchase of flowers. Margit would croon over them, but Rozsi, with a sober "Many tanks!" as if they were her right, would look long at herself in the glass, and pin one into her hair. Swithin ceased to wonder; he ceased to wonder at anything they did. One evening he found Boleskey deep in con-versation with a pale, dishevelled-looking person.

"Our friend Mr. Forsyte—Count D——," said Boleskey.

Swithin experienced a faint, unavoidable emotion; but looking at the Count's trousers, he thought: "Doesn't look much like one!" And with an ironic bow to the silent girls, he turned, and took his hat. But when he had reached the bottom of the dark stairs he heard footsteps. Rozsi came running down, looked out at the door, and put her hands up to her breast as if disappointed: suddenly with a quick glance round she saw him. Swithin caught her arm. She slipped away, and her face seemed to bubble with defiance or laughter; she ran up three steps, looked at him across her shoulder, and fled on up the stairs. Swithin went out bewildered and annoyed.

"What was she going to say to me?" he kept thinking. During these three weeks he had asked himself all sorts of questions: whether he were being made a fool of; whether she were in love with him; what he was doing there, and sometimes at night, with all his candles burning as if he wanted light, the breeze blowing on him through the window, his cigar, half-smoked, in his hand, he sat, an hour or more, staring at the wall. "Enough of this!" he thought every morn-ing. Twice he packed fully—once he ordered his travelling car-riage, but countermanded it the following day. What definitely he hoped, intended, resolved, he could not have said. He was always thinking of Rozsi, he could not read the riddle in her face—she held him in a vice, notwithstanding that everything about her threatened the very fetishes of his existence. And Boleskey! When-ever he looked at him he thought, "If he were only clean?" and mechanically fingered his own well-tied cravate. To talk with the fellow, too, was like being forced to look at things which had no place in the light of day. Freedom, equality, self-sacrifice!

"Why can't he settle down at some business," he thought, "instead of all this talk?" Boleskey's sudden diffidences, self-depreciation, fits of despair, irritated him. "Morbid beggar!" he would mutter; "thank God *I* haven't a thin skin." And proud too! Extraordinary! An impecunious fellow like that! One evening, moreover, Boleskey had returned home drunk. Swithin had hustled him away into his bedroom, helped him to undress, and stayed until he was asleep. "Too much of a good thing!" he thought, "before his own daughters, too!" It was after this that he ordered his travelling carriage. The other occasion on which he packed was one evening, when not only Boleskey, but Rozsi herself had picked chicken bones with her fingers.

Often in the mornings he would go to the Mirabell Garden to smoke his cigar; there, in stolid contemplation of the statues—rows of half-heroic men carrying off half-distressed females—he would spend an hour pleasantly, his hat tilted to keep the sun off his nose. The day after Rozsi had fled from him on the stairs, he came there as usual. It was a morning of blue sky and sunlight glowing on the old prim garden, on its yew-trees, and serio-comic statues, and walls covered with apricots and plums. When Swithin approached his usual seat, who should be sitting there but Rozsi!

"Good-morning," he stammered; "you knew this was my seat then?"

Rozsi looked at the ground. "Yes," she answered.

Swithin felt bewildered. "Do you know," he said, "you treat me very funnily?"

To his surprise Rozsi put her little soft hand down and touched his; then, without a word, sprang up and rushed away. It took him a minute to recover. There were people present; he did not like to run, but overtook her on the bridge, and slipped her hand beneath his arm.

"You shouldn't have done that," he said; "you shouldn't have run away from me, you know."

Rozsi laughed. Swithin withdrew his arm; a desire to shake her seized him. He walked some way before he said, "Will you have the goodness to tell me what you came to that seat for?"

Rozsi flashed a look at him. "To-morrow is the *fête*," she answered.

Swithin muttered, "Is that all?"

"If you do not take us, we cannot go."

"Suppose I refuse," he said sullenly, "there are plenty of others."

Rozsi bent her head, scurrying along. "No," she murmured, "if *you* do not go—I do not wish."

Swithin drew her hand back within his arm. How round and soft it was! He tried to see her face. When she was nearly home he said good-bye, not wishing, for some dark reason, to be seen with her. He watched till she had disappeared; then slowly retraced his steps to the Mirabell Garden. When he came to where she had been sitting, he slowly lighted his cigar, and for a long time after it was smoked out remained there in the silent presence of the statues.

VII

A crowd of people wandered round the booths, and Swithin found himself obliged to give the girls his arms. "Like a little Cockney clerk!" he thought. His indignation passed unnoticed; they talked, they laughed, each sight and sound in all the hurly-burly seemed to go straight into their hearts. He eyed them ironically— their eager voices, and little coos of sympathy seemed to him vulgar. In the thick of the crowd he slipped his arm out of Margit's, but, just as he thought that he was free, the unwelcome hand slid up again. He tried again, but again Margit reappeared, serene, and full of pleasant humour; and his failure this time appeared to him in a comic light. But when Rozsi leaned across him, the glow of her round cheek, her curving lip, the inscrutable grey gleam of her eyes, sent a thrill of longing through him. He was obliged to stand by while they parleyed with a gipsy, whose matted locks and skinny hands inspired him with a not unwarranted disgust. "Folly!" he muttered, as Rozsi held out her palm. The old woman mumbled, and shot a malignant look at him. Rozsi drew back her hand, and crossed herself. "Folly!" Swithin thought again; and seizing the girls' arms, he hurried them away.

"What did the old hag say?" he asked.

Rozsi shook her head.

"You don't mean that you believe?"

Her eyes were full of tears. "The gipsies are wise," she murmured.

"Come, what did she tell you?"

This time Rozsi looked hurriedly round, and slipped away into the crowd. After a hunt they found her, and Swithin, who was scared, growled: "You shouldn't do such things—it's not respectable."

On higher ground, in the centre of a clear space, a military band was playing. For the privilege of entering this charmed circle Swithin paid three *kronen,* choosing naturally the best seats. He ordered wine, too, watching Rozsi out of the corner of his eye as he poured it out. The protecting tenderness of yesterday was all lost in this medley. It was every man for himself, after all! The colour had deepened again in her cheeks, she laughed, pouting her lips. Suddenly she put her glass aside. "Thank you, very much," she said, "it is enough!"

Margit, whose pretty mouth was all smiles, cried, *"Lieber Gott!* is it not good—life?" It was not a question Swithin could undertake to answer. The band began to play a waltz. "Now they will dance. *Lieber Gott!* and are the lights not wonderful?" Lamps were flickering beneath the trees like a swarm of fireflies. There was a hum as from a gigantic beehive. Passers-by lifted their faces, then vanished into the crowd; Rozsi stood gazing at them spell-bound, as if their very going and coming were a delight.

The space was soon full of whirling couples. Rozsi's head began to beat time. "O Margit!" she whispered.

Swithin's face had assumed a solemn, uneasy expression. A man, raising his hat, offered his arm to Margit. She glanced back across her shoulder to reassure Swithin. "It is a friend," she said.

Swithin looked at Rozsi—her eyes were bright, her lips tremulous. He slipped his hand along the table and touched her fingers. Then she flashed a look at him—appeal, reproach, tenderness, all were expressed in it. Was she expecting him to dance? Did she want to mix with the riff-raff there; wish *him* to make an exhibition of himself in this hurly-burly? A voice said, "Good-evening!" Before them stood Kasteliz, in a dark coat tightly buttoned at the waist.

"You are not dancing, *Rozsi Kozsanony?"* (Miss Rozsi). "Let me, then, have the pleasure." He held out his arm. Swithin stared in front of him. In the very act of going she gave him a look that said as plain as words: "Will you not?" But for answer he turned his eyes away, and when he looked again she was gone. He paid the score and made his way into the crowd. But as he went she danced by close to him, all flushed and panting. She hung back as if to stop him, and he caught the glistening of tears. Then he lost sight of her again. To be deserted the first minute he was alone with her, and for that jackanapes with the small head and volcanic glances! It was too much! And suddenly it occurred to him that she was alone with Kasteliz—alone at night, and far from home. "Well," he thought, "what do I care?" and shouldered his way on through the crowd. It served him right for mixing with such people here. He left the fair, but the further he went, the more he nursed his rage, the more heinous seemed her offence, the sharper grew his jealousy. "A beggarly baron!" was his thought.

A figure came alongside—it was Boleskey. One look showed Swithin his condition. Drunk again! This was the last straw!

Unfortunately Boleskey had recognised him. He seemed violently excited. "Where—where are my daughters?" he began.

Swithin brushed past, but Boleskey caught his arm. "Listen—brother!" he said; "news of my country! After to-morrow——"

"Keep it to yourself!" growled Swithin, wrenching his arm free. He went straight to his lodgings, and, lying on the hard sofa of his unlighted sitting-room, gave himself up to bitter thoughts. But in spite of all his anger, Rozsi's supple-moving figure, with its pouting lips, and roguish appealing eyes, still haunted him.

VIII

Next morning there was not a carriage to be had, and Swithin was compelled to put off his departure till the morrow. The day was grey and misty; he wandered about with the strained, inquiring look of a lost dog in his eyes.

Late in the afternoon he went back to his lodgings. In a corner of the sitting-room stood Rozsi. The thrill of triumph, the sense of appeasement, the emotion, that seized on him, crept through to his lips in a faint smile. Rozsi made no sound, her face was hidden by her hands. And this silence of hers weighed on Swithin. She was forcing him to break it. What was behind her hands? His own face was visible! Why didn't she speak? Why was she here? Alone? That was not right surely.

Suddenly Rozsi dropped her hands; her flushed face was quivering—it seemed as though a word, a sign, even, might bring a burst of tears.

He walked over to the window. "I must give her time!" he thought;

then seized by unreasoning terror at this silence, spun around, and caught her by the arms. Rozsi held back from him, swayed forward and buried her face on his breast....

Half an hour later Swithin was pacing up and down his room. The scent of rose leaves had not yet died away. A glove lay on the floor; he picked it up, and for a long time stood weighing it in his hand. All sorts of confused thoughts and feelings haunted him. It was the purest and least selfish moment of his life, this moment after she had yielded. But that pure gratitude at her fiery, simple abnegation did not last; it was followed by a petty sense of triumph, and by uneasiness. He was still weighing the little glove in his hand, when he had another visitor. It was Kasteliz.

"What can I do for you?" Swithin asked ironically.

The Hungarian seemed suffering from excitement. Why had Swithin left his charges the night before? What excuse had he to make? What sort of conduct did he call this?

Swithin, very like a bull-dog at that moment, answered: What business was it of his?

The business of a gentleman! What right had the Englishman to pursue a young girl?

"Pursue?" said Swithin; "you've been spying, then?"

"Spying—I—Kasteliz—Maurus Johann—an insult!"

"Insult!" sneered Swithin; "d'you mean to tell me you weren't in the street just now?"

Kasteliz answered with a hiss, "If you do not leave the city I will make you, with my sword—do you understand?"

"And if you do not leave my room I will throw you out of the window!"

For some minutes Kasteliz spoke in pure Hungarian while Swithin waited, with a forced smile and a fixed look in his eye. He did not understand Hungarian.

"If you are still in the city to-morrow evening," said Kasteliz at last in English, "I will spit you in the street."

Swithin turned to the window and watched his visitor's retiring back with a queer mixture of amusement, stubbornness, and anxiety. "Well," he thought, "I suppose he'll run me through!" The thought was unpleasant; and it kept recurring, but it only served to harden his determination. His head was busy with plans for seeing Rozsi; his blood on fire with the kisses she had given him.

IX

Swithin was long in deciding to go forth next day. He had made up his mind not to go to Rozsi till five o'clock. "Mustn't make myself too cheap," he thought. It was a little past that hour when he at last sallied out, and with a beating heart walked towards Boleskey's. He looked up at the window, more than half expecting to see Rozsi there; but she was not, and he noticed with faint surprise that the window was not open; the plants, too, outside, looked singularly arid. He knocked. No one came. He beat a fierce tattoo. At last the door was opened by a man with a reddish beard, and one of those sardonic faces only to be seen on shoemakers of Teutonic origin.

"What do you want, making all this noise?" he asked in German.

Swithin pointed up the stairs. The man grinned, and shook his head.

"I want to go up," said Swithin.

The cobbler shrugged his shoulders, and Swithin rushed up-stairs. The rooms were empty. The furniture remained, but all signs of life were gone. One of his own bouquets, faded, stood in a glass; the ashes of a fire were barely cold; little scraps of paper strewed the hearth; already the room smelt musty. He went into the bedrooms, and with a feeling of stupefaction stood staring at the girls' beds, side by side against the wall. A bit of ribbon caught his eye; he picked it up and put it in his pocket—it was a piece of evidence that she had once existed. By the mirror some pins were dropped about; a little powder had been spilled. He looked at his own disquiet face and thought, "I've been cheated!"

The shoemaker's voice aroused him. "*Tausend Teufel! Eilen Sie, nur! Zeit is Geld! Kann nich' länger warten!*" Slowly he descended.

"Where have they gone?" asked Swithin painfully. "A pound for every English word you speak. A pound!" and he made an O with his fingers.

The corners of the shoemaker's lips curled. "*Geld! Mff! Eilen Sie, nur!*"

But in Swithin a sullen anger had begun to burn. "If you don't tell me," he said, "it'll be the worse for you."

"*Sind ein komischer Kerl!*" remarked the shoemaker. "*Hier ist meine Frau!*"

A battered-looking woman came hurrying down the passage, calling out in German, "Don't let him go!"

With a snarling sound the shoemaker turned his back, and shambled off.

The woman furtively thrust a letter into Swithin's hand, and furtively waited.

The letter was from Rozsi.

> "Forgive me"—it ran—"that I leave you and do not say good-bye. To-day our father had the call from our dear Father-town so long awaited. In two hours we are ready. I pray to the Virgin to keep you ever safe, and that you do not quite forget me.— Your unforgetting good friend,
>
> ROZSI."

When Swithin read it his first sensation was that of a man sinking in a bog; then his obstinacy stiffened. "I won't be done," he thought. Taking out a sovereign he tried to make the woman comprehend that she could earn it, by telling him where they had gone. He got her finally to write the words out in his pocket-book, gave her the sovereign, and hurried to the Goldene Alp, where there was a waiter who spoke English.

The translation given him was this:

"At three o'clock they start in a carriage on the road to Linz— they have bad horses—the Herr also rides a white horse."

Swithin at once hailed a carriage and started at full gallop on the road to Linz. Outside the Mirabell Garden he caught sight of Kasteliz and grinned at him. "I've sold *him* anyway," he thought; "for all their talk, they're no good, these foreigners!"

His spirits rose, but soon fell again. What chance had he of catching them? They had three hours' start! Still, the roads were heavy from the rain of the last two nights—they had luggage and bad horses; his own were good, his driver bribed—he might overtake them by ten o'clock! But did he want to? What a fool he had been not to bring his luggage; he would then have had a respectable position. What a brute he would look without a change of shirt, or anything to shave with! He saw himself with horror, all bristly, and in soiled linen. People would think him mad. "I've given myself away," flashed across him, "what the devil can I say to them?" and he stared sullenly at the driver's back. He read Rozsi's letter again;

it had a scent of her. And in the growing darkness, jolted by the swinging of the carriage, he suffered tortures from his prudence, tortures from his passion.

It grew colder and dark. He turned the collar of his coat up to his ears. He had visions of Piccadilly. This wild-goose chase appeared suddenly a dangerous, unfathomable business. Lights, fellowship, security! "Never again!" he brooded; "why won't they let me alone?" But it was not clear whether by "they" he meant the conventions, the Boleskeys, his passions, or those haunting memories of Rozsi. If he had only had a bag with him! What was he going to say? What was he going to get by this? He received no answer to these questions. The darkness itself was less obscure than his sensations. From time to time he took out his watch. At each village the driver made inquiries. It was past ten when he stopped the carriage with a jerk. The stars were bright as steel, and by the side of the road a reedy lake showed in the moonlight. Swithin shivered. A man on a horse had halted in the centre of the road. "Drive on!" called Swithin, with a stolid face. It turned out to be Boleskey, who, on a gaunt white horse, looked like some winged creature. He stood where he could bar the progress of the carriage, holding out a pistol.

"Theatrical beggar!" thought Swithin, with a nervous smile. He made no sign of recognition. Slowly Boleskey brought his lean horse up to the carriage. When he saw who was within he showed astonishment and joy.

"You?" he cried, slapping his hand on his attenuated thigh, and leaning over till his beard touched Swithin. "You have come? You followed us?"

"It seems so," Swithin grunted out.

"You throw in your lot with us. Is it possible? You—you are a knight-errant then!"

"Good God!" said Swithin. Boleskey, flogging his dejected steed, cantered forward in the moonlight. He came back, bringing an old cloak, which he insisted on wrapping round Swithin's shoulders. He handed him, too, a capacious flask.

"How cold you look!" he said. "Wonderful! Wonderful! you English!" His grateful eyes never left Swithin for a moment. They had come up to the heels of the other carriage now, but Swithin, hunched in the cloak, did not try to see what was in front of him. To the bottom of his soul he resented the Hungarian's gratitude. He remarked at last, with wasted irony:

"You're in a hurry, it seems!"

"If we had wings," Boleskey answered, "we would use them."

"Wings!" muttered Swithin thickly; "legs are good enough for me."

X

Arrived at the inn where they were to pass the night, Swithin waited, hoping to get into the house without a "scene," but when at last he alighted the girls were in the doorway, and Margit greeted him with an admiring murmur, in which, however, he seemed to detect irony. Rozsi, pale and tremulous, with a half-scared look, gave him her hand, and, quickly withdrawing it, shrank behind her sister. When they had gone up to their room Swithin sought Boleskey. His spirits had risen remarkably. "Tell the landlord to get us supper," he said; "we'll crack a bottle to our luck." He hurried on the landlord's preparations. The window of the room faced a wood, so near that he could almost touch the trees. The scent from the pines blew in on him. He turned away from that scented darkness, and began to draw the corks of wine-bottles. The sound seemed to conjure up Boleskey. He came in, splashed all over, smelling slightly of stables; soon after, Margit appeared, fresh and serene, but Rozsi did not come.

"Where is your sister?" Swithin said. Rozsi, it seemed, was tired. "It will do her good to eat," said Swithin. And Boleskey, murmuring, "She must drink to our country," went out to summon her, Margit followed him, while Swithin cut up a chicken. They came back without her. She had "a megrim of the spirit."

Swithin's face fell. "Look here!" he said, "*I'll* go and try. Don't wait for me."

"Yes," answered Boleskey, sinking mournfully into a chair; "try, brother, try—by all means, try."

Swithin walked down the corridor with an odd, sweet, sinking sensation in his chest; and tapped on Rozsi's door. In a minute, she peeped forth, with her hair loose, and wondering eyes.

"Rozsi," he stammered, "what makes you afraid of me, *now?*"

She stared at him, but did not answer.

"Why won't you come?"

Still she did not speak, but suddenly stretched out to him her bare arm. Swithin pressed his face to it. With a shiver, she whispered above him, "I will come," and gently shut the door.

Swithin stealthily retraced his steps, and paused a minute outside the sitting-room to regain his self-control.

The sight of Boleskey with a bottle in his hand steadied him.

"She is coming," he said. And very soon she did come, her thick hair roughly twisted in a plait.

Swithin sat between the girls; but did not talk, for he was really hungry. Boleskey too was silent, plunged in gloom; Rozsi was dumb; Margit alone chattered.

"You will come to our Father-town? We shall have things to show you. Rozsi, what things we will show him!" Rozsi, with a little appealing movement of her hands, repeated, "What things we will show you!" She seemed suddenly to find her voice, and with glowing cheeks, mouth full, and eyes bright as squirrels, they chattered reminiscences of the "dear Father-town," of "dear friends," of the "dear home."

"A poor place!" Swithin could not help thinking. This enthusiasm seemed to him common; but he was careful to assume a look of interest, feeding on the glances flashed at him from Rozsi's restless eyes.

As the wine waned Boleskey grew more and more gloomy, but now and then a sort of gleaming flicker passed over his face. He rose to his feet at last.

"Let us not forget," he said, "that we go perhaps to ruin, to death; in the face of all this we go, because our country needs— in this there is no credit, neither to me not to you, my daughters; but for this noble Englishman, what shall we say? Give thanks to God for a great heart. He comes—not for country, not for fame, not for money, but to help the weak and the oppressed. Let us drink, then, to him; let us drink again and again to heroic Forsyte!" In the midst of the dead silence, Swithin caught the look of suppliant mockery in Rozsi's eyes. He glanced at the Hungarian. Was he laughing at him? But Boleskey, after drinking up his wine, had sunk again into his seat; and there suddenly, to the surprise of all, he began to snore. Margit rose and, bending over him like a mother, murmured: "He is tired—it is the ride!" She raised him in her strong arms, and leaning on her shoulder Boleskey staggered from the room. Swithin and Rozsi were left alone. He slid his hand towards her hand that lay so close, on the rough tablecloth. It seemed to await his touch. Something gave way in him, and words came welling up; for the moment he forgot himself, forgot everything but that he was near her. Her head dropped on his shoulder, he breathed the perfume of her hair. "Good-night!" she whispered, and the whisper was like a kiss; yet before he could stop her she was gone. Her footsteps died away in the passage, but Swithin sat gazing intently at a single bright drop of spilt wine quivering on the table's edge. In that moment she, in her helplessness and emotion, was all in all to him—his life nothing; all the real things— his conventions, convictions, training, and himself—all seemed remote, behind a mist of passion and strange chivalry. Carefully with a bit of bread he soaked up the bright drop; and suddenly, he thought: "This is tremendous!" For a long time he stood there in the window, close to the dark pine-trees.

XI

In the early morning he awoke, full of the discomfort of this strange place and the medley of his dreams. Lying, with his nose peeping over the quilt, he was visited by a horrible suspicion. When he could bear it no longer, he started up in bed. What if it were all a plot to get him to marry her? The thought was treacherous, and inspired in him a faint disgust. Still, *she* might be ignorant of it! But she was so innocent? What innocent girl would have come to his room like that? What innocent girl? Her father, who pretended to be caring only for his country? It was not probable that any man was such a fool; it was all part of the game—a scheming rascal! Kasteliz, too—his threats! They intended him to marry her? And the horrid idea was strengthened by his reverence for marriage. It was the proper, the respectable condition; he was genuinely afraid of this other sort of *liaison*—it was somehow too primitive! And yet the thought of that marriage made his blood run cold. Considering that she had already yielded, it would be all the more monstrous! With the cold, fatal clearness of the morning light he now for the first time saw his position in its full bearings. And, like a fish pulled out of water, he gasped at what was disclosed. Sullen resentment against this attempt to force him settled deep into his soul.

He seated himself on the bed, holding his head in his hands, solemnly thinking out what such marriage meant. In the first place it meant ridicule, in the next place ridicule, in the last place ridicule. She would eat chicken bones with her fingers—those fingers his lips still burned to kiss. She would dance wildly with other men. She would talk of her "dear Father-town," and all the time her eyes would look beyond him, somewhere or other into some d——d place he knew nothing of. He sprang up and paced the room, and for a moment thought he would go mad.

They meant him to marry her! Even she—she meant him to marry her! Her tantalising inscrutability; her sudden little tendernesses; her quick laughter; her swift, burning kisses; even the movements of her hands; her tears—all were evidence against her. Not one of these things that Nature made her do counted on her side, but how they fanned his longing, his desire, and distress. He went to the glass and tried to part his hair with his fingers, but being rather fine, it fell into lank streaks. There was no comfort to be got from it. He drew his muddy boots on. Suddenly he thought: "If I could see her alone, I could arrive at some arrangement!" Then, with a sense of stupefaction, he made the discovery that no arrangement could possibly be made that would not be dangerous, even desperate. He seized his hat, and, like a rabbit that has been fired at, bolted from the room. He plodded along amongst the damp woods with his head down, and resentment and dismay in his heart. But, as the sun rose, and the air grew sweet with pine scent, he slowly regained a sort of equability. After all, she had already yielded; it was not as if——! And the tramp of his own footsteps lulled him into feeling that it would all come right. "Look at the thing practically," thought. The faster he walked the firmer became his conviction that he could still see it through. He took out his watch—it was past seven—he began to hasten back. In the yard of the inn his driver was harnessing the horses; Swithin went up to him.

"Who told you to put them in?" he asked.

The driver answered, "*Der Herr.*"

Swithin turned away. "In ten minutes," he thought, "I shall be in that carriage again, with this going on in my head! Driving away from England, from all I'm used to—driving to—what?" Could he face it? Could he face all that he had been through that morning; face it day after day, night after night? Looking up, he saw Rozsi at her open window gazing down at him; never had she looked sweeter, more roguish. An inexplicable terror seized on him; he ran across the yard and jumped into his carriage. "To Salzburg!" he cried; "drive on!" And rattling out of the yard without a look behind, he flung a sovereign at the hostler. Flying back along the road faster even than he had come, with pale face, and eyes blank and staring like a pug-dog's, Swithin spoke no single word; nor, till he had reached the door of his lodgings, did he suffer the driver to draw rein.

XII

Towards evening, five days later, Swithin, yellow and travel-worn, was ferried in a gondola to Danielli's Hotel. His brother, who was on the steps, looked at him with an apprehensive curiosity.

"Why, it's you!" he mumbled. "So you've got here safe?"

"Safe?" growled Swithin.

James replied, "I thought you wouldn't leave your friends!" Then, with a jerk of suspicion, "You haven't brought your friends?"

"What friends?" growled Swithin.

James changed the subject. "You don't look the thing," he said.

"Really!" muttered Swithin; "what's that to you?"

He appeared at dinner that night, but fell asleep over his coffee. Neither Traquair nor James asked him any further question, nor did they allude to Salzburg; and during the four days which con-cluded the stay in Venice Swithin went about with his head up, but his eyes half-closed like a dazed man. Only after they had taken ship at Genoa did he show signs of any healthy interest in life, when, finding that a man on board was perpetually strumming, he locked the piano up and pitched the key into the sea.

That winter in London he behaved much as usual, but fits of moroseness would seize on him, during which he was not pleasant to approach.

One evening when he was walking with a friend in Piccadilly, a girl coming from a side-street accosted him in German. Swithin, after staring at her in silence for some seconds, handed her a five-pound note, to the great amazement of his friend; nor could he himself have explained the meaning of this freak of generosity.

Of Rozsi he never heard again....

•

This, then, was the substance of what he remembered as he lay ill in bed. Stretching out his hand he pressed the bell. His valet appeared, crossing the room like a cat; a Swede, who had been with Swithin many years; a little man with a dried face and fierce moustache, morbidly sharp nerves, and a queer devotion to his master.

Swithin made a feeble gesture. "Adolf," he said, "I'm very bad."

"Yes, sir!"

"Why do you stand there like a cow?" asked Swithin; "can't you see I'm very bad?"

"Yes, sir!" The valet's face twitched as though it masked the dance of obscure emotions.

"I shall feel better after dinner. What time is it?"

"Five o'clock."

"I thought it was more. The afternoons are very long."

"Yes, sir!"

Swithin sighed, as though he had expected the consolation of denial.

"Very likely I shall have a nap. Bring up hot water at half-past six and shave me before dinner."

The valet moved towards the door. Swithin raised himself.

"What did Mr. James say to you!"

"He said you ought to have another doctor; two doctors, he said, better than one. He said, also, he would look in again on his way 'home.'"

Swithin grunted, "Umph! What else did he say?"

"He said you didn't take care of yourself."

Swithin glared.

"Has anybody else been to see me?"

The valet turned away his eyes. "Mrs. Thomas Forsyte came last Monday fortnight."

"How long have I been ill?"

"Five weeks on Saturday."

"Do you think I'm very bad?"

Adolf's face was covered suddenly with crow's-feet. "You have no business to ask me question like that! I am not paid, sir, to answer question like that."

Swithin said faintly: "You're a peppery fool! Open a bottle of champagne!"

Adolf took a bottle of champagne from a cupboard and held nippers to it. He fixed his eyes on Swithin. "The doctor said——"

"Open the bottle!"

"It is not——"

"Open the bottle—or I give you warning."

Adolf removed the cork. He wiped a glass elaborately, filled it, and bore it scrupulously to the bedside. Suddenly twirling his moustaches, he wrung his hands, and burst out: "It is poison."

Swithin grinned faintly. "You foreign fool!" he said. "Get out!" The valet vanished.

"He forgot himself!" thought Swithin. Slowly he raised the glass, slowly put it back, and sank gasping on his pillows. Almost at once he fell asleep.

He dreamed that he was at his club, sitting after dinner in the crowded smoking-room, with its bright walls and trefoils of light. It was there that he sat every evening, patient, solemn, lonely, and sometimes fell asleep, his square, pale old face nodding to one side. He dreamed that he was gazing at the picture over the fireplace, of an old statesman with a high collar, supremely finished face, and sceptical eyebrows—the picture, smooth, and reticent as sealing-wax, of one who seemed for ever exhaling the narrow wisdom of final judgments. All round him, his fellow-members were chattering. Only he himself, the old sick member, was silent. If fellows only knew what it was like to sit by yourself and feel ill all the time! What they were saying he had heard a hundred times. They were talking of investments, of cigars, horses, actresses, machinery. What was that? A foreign patent for cleaning boilers? There was no such thing; boilers couldn't be cleaned, any fool knew that! If an Englishman couldn't clean a boiler, no foreigner could clean one. He appealed to the old statesman's eyes. But for once those eyes seemed hesitating, blurred, wanting in finality. They vanished. In their place were Rozsi's little deep-set eyes, with their wide and far-off look; and as he gazed they seemed to grow bright as steel, and to speak to him. Slowly the whole face grew to be there, floating on the dark background of the picture; it was pink, aloof, unfathomable, enticing, with its fluffy hair and quick lips, just as he had last seen it. "Are you looking for something?" she seemed to say: "I could show you."

"I have everything safe enough," answered Swithin, and in his sleep he groaned.

He felt the touch of fingers on his forehead. "I'm dreaming," he thought in his dream.

She had vanished; and far away, from behind the picture, came a sound of footsteps.

Aloud, in his sleep, Swithin muttered: "I've missed it."

Again he heard the rustling of those light footsteps, and close in his ear a sound, like a sob. He awoke; the sob was his own. Great drops of perspiration stood on his forehead. "What is it?" he thought; "what have I lost?" Slowly his mind travelled over his investments; he could not think of any single one that was unsafe. What was it, then, that he had lost? Struggling on his pillows, he clutched the wine-glass. His lips touched the wine. "This isn't the 'Heidseck'!" he thought angrily, and before the reality of that displeasure all the dim vision passed away. But as he bent to drink, something snapped, and, with a sigh, Swithin Forsyte died above the bubbles....

•

When James Forsyte came in again on his way home, the valet, trembling, took his hat and stick.

"How's your master?"

"My master is dead, sir!"

"Dead! He can't be! I left him safe an hour ago!"

On the bed Swithin's body was doubled like a sack; his hand still grasped the glass.

James Forsyte paused. "Swithin!" he said, and with his hand to his ear he waited for an answer; but none came, and slowly in the glass a last bubble rose and burst.

Pearl S. Buck

THE LOVERS

NOBEL PRIZE 1938

After a gap of eight years, Pearl S. Buck (1892–1973) became the second American and the first woman to win the Nobel Prize for literature. Although she was born in the tiny town of Hillsboro, West Virginia, she spent part of her life in China, where her parents worked as Presbyterian missionaries. She earned undergraduate and graduate degrees from Randolph-Macon Women's College and Cornell University and embarked on a career in teaching, spending the years from 1925 to 1931 at Nanking and Chung Yang Universities in China, a country she left only in 1935, several years after the Japanese invasion. A Pultizer Prize in 1932 preceded her receipt of the Nobel.

Ms. Buck will always be remembered for her classic novel The Good Earth, *which presented a moving, romantic view of Chinese life that Western readers found fascinating. Her strongest quality was her ability to involve the reader in the lives of her characters, and she specialized in intelligent female protagonists. And while most critics feel that she was one of the weakest writers to win the Nobel Prize, at her best (as in her many volumes of short fiction) she was very good indeed, and made a major contribution to the task of describing a culture in conflict.*

GILES BREDON HESITATED AT the corner of the street. From here he had always caught the first glimpse of his house when he had been away and was coming home again. It stood in the large square lawn, a solid old brick structure, the place where he was born, but it was no longer home. He had not seen it for more than a year, not since the day that he had packed his bags and left Lesley, his wife, standing in the living room, looking at him in silence. It was his last sight of her, and whenever he thought of her, he saw her as she had been at that moment, her dark eyes large and tragic, red stubborn mouth, ivory pale face against the soft straight black hair. She had said not a word when he stalked out of the room. At the threshold he had hesitated.

"Aren't you going to say anything?" he had demanded.

She shook her head and he had slammed out of the door.

Since then their communication had been through lawyers. Once a month he had paid the household bills and her personal allowance. When Judith, their only child, came to visit him in town at the apartment he was renting, he asked no questions concerning her mother, and Judith, chattering to him apparently about everything, never spoke her name. He had tried to make each visit interesting, notable for some amusement or person, hoping, as he recognized, half ruefully, that Judith would tell her mother that she had had a good time with him.

Then a week ago Colton Bates, his lawyer, had insisted on a meeting between what he called "the estranged pair." This meant simply that he, Giles, had to see his wife, Lesley, once more. At least he supposed that she was still his wife? At what moment did a man and woman cease to be husband and wife?

The day was fine, a warm wind blew from the south, and the flowering shrubs on every lawn proclaimed the spring. He was walking toward his house now. If the divorce went through he supposed the house would no longer be his. No, damn Lesley, that he could not bear. He would give the house to Judith, allowing her mother only the right to live in it. Lesley might be too proud to stay on such terms.

The trouble was that he and Lesley had married too young. He had been graduated from Harvard one day and married the next, like a fool! Their parents had not approved such romantic haste, but he and Lesley had been desperately in love. At that, he now wondered, how much of it had been real love? Both of them wanted to be independent of the formal old life in two formal old houses. Love had been confused with independence. He grinned sardonically at the thought.

"Why, Giles Bredon!" He was startled by a loud cheerful voice, and he looked across the pavement into a woman's face.

"Hello, Kit," he said.

It was Katharine Baker, a neighbor, and she was down on her knees, planting something or other, as usual. George Baker, her husband, was a dull fellow, successful in the wholesale furniture business. Kit sat back on her heels and the sun shone down on her sunburned cheeks.

"Are you coming home again, Giles?"

"Only to talk lawyer business with Lesley," he said. Better to be frank and ruthless, else Kit would spread false good news over the whole neighborhood!

"Oh, Giles!" Her honest grey eyes were sad with reproach. "Lesley is so lovely—"

"There's nothing you can tell me about Lesley that I don't know," he said firmly.

"Giles, forgive me—there isn't anyone else, is there?" she pleaded.

"Nobody else for either of us," Giles said.

"Then what—"

"Then nothing," he said. "We have simply grown apart."

He smiled, tipped his hat and walked on. She would convey that speech everywhere. "My dear, I asked Giles myself and he said they had simply grown apart."

Well, it was the truth, so let it stand. He was at his own front door now. The place looked well kept, Lesley would see to that always. She was a good manager. The door stood open. She liked the cool fresh air, and he liked the warmth. Many a time he had shut this door.

Should he go in? It seemed absurd to ring the doorbell of his own house, but he rang it. He waited and no one came. The house was silent. He rang the bell again. Then he heard Lesley's voice calling from the upstairs hall.

"Please come in, Giles. I'll be down in a minute. Just go into the living room."

He went in, took off his hat and topcoat and put them in the closet under the stairs, then crossing the hall he entered the familiar place. He was shocked at the change. He had walked out of it a year ago, leaving it the big old-fashioned room that he had known since his earliest memory. What had Lesley done? The famous flowered wallpaper that his father had brought from Paris was gone. The walls were a strange white, an off-white that tinged on grey, the old dark green velvet hangings were changed to crisp yellow new ones, and instead of the brocades the furniture was covered with some rough material, the same strange white again. The long couch was cherry-red and so were two of the chairs. He sat down in another chair that he remembered as blue, which was now white, and felt aggrieved. Lesley had no right—

She came in, composed and fresh, looking exactly as usual. He stood up, confused. How does a man greet a woman who is his wife, or was, and still was, legally—should he kiss her? She settled it by coming to him and kissing him on the cheek lightly, almost carelessly.

"Well, Giles—"

She sat down in a cherry-red chair, and looked, he had to admit, very handsome in her black and white suit. No, handsome was too hard a word. She was beautiful.

"How are you, Lesley?" he asked.

"Very well, thank you," she said in her usual clear voice.

She was forty-four years old, he grumbled to himself and he felt that he looked ten years older than she was, after this year. Whereas she—but women were tough, he supposed. She didn't feel things the way he did. And, after all, she had the house and Judy, while he had lived alone in a damned apartment. He refused to remember for the moment that he had told himself often how much he enjoyed living in town alone.

"I suppose you have seen Colton Bates?" Lesley asked.

"He told me I'd better talk to you before we drew up the papers," he said.

And women were damned cold, he told himself. While he had been feeling sad, Lesley had been thinking about the lawyer.

"What grounds are you going to give for wanting a divorce?" he demanded belligerently.

Lesley opened her dark eyes at him. "I thought it was agreed— mental cruelty."

He had agreed, months ago, but now when he heard the words on her lips he instantly rebelled.

"Silly nonsense," he said. "It's the excuse people give when they haven't any excuse. You know there's been no mental cruelty."

"I don't know," she said. "It depends on what one means by cruelty. We were both cruel, perhaps. I mean—we weren't happy."

He agreed gloomily. "I don't know what was the matter with us."

"Nothing I did pleased you," she said.

"Nonsense," he said. He crossed and uncrossed his legs. "You criticized me for every little thing."

"Bicker-bicker," she said.

He scrutinized her face. Was she angry? No, she was curiously calm. Bicker-bicker was right. Their mutual irritation had penetrated into the depth of their relationship, destroying all unity.

They were silent. He perceived that she felt him looking at her and so she kept her eyes fixed on the window.

"It's cold in here," he said.

The moment he said the words he wished that he had not, although he had spoken thoughtlessly and not meaning in the least to recall the times that he had said exactly the same thing. She would retort, "I like the fresh air. You always want everything so hot."

But she did not. Instead, as though he were a guest, she rose and shut the front door and sat down again.

"The sunshine is warm," she said, "but there is a slight chill in the air."

He made an effort. "Well, it's mental cruelty then, is it?"

"Call it incompatibility, if you like," she said, "but that's rather old-fashioned, I believe. It's the same thing."

"It sounds silly to say people are incompatible when they have been married long enough to raise a child. In fact, the whole thing is pretty silly when it's put into words, except that—" he trailed off, leaving the sentence, unfinished.

"It is," she said reasonably, taking it up, "but it is also the fact that for some reason or other we are happier apart. Aren't you?"

"Aren't I what?" he asked, not listening. He kept staring at her. She was the woman he knew so well—and she wasn't. Just what—and why—was the difference? There was a charm about her that he had forgotten while they lived together. Now, seeing her after separation, he recognized it again.

"Happier without me," she said with a touch of old impatience. He had a habit of leaving sentences unfinished and not listening, and he remembered this guiltily.

"In some ways," he conceded, but not as happy, he felt, as he had thought he was. Now that he sat here, even though the room was strange, he felt a rush of old habit. The house, the life in it, his bedroom upstairs—and here—the way they used to spend Sunday mornings lounging around, newspaper all over the floor, breakfast when he felt like it, planning the spring garden—

"How is the tulip bed?" he asked. The tulips had been his pride, always blooming first before anybody's.

"They should be replanted next year," she said.

He leaned forward, forgetting. "Now, Lesley, they must be Holland bulbs. I'd better make out the list for you—"

She looked surprised. "Why, all right—but I planned to be in Florida next winter, Giles. Judith goes to college in September and I'll be alone—unless you want the house? I'd rather like to move into town, I think—take an apartment, perhaps."

He was suddenly angry. "You'll find an apartment very cramped after a big house like this."

"Then you take the house," she said stubbornly.

"See here, Lesley," he said, "a man in a house is very different from a woman in a house. I have to be at my office all day."

"Get a housekeeper," she said succinctly. "That's about all I am now, anyway."

"Oh, come," he protested. "You are the mistress of a handsome establishment and you know it. Don't be sorry for yourself."

What she might have retorted to this he did not know. He was ashamed of himself and was saved from proper punishment by Judith, running down the stairs and into the room between them, the wide skirt of her white dress flying out like wings behind her.

"Dad!" she cried. "Oh Dad, how swell to see you here!" She enveloped him in soft bare arms. Soft? They were as strong as steel around his neck. She subsided on his lap and turned her face to her mother. Her eyes were bright blue, like his.

"Mother, have you told him?"

"We've been talking business," her mother said.

"You haven't told him!" Judith cried.

"Told me what?" he demanded.

She returned to him, clutching him again around the neck. He felt her fresh cheek against his lips.

"Dad, I'm in love!"

Against her cheek he mumbled. "Nonsense—"

"Not nonsense," she said, removing her cheek. "It's true—I'm in love—I'm in love—"

"Stop it," he said. "It sounds like a routine. Now tell me all about it."

His eyes met Lesley's, and he saw a secret smile in those dark depths.

"Love has hit Judith hard," she said. "It's the first time. Ah well!"

"Mother, don't be cynical," Judith commanded.

"You look such a child sitting there on your father's lap," Lesley retorted, amused.

Judith rose instantly, flounced her skirts and sat down in the other cherry-red chair.

"I haven't seen Dad for a week," she said furiously.

"I am not criticizing," her mother said mildly.

"You are," Judith cried in the same furious voice. Her cheeks, always cream pale, flushed pink and her blue eyes shone under a frown. "You're as cynical as you can be. You don't believe in love!"

"Come, come, Judy," Giles said. "You haven't even told me the fellow's name." He was rather enjoying the scene between his wife and his daughter. It brought him into the family again.

"It's only William Baker," Lesley said.

"Mother," Judith cried, "you know he wants to be called Bill! And how dare you say 'only'?"

"What—George and Kit's boy?" Giles asked, unbelieving. "Is he big enough to fall in love with? Last time I saw him he was still wearing—"

"Oh, shut up," Judith said and burst into tears.

Her parents looked at each other over her bent head and each caught remorse in the other's look.

"The first time is so hard," Lesley said in a feeling voice.

"Don't I remember," Giles said, gazing into her eyes. "I stopped eating and sleeping, and I camped under your window even after we had said good night twenty times or so."

Judith lifted her head. "Don't you dare compare Bill and me to you two! We're serious!"

Her face, still pink and white, was fierce.

"Darling," Lesley said. "We are only remembering. So will you some day."

"I won't," Judith said. "I shan't need to remember—I'll be living with Bill—and—and—our children—forever!"

Giles felt a sharp quickening about his heart. Anger? Pain? He did not know which.

"So we thought," he said.

His daughter flouted the idea. "Thought!" she echoed, scornfully. "Bill and I don't just think—we know!"

"Just what do you know?" Lesley asked. Her own cheeks were suddenly quite pink, and Giles, watching her, saw what he had never noticed before, that while Judith had his coloring, actually she looked like her mother. Lesley had been just such a fiery girl.

"You make me think of your mother, Judy," he said. "I remember a scene in this very room, as a matter of fact—not this furniture of course. Her parents and mine met here one evening to tell us that we were too young to be in love. God—there's a song about that now, isn't there, 'too young to love'! Well, they were right."

Judy stopped crying. She wiped her eyes, producing a small white handkerchief from inside her wide belt and mopping her face with it. "Maybe you and Mother were too young to love," she said. Her voice trembled. She was looking from one parent to the other. "Sometimes I think you'll never grow up. Bill and I are much older than you two in lots of ways. We were talking about it the other day. There's been so much to make us grow up—the war and—and everything the way it is now. We haven't loved in the easy way you did, thinking everything was going to be peaceful and happy ever after. We already know it isn't." She turned to her mother. "And that's what we know, Mother. And we know we can take it, if we're together, Bill and I."

Lesley lost her own temper, promptly concealing the fact as usual under icelike calm.

"You are being very childish without knowing it, Judith," she said. "You understand nothing about marriage. The qualities in Bill that you now think are wonderful will probably become—tiresome—as time goes on."

"If they are," Judith said, "nobody will know it. I'll stick to my bargain. I won't run out on him. I'll be too proud."

A piercing whistle rose outside the open window. It hung in the air, a corkscrew of sound, prolonged and shrill.

"Is that Bill?" Giles inquired.

He need not have asked. His daughter changed under his very eyes. Fury faded from her face, her eyes grew tender, her cheeks pale. She rose and floated out of the room, her full skirts swirling about her. She breathed out ecstasy and it hung in the air like a perfume.

He walked to the window, scarcely knowing that he did, and from there he saw the love scene, as old as humanity and new as today. A tall lean boy stepped over the side of a worn and winded-looking car, and striding up the walk, he met the girl at the door. There he took her in his arms. They kissed long and fervently, and Giles felt a queer faintness at the sight of his daughter's golden hair lying upon the shoulder of the boy's dark blue coat, and then remembered that this same faintness had attacked him about the heart when he and Lesley had first kissed so long ago.

"Have you told your folks?" The boy lifted his head to ask the question.

"Yes," Judith said.

He could hear their voices clearly, as though they did not care whether they were heard.

"I told them," Judith said, not drawing away, her face still uplifted.

"What did they say?" Bill asked.

"Does it matter?" Judy asked.

They were gazing into each other's eyes.

"No," he said, and bent his head. Again they kissed.

This time, Giles told himself, he could not bear it. He stepped back, and stumbled against Lesley. She had tiptoed to the window behind him and over his shoulder had been watching the same scene.

"I'm sorry," he said, recovering himself.

"I'm not hurt," she said.

Each stepped back, too conscious of the moment's contact. They sat down, silent and listening, and Giles turned his head to the window.

"Isn't she going to bring him in?" he asked.

"I don't know," Lesley said. "She's so strange. She's cut herself off from us."

"We don't matter now," Giles said ruthlessly.

Lesley did not answer. Her hands were crossed on her lap, and she sat pensively looking at her rings.

"You are still wearing your wedding ring," he remembered irrelevantly.

"I thought I'd keep wearing it, if you don't mind," she replied.

"It will save explanations, perhaps, when I'm travelling."

"As a matter of fact, you're still married," he said.

She flashed her dark eyes at him. "Are you trying to be cynical or helpful?"

He evaded this potential tinder. "They're getting in the car now," he said, looking at the window.

"Are they?" she said indifferently.

He was irritated. "See here, Lesley, we ought to do something— say something, at least, about this affair. After all, I didn't kiss you—like that—until we were regularly engaged."

"We were old-fashioned," she said in the same voice, indifferent and musing.

"They've changed their minds," he said, still watching. "They're coming in."

She did not reply and he lit a cigarette. Almost immediately they were at the door, the tall brown-haired boy, his thin face set and white. Not a handsome boy, Giles thought, much too tall and slender, but the army would fill him out. Of course marriage was absurd when there was the army ahead! By the time the boy got back Judith would be in love with someone else. If he had been separated from Lesley at the same age—

"Bill wants to talk with you, Dad," Judith announced from the door. Her voice was sharp, feminine, adult.

"Come in," Giles said. He held out his hand, and did not rise. "I wouldn't have known you, Bill—haven't seen you for a while, have I?"

"No, sir. I've been at college."

They shook hands. The boy's hand was bony but warm and firm.

"You've changed by several feet," Giles said, trying to be affable.

Bill grinned. "I've done some growing," he admitted.

"Hello, Bill," Lesley said in a low voice.

"Hello, Mrs. Bredon," Bill said. "It hasn't been many hours since two o'clock this morning."

"Very few," Lesley said.

Bill turned to Giles. "Judy and I were at a dance last night, sir. That's when we decided."

Giles felt paternalistic and despised himself and said nothing. Bill went on calmly, damnably calm, Giles thought, remembering his own sweating agony a generation ago in this very room, his parents sitting in these two chairs, now cherry-red, and Lesley's parents on the couch, her father wearing a formal cutaway and striped trousers because he was on his way to a directors' meeting at the bank, and her mother, he remembered, in a dove-grey dress of some sort. Lesley, sitting on the hassock by the window, had been in white the way Judith was now, and looking like an angel. He could remember how sick he felt with love that day, an actual nausea, a faintness in the breast, his voice weak when he wanted it strong, and he had sweated like a porpoise while she waited for him to defend her.

"I want you to know." His voice had actually squeaked, "Lesley and I are engaged."

"Really and truly engaged," she had echoed, almost in a whisper.

Bill was talking. Giles brought his reluctant mind back into the present.

"Judy needs security," Bill was saying, "and I can give it to her. We both believe in real love—lasting love, that is."

"Bill needs security, too," Judith put in. Her voice was still sharp, feminine, adult. "He has to go into the army. He's had his notice—twenty-one days. If we're married, he'll feel secure."

Lesley came out of her dreamy silence. "Marriage doesn't mean security—not any more."

"It's going to mean that in our case," Bill said definitely.

"This isn't just romance," Judith said with grimness. "It's love."

"Good God," Giles said. He lit another cigarette.

"Have you any objection, sir?" Bill said.

"Objection?" Giles repeated. "To what?"

"To me," Bill said.

"None in the least," Giles said. "After all, I've known you since you were born, practically, your family and so on. You're both too young, but I suppose you know that."

"I don't think being young has anything to do with it, sir," Bill said. "Not when you need security. You had it, sir, in your generation, I mean. I guess that's why you've thrown it overboard so easily."

Giles felt his collar suddenly tight. "What do you mean by that?" he demanded.

"It's a different world," Bill said. "Judy and I have to make our own security or there isn't any."

"We aren't complaining," Judith said. "We have to take it as we find it. But we don't want our children to—to go through what we have. We want them to be secure because we are."

Giles, listening to this speech, was about to say something scornful concerning young preachers when he saw his daughter's knees visibly trembling under her skirts. A child, after all, in spite of her being in love—his child!

"Who am I to tell you what to do?" he said suddenly. "Get married if you think it's what you want."

"Oh, go away," Lesley said under her breath. "Please go away, everybody!"

The girl and boy rose at once. Judith went to her mother and kissed her, then to her father, and kissed him. Then she caught Bill's hand and hand in hand they went to the door. There he turned.

"Goodbye, Mr. and Mrs. Bredon," he said.

Giles did not reply. He lit another cigarette and sat smoking it in silence. Lesley got up and moved about the room and sat down again. Outside the car snorted loudly and rattled away.

"Do you suppose they will run off and get married now, the fools?" Giles asked.

"Maybe they won't be as silly as we were," Lesley said. They remembered, silent and apart, that noontime scene in the tiny office of a justice of the peace. He remembered, too, the rush of freedom that swept him heavenward when they were pronounced man and wife. He had put his right arm about Lesley's shoulders and caught her with him out into the sunshine of that day.

"Nobody can part us now," he had said. "We are free and alone, man and wife!"

They had rattled off in an old jalopy of a car, too, something that he had put together himself, and had left behind when he went to college. But it had served their purpose until he had bought his first new car when they had been married a year.

"If they aren't as silly as we were, they'll be missing a lot," he muttered.

"Hadn't we better begin to talk business?" she asked.

He made an effort and felt himself entangled in a net of memory. That first night they had stayed in a country inn. He closed his eyes and leaned his head back. They had been absurdly ignorant, but brave with love. He had not thought of it in years.

"About this house," Lesley said. "I don't want it."

He opened his eyes and said harshly, "I certainly don't want it. What would I do with it—living alone?"

"Judith and Bill might be willing to live here with you," she suggested.

"I couldn't stand it," he retorted. "When we were young it was only our parents who were self-righteous. Now it's the young people who are so damned self-righteous."

She spoke with her first warmth. "Aren't they! I assure you, it has been no easy task to live with Judith day in and day out. She had acted as though the collapse of the world were my individual doing. She and Bill, I suppose, will set it all right again. Maybe!"

"Maybe," he agreed. "Anyway, it's their turn. Let them have the world. I'm sick of it."

"So am I," she said heartily.

They were gazing at each other quite happily in unconscious agreement.

"I want to live with my own generation," he went on. "Someone who knows what I'm talking about."

"I feel the same way," she said.

His eyes fell on the cherry-red chairs.

"What in hell made you change this room?" he demanded.

"I didn't want to," she said. "It was Judy's idea."

"You shouldn't have given in," he argued. "After all, it isn't her house—not yet."

"You had moved out," she reminded him.

"You told me to go," he reminded her in turn.

Reluctantly they smiled at each other, his smile grew into a grin, and she laughed.

"Oh dear," she said, wiping her eyes. "I haven't had anything to laugh at for a long time."

He crushed his cigarette and leaned forward, elbows on his knees. His voice was bold and bright. "Why don't we run away again, the way we did before?"

She broke into waves of new laughter. "Oh, Giles, away from this same room—again?"

"Hideous, isn't it?" he said.

"Oh, I don't care," she said recklessly. "What's a house? Let Judy do what she likes with it."

"Let's make our own," he said ardently. He felt a new and sudden exhilaration, a fire in his heart again! "I've always wanted to build a house with extra bedrooms, lots of living room and terraces, and somewhere on a mountainside where we won't have to draw the curtains at night because there will be no one to look in."

"I've always hated this house," she confessed. "I hated it when your parents lived here, and I've hated it even more now that it's changed to suit Judy."

"Oh damn it," he said, "let's get away from them all!"

Insight, unusual and astonishing, illumined his face. He pounded the arms of his chair with his clenched fists. "Look here, Lesley—they're alike, these kids and their grandparents, both yelling for security. We know there isn't any, and we don't care!"

He crossed the room in three long strides and pulled her to her feet. "We've still got plenty of time," he said.

He swept her into his arms. Oh God, whoever said anything about young love? This was a thousand times better, to feel her back in his arms again, fitting him with all the experiences of the years. This, this was love!

"I can't live without you," he muttered, his cheek upon her hair.

"I've tried to live without you," she said in a small still voice, "it's too lonely."

"So now we know," he said.

The telephone rang, she tried to draw away and he held her fast. "Let's not have a telephone in our house."

"Let's not," she said.

But she flew to answer it. She listened, the receiver at her ear.

"Judy!" she whispered to him, and she told him the news, answering Judy, while she gazed at him.

"You're going to be married right away? Oh Judy—no wedding? We can't blame you, since we did exactly the same thing—didn't you know? Oh yes, we ran away and got married. What—you're going to live happy ever after, not like us? You may be surprised, Judy, very surprised! A week's honeymoon? Well, be happy, darling...Yes, he's still here."

She motioned to him and he came and took the receiver from her.

"Judy!" he shouted. "You ought to be ashamed of yourself! What have I done to get this treatment? Of course I'm angry! I haven't even given my consent—nobody asked for it! Well, it's up to you and Bill to make a go of it now, after all your boasting! What's that? Put him on, then!"

Bill's voice was at his ear. "I'm sorry we felt obliged to take things in our own hands, sir. We both felt we ought to tell you."

"Well, it's your responsibility. I wash my hands, etc!" He tried not to allow gaiety in his voice.

"I'll be responsible, sir," Bill said. His voice was serious, too serious.

"I don't need to tell you that Judy has a nice little temper of her own when she's crossed," Giles said with a touch of malice.

"I know," Bill said.

"Don't be too patient," Giles retorted. "And good luck!"

He hung up quickly and faced Lesley.

"We're free," he said.

"Free," she echoed.

They stood face to face for a moment, not touching. Slowly a smile crept up from their hearts and into their eyes to spread like sunshine over their lively faces. She stepped toward him and he took her in his arms, and in common accord, without a word, they began to dance. It was a medley of a dance, waltz and minuet and jive, he improvising, she following, embellishing while she yielded.

"Reckless," he murmured, "a reckless pair, and mad with love!"

William Faulkner

BARN BURNING

NOBEL PRIZE 1949

The third American to win the Nobel Prize for literature, William Faulkner (1897–1962) was born in New Albany, Mississippi, although he lived in Oxford, Mississippi, from the age of five. A full-time writer from his late twenties, he also worked as a Hollywood screenwriter for some nine years between 1932 and 1945. Among America's most honored writers, he won the O. Henry Award, the Howells Medal, the National Book Award, the American Academy of Arts and Letters Gold Medal, and two Pulitzer Prizes in addition to the Nobel.

Perhaps the finest regional writer in American history, Faulkner effectively captured the minds, dialects, and souls of poor (and not so poor) Southern whites in his many novels and stories, especially in the marvelous tales of the folk of Yoknapatawpha County, his model for an examination of humankind. Few writers have reflected a society in transition as well as Faulkner, and many argue that he is the finest novelist yet developed in this country. Anyone who has read such books as Sanctuary *(1931),* Absalom, Absalom! *(1936), and* Intruder in the Dust *(1948) would be likely to agree with this evaluation.*

THE STORE IN WHICH the Justice of the Peace's court was
sitting smelled of cheese. The boy, crouched on his nail keg at the
back of the crowded room, knew he smelled cheese, and more:
from where he sat he could see the ranked shelves close-packed
with the solid, squat, dynamic shapes of tin cans whose labels his
stomach read, not from the lettering which meant nothing to his
mind but from the scarlet devils and the silver curve of fish—this,
the cheese which he knew he smelled and the hermetic meat which
his intestines believed he smelled coming in intermittent gusts momentary and brief between the other constant one, the smell and
sense just a little of fear because mostly of despair and grief, the
old fierce pull of blood. He could not see the table where the Justice
sat and before which his father and his father's enemy (*our enemy*
he thought in that despair; *ourn! mine and hisn both! He's my father!*)
stood, but he could hear them, the two of them that is, because his
father had said no word yet:

"But what proof have you, Mr. Harris?"

"I told you. The hog got into my corn. I caught it up and sent
it back to him. He had no fence that would hold it. I told him so,
warned him. The next time I put the hog in my pen. When he
came to get it I gave him enough wire to patch up his pen. The
next time I put the hog up and kept it. I rode down to his house
and saw the wire I gave him still rolled on to the spool in his yard.
I told him he could have the hog when he paid me a dollar pound
fee. That evening a nigger came with the dollar and got the hog.
He was a strange nigger. He said, 'He say to tell you wood and hay
kin burn.' I said. 'What?' 'That whut he say to tell you,' the nigger
said. 'Wood and hay kin burn.' That night my barn burned. I got
the stock out but I lost the barn."

"Where is the nigger? Have you got him?"

"He was a strange nigger, I tell you. I don't know what became
of him."

"But that's not proof. Don't you see that's not proof?"

"Get that boy up here. He knows." For a moment the boy thought
too that the man meant his older brother until Harris said, "Not
him. The little one. The boy," and, crouching, small for his age,
small and wiry like his father, in patched and faded jeans even too
small for him, with straight, uncombed, brown hair and eyes gray
and wild as storm scud, he saw the men between himself and the
table part and become a lane of grim faces, at the end of which he

saw the Justice, a shabby, collarless, graying man in spectacles, beckoning him. He felt no floor under his bare feet; he seemed to walk beneath the palpable weight of the grim turning faces. His father, stiff in his black Sunday coat donned not for the trial but for the moving, did not even look at him. *He aims for me to lie*, he thought, again with that frantic grief and despair. *And I will have to do hit.*

"What's your name, boy?" the Justice said.

"Colonel Sartoris Snopes," the boy whispered.

"Hey?" the Justice said. "Talk louder. Colonel Sartoris? I reckon anybody named for Colonel Sartoris in this country can't help but tell the truth, can they?" The boy said nothing. *Enemy! Enemy!* he thought; for a moment he could not even see, could not see that the Justice's face was kindly nor discern that his voice was troubled when he spoke to the man named Harris: "Do you want me to question this boy?" But he could hear, and during those subsequent long seconds while there was absolutely no sound in the crowded little room save that of quiet and intent breathing it was as if he had swung outward at the end of a grape vine, over a ravine, and at the top of the swing had been caught in a prolonged instant of mesmerized gravity, weightless in time.

"No!" Harris said violently, explosively. "Damnation! Send him out of here!" Now time, the fluid world, rushed beneath him again, the voices coming to him again through the smell of cheese and sealed meat, the fear and despair and the old grief of blood:

"This case is closed. I can't find against you, Snopes, but I can give you advice. Leave this country and don't come back to it."

His father spoke for the first time, his voice cold and harsh, level, without emphasis: "I aim to. I don't figure to stay in a country among people who..." he said something unprintable and vile, addressed to no one.

"That'll do," the Justice said. "Take your wagon and get out of this country before dark. Case dismissed."

His father turned, and he followed the stiff black coat, the wiry figure walking a little stiffly from where a Confederate provost's man's musket ball had taken him in the heel on a stolen horse thirty years ago, followed the two backs now, since his older brother had appeared from somewhere in the crowd, no taller than the father but thicker, chewing tobacco steadily, between the two lines of grim-faced men and out of the store and across the worn gallery and down the sagging steps and among the dogs and half-grown boys in the mild May dust, where as he passed a voice hissed:

"Barn burner!"

Again he could not see, whirling; there was a face in a red haze, moonlike, bigger than the full moon, the owner of it half again his size, he leaping in the red haze toward the face, feeling no blow, feeling no shock when his head struck the earth, scrabbling up and leaping again, feeling no blow this time either and tasting no blood, scrabbling up to see the other boy in full flight and himself already leaping into pursuit as his father's hand jerked him back, the harsh, cold voice speaking above him: "Go get in the wagon."

It stood in a grove of locusts and mulberries across the road. His two hulking sisters in their Sunday dresses and his mother and her sister in calico and sunbonnets were already in it, sitting on and among the sorry residue of the dozen and more movings which even the boy could remember—the battered stove, the broken beds and chairs, the clock inlaid with mother-of-pearl, which would not run, stopped at some fourteen minutes past two o'clock of a dead and forgotten day and time, which had been his mother's dowry. She was crying, though when she saw him she drew her sleeve across her face and began to descend from the wagon. "Get back," the father said.

"He's hurt. I got to get some water and wash his..."

"Get back in the wagon," his father said. He got in too, over the tail-gate. His father mounted to the seat where the older brother already sat and struck the gaunt mules two savage blows with the peeled willow, but without heat. It was not even sadistic; it was exactly that same quality which in later years would cause his descendants to over-run the engine before putting a motor car into motion, striking and reining back in the same movement. The wagon went on, the store with its quiet crowd of grimly watching men dropped behind; a curve in the road hid it. *Forever* he thought. *Maybe he's done satisfied now, now that he has...* stopping himself, not to say it aloud even to himself. His mother's hand touched his shoulder.

"Does hit hurt?" she said.

"Naw," he said. "Hit don't hurt. Lemme be."

"Can't you wipe some of the blood off before hit dries?"

"I'll wash to-night," he said. "Lemme be, I tell you."

The wagon went on. He did not know where they were going.

None of them ever did or ever asked, because it was always somewhere, always a house of sorts waiting for them a day or two days
or even three days away. Likely his father had already arranged to
make a crop on another farm before he...Again he had to stop
himself. He (the father) always did. There was something about
his wolflike independence and even courage when the advantage
was at least neutral which impressed strangers, as if they got from
his latent ravening ferocity not so much a sense of dependability
as a feeling that his ferocious conviction in the rightness of his own
actions would be of advantage to all whose interest lay with his.

That night they camped, in a grove of oaks and beeches where
a spring ran. The nights were still cool and they had a fire against
it, of a rail lifted from a nearby fence and cut into lengths—a small
fire, neat, niggard almost, a shrewd fire; such fires were his father's
habit and custom always, even in freezing weather. Older, the boy
might have remarked this and wondered why not a big one; why
should not a man who had not only seen the waste and extravagance
of war, but who had in his blood an inherent voracious prodigality
with material not his own, have burned everything in sight? Then
he might have gone a step farther and thought that that was the
reason: that niggard blaze was the living fruit of nights passed
during those four years in the woods hiding from all men, blue or
gray, with his strings of horses (captured horses, he called them).
And older still, he might have divined the true reason: that the
element of fire spoke to some deep mainspring of his father's being,
as the element of steel or of powder spoke to other men, as the
one weapon for the preservation of integrity, else breath were not
worth the breathing, and hence to be regarded with respect and
used with discretion.

But he did not think this now and he had seen those same niggard
blazes all his life. He merely ate his supper beside it and was already
half asleep over his iron plate when his father called him, and once
more he followed the stiff back, the stiff and ruthless limp, up the
slope and on to the starlit road where, turning, he could see his
father against the stars but without face or depth—a shape black,
flat, and bloodless as though cut from tin in the iron folds of the
frockcoat which had not been made for him, the voice harsh like
tin and without heat like tin:

"You were fixing to tell them. You would have told him." He
didn't answer. His father struck him with the flat of his hand on

the side of the head, hard but without heat, exactly as he had struck the two mules at the store, exactly as he would strike either of them with any stick in order to kill a horse fly, his voice still without heat or anger. "You're getting to be a man. You got to learn. You got to learn to stick to your own blood or you ain't going to have any blood to stick to you. Do you think either of them, any man there this morning, would? Don't you know all they wanted was a chance to get at me because they knew I had them beat? Eh?" Later, twenty years later, he was to tell himself, "If I had said they wanted only truth, justice, he would have hit me again." But now he said nothing. He was not crying. He just stood there. "Answer me," his father said.

"Yes," he whispered. His father turned.

"Get on to bed. We'll be there tomorrow."

To-morrow they were there. In the early afternoon the wagon stopped before a paintless two-room house identical almost with the dozen others it had stopped before even in the boy's ten years, and again, as on the other dozen occasions, his mother and aunt got down and began to unload the wagon, although his two sisters and his father and brother had not moved.

"Likely hit ain't fitten for hawgs," one of the sisters said.

"Nevertheless, fit it will and you'll hog it and like it," his father said. "Get out of them chairs and help your Ma unload."

The two sisters got down, big, bovine, in a flutter of cheap ribbons, one of them drew from the jumbled wagon bed a battered lantern, the other a worn broom. His father handed the reins to the older son and began to climb stiffly over the wheel. "When they get unloaded, take the team to the barn and feed them." Then he said, and at first the boy thought he was still speaking to his brother: "Come with me."

"Me?" he said.

"Yes," his father said. "You."

"Abner," his mother said. His father paused and looked back— the harsh level stare beneath the shaggy, graying, irascible brows.

"I reckon I'll have a word with the man that aims to begin to-morrow owning me body and soul for the next eight months."

They went back up the road. A week ago—or before last night, that is—he would have asked where they were going, but not now. His father had struck him before last night but never before had he paused afterward to explain why; it was as if the blow and the following calm, outrageous voice still rang, repercussed, divulging nothing to him save the terrible handicap of being young, the light weight of his few years, just heavy enough to prevent his soaring free of the world as it seemed to be ordered but not heavy enough to keep him footed solid in it, to resist it and try to change the course of its events.

Presently he could see the grove of oaks and cedars and the other flowering trees and shrubs where the house would be, though not the house yet. They walked beside a fence massed with honeysuckle and Cherokee roses and came to a gate swinging open between two brick pillars, and now, beyond a sweep of drive, he saw the house for the first time and at that instant he forgot his father and the terror and despair both, and even when he remembered his father again (who had not stopped) the terror and despair did not return. Because, for all the twelve movings, they had sojourned until now in a poor country, a land of small farms and fields and houses, and he had never seen a house like this before. *Hit's big as a courthouse* he thought quietly, with a surge of peace and joy whose reason he could not have thought into words, being too young for that: *They are safe from him. People whose lives are a part of this peace and dignity are beyond his touch, be no more to them than a buzzing wasp: capable of stinging for a little moment but that's all; the spell of this peace and dignity rendering even the barns and stable and cribs which belong to it impervious to the puny flames he might contrive*... this, the peace and joy, ebbing for an instant as he looked again at the stiff black back, the stiff and implacable limp of the figure which was not dwarfed by the house, for the reason that it had never looked big anywhere and which now, against the serene columned backdrop, had more than ever that impervious quality of something cut ruthlessly from tin, depthless, as though, sidewise to the sun, it would cast no shadow. Watching him, the boy remarked the absolutely undeviating course which his father held and saw the stiff foot come squarely down in a pile of fresh droppings where a horse had stood in the drive and which his father could have avoided by a simple change of stride. But it ebbed only for a moment, though he could not have thought this into words either, walking on in the spell of the house, which he could even want but without envy, without sorrow, certainly never with that ravening and jealous rage which unknown to him walked in the ironlike black coat before him: *Maybe he will feel it too. Maybe it will even change him now from what maybe he couldn't help but be.*

They crossed the portico. Now he could hear his father's stiff foot as it came down on the boards with clocklike finality, a sound out of all proportion to the displacement of the body it bore and which was not dwarfed either by the white door before it, as though it had attained to a sort of vicious and ravening minimum not to be dwarfed by anything—the flat, wide, black hat, the formal coat of broadcloth which had once been black but which had now that friction-glazed greenish cast of the bodies of old house flies, the lifted sleeve which was too large, the lifted hand like a curled claw. The door opened so promptly that the boy knew the Negro must have been watching them all the time, an old man with neat grizzled hair, in a linen jacket, who stood barring the door with his body, saying, "Wipe yo foots, white man, fo you come in here. Major ain't home nohow."

"Get out of my way, nigger," his father said, without heat too, flinging the door back and the Negro also and entering, his hat still on his head. And now the boy saw the prints of the stiff foot on the doorjamb and saw them appear on the pale rug behind the machinelike deliberation of the foot which seemed to bear (or transmit) twice the weight which the body compassed. The Negro was shouting "Miss Lula! Miss Lula!" somewhere behind them, then the boy, deluged as though by a warm wave by a suave turn of carpeted stair and a pendant glitter of chandeliers and a mute gleam of gold frames, heard the swift feet and saw her too, a lady— perhaps he had never seen her like before either—in a gray, smooth gown with lace at the throat and an apron tied at the waist and the sleeves turned back, wiping cake or biscuit dough from her hands with a towel as she came up the hall, looking not at his father at all but at the tracks on the blond rug with an expression of incredulous amazement.

"I tried," the Negro cried. "I tole him to . . ."

"Will you please go away?" she said in a shaking voice. "Major de Spain is not at home. Will you please go away?"

His father had not spoken again. He did not speak again. He did not even look at her. He just stood stiff in the center of the rug, in his hat, the shaggy iron-gray brows twitching slightly above the pebble-colored eyes as he appeared to examine the house with brief deliberation. Then with the same deliberation he turned; the boy watched him pivot on the good leg and saw the stiff foot drag round the arc of the turning, leaving a final long and fading smear. His father never looked at it, he never once looked down at the rug. The Negro held the door. It closed behind them, upon the hysteric and indistinguishable woman-wail. His father stopped at the top of the steps and scraped his boot clean on the edge of it. At the gate he stopped again. He stood for a moment, planted stiffly on the stiff foot, looking back at the house. "Pretty and white, ain't it?" he said. "That's sweat. Nigger sweat. Maybe it ain't white enough yet to suit him. Maybe he wants to mix some white sweat with it."

Two hours later the boy was chopping wood behind the house within which his mother and aunt and the two sisters (the mother and aunt, not the two girls, he knew that; even at this distance and muffled by walls the flat loud voices of the two girls emanated an incorrigible idle inertia) were setting up the stove to prepare a meal, when he heard the hooves and saw the linen-clad man on a fine sorrel mare, whom he recognized even before he saw the rolled rug in front of the Negro youth following on a fat bay carriage horse—a suffused, angry face vanishing, still at full gallop, beyond the corner of the house where his father and brother were sitting in the two tilted chairs; and a moment later, almost before he could have put the axe down, he heard the hooves again and watched the sorrel mare go back out of the yard, already galloping again. Then his father began to shout one of the sisters' names, who presently emerged backward from the kitchen door dragging the rolled rug along the ground by one end while the other sister walked behind it.

"If you ain't going to tote, go on and set up the wash pot," the first said.

"You, Sarty!" the second shouted. "Set up the wash pot!" His father appeared at the door, framed against that shabbiness, as he had been against that other bland perfection, impervious to either, the mother's anxious face at his shoulder.

"Go on," the father said. "Pick it up." The two sisters stooped, broad, lethargic; stooping, they presented an incredible expanse of pale cloth and a flutter of tawdry ribbons.

"If I thought enough of a rug to have to git hit all the way from France I wouldn't keep hit where folks coming in would have to tromp on hit," the first said. They raised the rug.

"Abner," the mother said. "Let me do it."

"You go back and git dinner," his father said. "I'll tend to this."

From the woodpile through the rest of the afternoon the boy watched them, the rug spread flat in the dust beside the bubbling wash-pot, the two sisters stooping over it with that profound and lethargic reluctance, while the father stood over them in turn, implacable and grim, driving them though never raising his voice again. He could smell the harsh homemade lye they were using; he saw his mother come to the door once and look toward them with an expression not anxious now but very like despair; he saw his father turn, and he fell to with the axe and saw from the corner of his eye his father raise from the ground a flattish fragment of field stone and examine it and return to the pot, and this time his mother actually spoke: "Abner. Abner. Please don't. Please, Abner."

Then he was done too. It was dusk; the whippoorwills had already begun. He could smell coffee from the room where they would presently eat the cold food remaining from the mid-afternoon meal, though when he entered the house he realized they were having coffee again probably because there was a fire on the hearth, before which the rug now lay spread over the backs of the two chairs. The tracks of his father's foot were gone. Where they had been were now long, water-cloudy scoriations resembling the sporadic course of a lilliputian mowing machine.

It still hung there while they ate the cold food and then went to bed, scattered without order or claim up and down the two rooms, his mother in one bed, where his father would later lie, the older brother in the other, himself, the aunt, and the two sisters on pallets on the floor. But his father was not in bed yet. The last thing the boy remembered was the depthless, harsh silhouette of the hat and coat bending over the rug and it seemed to him that he had not even closed his eyes when the silhouette was standing over him, the fire almost dead behind it, the stiff foot prodding him awake. "Catch up the mule," his father said.

When he returned with the mule his father was standing in the black door, the rolled rug over his shoulder. "Ain't you going to ride?" he said.

"No. Give me your foot."

He bent his knee into his father's hand, the wiry, surprising power flowed smoothly, rising, he rising with it, on to the mule's bare back (they had owned a saddle once; the boy could remember it though not when or where) and with the same effortlessness his father swung the rug up in front of him. Now in the starlight they retraced the afternoon's path, up the dusty road rife with honeysuckle, through the gate and up the black tunnel of the drive to the lightless house, where he sat on the mule and felt the rough warp of the rug drag across his thighs and vanish.

"Don't you want me to help?" he whispered. His father did not answer and now he heard again that stiff foot striking the hollow portico with that wooden and clocklike deliberation, that outrageous overstatement of the weight it carried. The rug, hunched, not flung (the boy could tell that even in the darkness) from his father's shoulder struck the angle of wall and floor with a sound unbelievably loud, thunderous, then the foot again, unhurried and enormous; a light came on in the house and the boy sat, tense, breathing steadily and quietly and just a little fast, though the foot itself did not increase its beat at all, descending the steps now; now the boy could see him.

"Don't you want to ride now?" he whispered. "We kin both ride now," the light within the house altering now, flaring up and sinking. *He's coming down the stairs now,* he thought. He had already ridden the mule up beside the horse block; presently his father was up behind him and he doubled the reins over and slashed the mule across the neck, but before the animal could begin to trot the hard, thin arm came round him, the hard, knotted hand jerking the mule back to a walk.

In the first red rays of the sun they were in the lot, putting plow gear on the mules. This time the sorrel mare was in the lot before he heard it at all, the rider collarless and even bareheaded, trembling, speaking in a shaking voice as the woman in the house had done, his father merely looking up once before stooping again to the hame he was buckling, so that the man on the mare spoke to his stooping back:

"You must realize you have ruined that rug. Wasn't there anybody here, any of your women..." he ceased, shaking, the boy watching him, the older brother leaning now in the stable door, chewing, blinking slowly and steadily at nothing apparently. "It cost a hundred dollars. But you never had a hundred dollars. You never will. So I'm going to charge you twenty bushels of corn against your crop. I'll add it in your contract and when you come to the commissary you can sign it. That won't keep Mrs. de Spain quiet but maybe it will teach you to wipe your feet off before you enter her house again."

Then he was gone. The boy looked at his father, who still had not spoken or even looked up again, who was now adjusting the logger-head in the hame.

"Pap," he said. His father looked at him—the inscrutable face, the shaggy brows beneath which the gray eyes glinted coldly. Suddenly the boy went toward him, fast, stopping as suddenly. "You done the best you could!" he cried. "If he wanted hit done different why didn't he wait and tell you how? He won't git no twenty bushels! He won't git none! We'll gether hit and hide hit! I kin watch..."

"Did you put the cutter back in that straight stock like I told you?"

"No, sir," he said.

"Then go do it."

That was Wednesday. During the rest of that week he worked steadily, at what was within his scope and some which was beyond it, with an industry that did not need to be driven nor even commanded twice; he had this from his mother, with the difference that some at least of what he did he liked to do, such as splitting wood with the half-size axe which his mother and aunt had earned, or saved money somehow, to present him with at Christmas. In company with the two older women (and on one afternoon, even one of the sisters), he built pens for the shoat and the cow which were a part of his father's contract with the landlord, and one afternoon, his father being absent, gone somewhere on one of the mules, he went to the field.

They were running a middle buster now, his brother holding the plow straight while he handled the reins, and walking beside the straining mule, the rich black soil shearing cool and damp against his bare ankles, he thought *Maybe this is the end of it. Maybe even that twenty bushels that seems hard to have to pay for just a rug will be a cheap price for him to stop forever and always from being what he used to be;* thinking, dreaming now, so that his brother had to speak sharply to him to mind the mule: *Maybe he even won't collect the twenty bushels. Maybe it will all add up and balance and vanish—corn, rug, fire; the terror and grief, the being pulled two ways like between two teams of horses—gone, done with for ever and ever.*

Then it was Saturday; he looked up from beneath the mule he was harnessing and saw his father in the black coat and hat. "Not that," his father said. "The wagon gear." And then, two hours later, sitting in the wagon bed behind his father and brother on the seat, the wagon accomplished a final curve, and he saw the weathered paintless store with its tattered tobacco- and patent-medicine posters and the tethered wagons and saddle animals below the gallery. He mounted the gnawed steps behind his father and brother, and there again was the lane of quiet, watching faces for the three of them to walk through. He saw the man in spectacles sitting at the plank table and he did not need to be told this was a Justice of the Peace; he sent one glare of fierce, exultant, partisan defiance at the man in collar and cravat now, whom he had seen but twice before in his life, and that on a galloping horse, who now wore on his face an expression not of rage but of amazed unbelief which the boy could not have known was at the incredible circumstance of being sued by one of his own tenants, and came and stood against his father and cried at the Justice: "He ain't done it! He ain't burnt..."

"Go back to the wagon," his father said.

"Burnt?" the Justice said. "Do I understand this rug was burned too?"

"Does anybody here claim it was?" his father said. "Go back to the wagon." But he did not, he merely retreated to the rear of the room, crowded as that other had been, but not to sit down this time, instead, to stand pressing among the motionless bodies, listening to the voices:

"And you claim twenty bushels of corn is too high for the damage you did to the rug?"

"He brought the rug to me and said he wanted the tracks washed out of it. I washed the tracks out and took the rug back to him."

"But you didn't carry the rug back to him in the same condition it was in before you made the tracks on it."

His father did not answer, and now for perhaps half a minute there was no sound at all save that of breathing, the faint, steady suspiration of complete and intent listening.

"You decline to answer that, Mr. Snopes?" Again his father did not answer. "I'm going to find against you, Mr. Snopes. I'm going to find that you were responsible for the injury to Major de Spain's rug and hold you liable for it. But twenty bushels of corn seems a little high for a man in your circumstances to have to pay. Major de Spain claims it cost a hundred dollars. October corn will be worth about fifty cents. I figure that if Major de Spain can stand a ninety-five dollar loss on something he paid cash for, you can stand a five-dollar loss you haven't earned yet. I hold you in damages to Major de Spain to the amount of ten bushels of corn over and above your contract with him, to be paid to him out of your crop at gathering time. Court adjourned."

It had taken no time hardly, the morning was but half begun. He thought they would return home and perhaps back to the field, since they were late, far behind all other farmers. But instead his father passed on behind the wagon, merely indicating with his hand for the older brother to follow with it, and crossed the road toward the blacksmith shop opposite, pressing on after his father, overtaking him, speaking, whispering up at the harsh, calm face beneath the weathered hat: "He won't git no ten bushels neither. He won't git one. We'll..." until his father glanced for an instant down at him, the face absolutely calm, the grizzled eyebrows tangled above the cold eyes, the voice almost pleasant, almost gentle:

"You think so? Well, we'll wait till October anyway."

The matter of the wagon—the setting of a spoke or two and the tightening of the tires—did not take long either, the business of the tires accomplished by driving the wagon into the spring branch behind the shop and letting it stand there, the mules nuzzling into the water from time to time, and the boy on the seat with the idle reins, looking up the slope and through the sooty tunnel of the shed where the slow hammer rang and where his father sat on an upended cypress bolt, easily, either talking or listening, still sitting there when the boy brought the dripping wagon up out of the branch and halted it before the door.

"Take them on to the shade and hitch," his father said. He did so and returned. His father and the smith and a third man squatting on his heels inside the door were talking, about crops and animals; the boy, squatting too in the ammoniac dust and hoof-parings and scales of rust, heard his father tell a long and unhurried story out of the time before the birth of the older brother even when he had been a professional horsetrader. And then his father came up beside him where he stood before a tattered last year's circus poster on the other side of the store, gazing rapt and quiet at the scarlet horses, the incredible poisings and convolutions of tulle and tights and the painted leers of comedians, and said, "It's time to eat."

But not at home. Squatting beside his brother against the front

wall, he watched his father emerge from the store and produce
from a paper sack a segment of cheese and divide it carefully and
deliberately into three with his pocket knife and produce crackers
from the same sack. They all three squatted on the gallery and ate,
slowly, without talking; then in the store again, they drank from a
tin dipper tepid water smelling of the cedar bucket and of living
beech trees. And still they did not go home. It was a horse lot this
time, a tall rail fence upon and along which men stood and sat and
out of which one by one horses were led, to be walked and trotted
and then cantered back and forth along the road while the slow
swapping and buying went on and the sun began to slant westward,
they—the three of them—watching and listening, the older brother
with his muddy eyes and his steady, inevitable tobacco, the father
commenting now and then on certain of the animals, to no one in
particular.

It was after sundown when they reached home. They ate supper
by lamplight, then, sitting on the doorstep, the boy watched the
night fully accomplish, listening to the whippoorwills and the frogs,
when he heard his mother's voice: "Abner! No! No! Oh, God. Oh,
God. Abner!" and he rose, whirled, and saw the altered light through
the door where a candle stub now burned in a bottle neck on the
table and his father, still in the hat and coat, at once formal and
burlesque as though dressed carefully for some shabby and ceremonial violence, emptying the reservoir of the lamp back into the
five-gallon kerosene can from which it had been filled, while the
mother tugged at his arm until he shifted the lamp to the other
hand and flung her back, not savagely or viciously, just hard, into
the wall, her hands flung out against the wall for balance, her mouth
open and in her face the same quality of hopeless despair as had
been in her voice. Then his father saw him standing in the door.

"Go to the barn and get that can of oil we were oiling the wagon
with," he said. The boy did not move. Then he could speak.

"What..." he cried. "What are you..."

"Go get that oil," his father said. "Go."

Then he was moving, running, outside the house, toward the
stable: this the old habit, the old blood which he had not been
permitted to choose for himself, which had been bequeathed him
willy nilly and which had run for so long (and who knew where,
battening on what of outrage and savagery and lust) before it came
to him. *I could keep on,* he thought. *I could run on and on and never*

look back, never need to see his face again. Only I can't. I can't, the rusted can in his hand now, the liquid sploshing in it as he ran back to the house and into it, into the sound of his mother's weeping in the next room, and handed the can to his father.

"Ain't you going to even send a nigger?" he cried. "At least you sent a nigger before!"

This time his father didn't strike him. The hand came even faster than the blow had, the same hand which had set the can on the table with almost excruciating care flashing from the can toward him too quick for him to follow it, gripping him by the back of his shirt and on to tiptoe before he had seen it quit the can, the face stooping at him in breathless and frozen ferocity, the cold, dead voice speaking over him to the older brother who leaned against the table, chewing with that steady, curious, sidewise motion of cows:

"Empty the can into the big one and go on. I'll catch up with you."

"Better tie him up to the bedpost," the brother said.

"Do like I told you," the father said. Then the boy was moving, his bunched shirt and the hard, bony hand between his shoulder-blades, his toes just touching the floor, across the room and into the other one, past the sisters sitting with spread heavy thighs in the two chairs over the cold hearth, and to where his mother and aunt sat side by side on the bed, the aunt's arms about his mother's shoulders.

"Hold him," the father said. The aunt made a startled movement. "Not you," the father said. Lennie. Take hold of him. I want to see you do it." His mother took him by the wrist. "You'll hold him better than that. If he gets loose don't you know what he is going to do? He will go up yonder." He jerked his head toward the road. "Maybe I'd better tie him."

"I'll hold him," his mother whispered.

"See you do then." Then his father was gone, the stiff foot heavy and measured upon the boards, ceasing at last.

Then he began to struggle. His mother caught him in both arms, he jerking and wrenching at them. He would be stronger in the end, he knew that. But he had no time to wait for it. "Lemme go!" he cried. "I don't want to have to hit you!"

"Let him go!" the aunt said. "If he don't go, before God, I am going up there myself!"

"Don't you see I can't?" his mother cried. "Sarty! Sarty! No! No! Help me, Lizzie!"

Then he was free. His aunt grasped at him but it was too late. He whirled, running, his mother stumbled forward on to her knees behind him, crying to the nearer sister: "Catch him, Net! Catch him!" But that was too late too, the sister (the sisters were twins, born at the same time, yet either of them now gave the impression of being, encompassing as much living meat and volume and weight as any other two of the family) not yet having begun to rise from the chair, her head, face, alone merely turned, presenting to him in the flying instant an astonishing expanse of young female features untroubled by any surprise even, wearing only an expression of bovine interest. Then he was out of the room, out of the house, in the mild dust of the starlit road and the heavy rifeness of honeysuckle, the pale ribbon unspooling with terrific slowness under his running feet, reaching the gate at last and turning in, running, his heart and lungs drumming, on up the drive toward the lighted house, the lighted door. He did not knock, he burst in, sobbing for breath, incapable for the moment of speech; he saw the astonished face of the Negro in the linen jacket without knowing when the Negro had appeared.

"De Spain!" he cried, panted. "Where's..." then he saw the white man too emerging from a white door down the hall. "Barn!" he cried. "Barn!"

"What?" the white man said. "Barn?"

"Yes!" the boy cried. "Barn!"

"Catch him!" the white man shouted.

But it was too late this time too. The Negro grasped his shirt, but the entire sleeve, rotten with washing, carried away, and he was out that door too and in the drive again, and had actually never ceased to run even while he was screaming into the white man's face.

Behind him the white man was shouting, "My horse! Fetch my horse!" and he thought for an instant of cutting across the park and climbing the fence into the road, but he did not know the park nor how high the vine-massed fence might be and he dared not risk it. So he ran on down the drive, blood and breath roaring; presently he was in the road again though he could not see it. He could not hear either: the galloping mare was almost upon him before he heard her, and even then he held his course, as if the very urgency of his wild grief and need must in a moment more find him wings, waiting until the ultimate instant to hurl himself aside and into the weed-choked roadside ditch as the horse thundered past and on, for an instant in furious silhouette against the stars, the tranquil early summer night sky which, even before the shape of the horse and rider vanished, stained abruptly and violently upward: a long, swirling roar incredible and soundless, blotting the stars, and he springing up and into the road again, running again, knowing it was too late yet still running even after he heard the shot and, an instant later, two shots, pausing now without knowing he had ceased to run, crying "Pap! Pap!", running again before he knew he had begun to run, stumbling, tripping over something and scrabbling up again without ceasing to run, looking backward over his shoulder at the glare as he got up, running on among the invisible trees, panting, sobbing, "Father! Father!"

At midnight he was sitting on the crest of a hill. He did not know it was midnight and he did not know how far he had come. But there was no glare behind him now and he sat now, his back toward what he had called home for four days anyhow, his face toward the dark woods which he would enter when breath was strong again, small, shaking steadily in the chill darkness, hugging himself into the remainder of his thin, rotten shirt, the grief and despair now no longer terror and fear but just grief and despair. *Father. My father,* he thought. "He was brave!" he cried suddenly, aloud but not loud, no more than a whisper: "He was! He was in the war! He was in Colonel Sartoris' cav'ry!" not knowing that his father had gone to that war a private in the fine old European sense, wearing no uniform, admitting the authority of and giving fidelity to no man or army or flag, going to war as Malbrouck himself did: for booty—it meant nothing and less than nothing to him if it were enemy booty or his own.

The slow constellations wheeled on. It would be dawn and then sun-up after a while and he would be hungry. But that would be to-morrow and now he was only cold, and walking would cure that. His breathing was easier now and he decided to get up and go on, and then he found that he had been asleep because he knew it was almost dawn, the night almost over. He could tell that from the whippoorwills. They were everywhere now among the dark trees below him, constant and inflectioned and ceaseless, so that, as the instant for giving over to the day birds drew nearer and nearer,

there was no interval at all between them. He got up. He was a
little stiff, but walking would cure that too as it would the cold, and
soon there would be the sun. He went on down the hill, toward
the dark woods within which the liquid silver voices of the birds
called unceasing—the rapid and urgent beating of the urgent and
quiring heart of the late spring night. He did not look back.

Bertrand Russell

THE INFRA-REDIOSCOPE

NOBEL PRIZE 1950

Bertrand Arthur William Russell, 3rd Earl Russell (1872– 1970) was born in Trelleck, Wales, and graduated from Cambridge in 1894. A brilliant mathematician, philosopher, and social activist, he spent most of the rest of his life in various academic posts even though his strong views about pacifism, religion, and free love often landed him in trouble.

He should have been awarded a Nobel Prize in mathematics or philosophy for such works as The Principles of Mathematics *(1902),* Principia Mathematica *(coauthored in three volumes with Alfred North Whitehead, 1910–1913),* Introduction to Mathematical Philosophy *(1919), and* Our Knowledge of the External World *(1926). But since such categories did not exist, he seems to have been given the 1950 Nobel Prize for Literature "for his varied and significant writings championing humanitarian ideals and freedom of thought" as a form of compensation.*

I

LADY MILLICENT PINTURQUE, KNOWN to her friends as the lovely Millicent, was sitting alone in her armchair in her luxurious boudoir. All the chairs and sofas were soft; the electric light was softly shaded; beside her, on a small table, stood what appeared to be a large doll with voluminous skirts. The walls were covered with water colors, all signed "Millicent," representing romantic scenes in the Alps and the Italian shores of the Mediterranean, in the islands of Greece, and in Teneriffe. Another water color was in her hands, and she was scrutinizing it with minute care. At last she reached out her hand to the doll, and touched a button. The doll opened in the middle, and revealed a telephone in its entrails. She lifted the receiver. Her movements, although they showed what was evidently an habitual grace, displayed a certain tenseness of manner, suggesting an important decision just arrived at. She called a number, and when it had been obtained she said: "I wish to speak with Sir Bulbus."

Sir Bulbus Frutiger was known to all the world as the editor of the *Daily Lightning,* and as one of the great powers in our land, no matter what party might be nominally in office. He was protected from the public by a secretary and six secretary's secretaries. Few ventured to call him on the telephone, and of these few only an infinitesimal proportion reached him. His lucubrations were too important to be interrupted. It was his mission to preserve an imperturbable calm, while developing schemes for destroying the calm of all his readers. But in spite of this wall of protection, he answered instantly to the call of Lady Millicent.

"Yes, Lady Millicent?" he said.

"All is ready," she answered, and replaced the receiver.

II

Much preparation had preceded these brief words. The lovely Millicent's husband, Sir Theophilus Pinturque, was one of the leaders in the world of finance, an immensely rich man, but not, though this grieved him, without rivals in the world that he wished to dominate. There were still men who could meet him on equal terms and who, in a financial contest, had reasonable chances of victory. His character was Napoleonic, and he sought for means by which his superiority could become unchallenged and unquestionable. He recognized that the power of finance was not the only great power in the modern world. There are, he reflected, three others: one is the power of the Press; one is the power of advertising; and one, too often underestimated by men in his profession, is the power of science. He decided that victory would require a combination of these four powers, and with this end in view, he formed a secret committee of four.

He himself was the chairman. Next in power and dignity was Sir Bulbus Frutiger, who had a slogan: "Give the public what it wants." This slogan governed all his vast chain of newspapers. The third member of the syndicate was Sir Publius Carper, who controlled the advertising world. Those who, in compelled, though temporary, idleness went up and down escalators, imagined that the men whose advertisements they read, because they had nothing else to do, were rivals. This was a mistake. All the advertisements came to a central pool, and in that central pool their distribution was decided by Sir Publius Carper. If he wished your dentrifice to be known, it would be known; if he wished it ignored, it would be ignored, however excellent. It rested with him to make or mar the fortunes of those who were unwise enough to produce consumable commodities — instead of recommending them. Sir Publius had a certain kindly contempt for Sir Bulbus. He thought Sir Bulbus's slogan too submissive altogether. His slogan was: "Make the public want what you give it." In this he was amazingly successful. Wines of unspeakable nastiness sold in vast numbers because, when he told the public that they were delicious, the public had not the courage to doubt his word. Seaside resorts where hotels were filthy, the lodgings dingy, and the sea, except at extreme high tide, a sea of mud, acquired through the activities of Sir Publius a reputation for ozone, stormy seas, and invigorating Atlantic breezes. Political parties at General Elections made use of the inventiveness of his employees, which was at the service of all (except Communists) who could afford his prices. No sensible man who knew the world would dream of launching a campaign without the support of Sir Publius.

Sir Bulbus and Sir Publius, though frequently joined in their public campaigns, were in appearance very different from each other. Both were *bons viveurs,* but while Sir Bulbus looked the part, having a considerable corporation and a cheerful, eupeptic appearance, Sir Publius was lean and ascetic-looking. Anybody who did not know who he was would imagine him an earnest seeker after some mystic vision. Never could his portrait be used to advertise any article of food or drink. Nevertheless, when, as not infrequently occurred, the two men dined together, to plan a new conquest or a change of policy, they agreed remarkably with each other. Each understood the workings of the other's mind; each respected the other's ambitions; each felt the need of the other to complete his designs. Sir Publius would point out how much Sir Bulbus owed to the picture which appeared on every hoarding of the moron who does not read the *Daily Lightning*, pointed at with contempt by a well-dressed crowd of handsome men and lovely women, each supplied with his or her copy of that great newspaper. And Sir Bulbus would retort: "Yes, but where would you be, but for my great campaign to secure control of the Canadian forests? Where would you be without paper, and where would you get the paper, but for the masterly policy which I have pursued in that great Transatlantic Dominion?" Such friendly quips would occupy them until the dessert; after that, both would become serious, and their cooperation would be intense and creative.

Pendrake Markle, the fourth member of the secret syndicate, was somewhat different from the other three. Sir Bulbus and Sir Publius had had some doubts as to his admission, but their doubts had been overruled by Sir Theophilus. Their doubts were not unreasonable. In the first place, unlike the other three, he had not been honored with a knighthood. There were, however, even graver objections to him. Nobody denied that he was brilliant, but solid men suspected that he was unsound. His was not the sort of name that would be put on a prospectus to tempt country investors. Sir Theophilus, however, insisted upon including him, because of his extreme fertility in unorthodox invention, and also because, unlike some other men of science, he was not hampered by an undue scrupulosity.

He had a grudge against the human race, which was intelligible to those who knew his history. His father was a Nonconformist minister of the most exemplary piety, who used to explain to him when he was a little boy how right it was of Elisha to curse the children who, as a result of his curse, were torn to pieces by she-bears. In all ways his father was a relic of a bygone age. Respect for the Sabbath, and a belief in the literal inspiration of every word of the Old and New Testaments, dominated all his converse in the home. The boy, already intelligent, once ventured in a rash moment to ask his father whether it was impossible to be a good Christian if one did not believe that the hare chews the cud. His father thrashed him so unmercifully that he could not sit down for a week.

In spite of this careful upbringing, he refused to gratify the parental desire that he should become himself a Noncomformist minister. By means of scholarships he managed to work his way through the university, where he obtained the highest honors. His first piece of research was stolen from him by his professor, who was awarded a Royal Society Medal on the strength of it. When he attempted to make his grievance known, no one believed him, and he was thought to be an ill-conditioned boor. As a result of this experience and of the suspicion with which his protests caused him to be regarded, he became a cynic and a misanthropist. He took care, however, henceforth, that no one should steal his inventions or discoveries. There were nasty stories, never substantiated, of shady dealings in regard to patents. The stories varied, and no one knew what foundation they had in fact. However that may be, he acquired at last enough money to make for his own use a private laboratory, to which no possible rivals were allowed access. Gradually his work began to win reluctant recognition. At last the Government approached him with a request that he should devote his talents to improving bacteriological warfare. He refused this request on a ground which was universally considered exceedingly strange, namely that he knew nothing about bacteriology. It was suspected, however, that his real reason was a hatred of all the forces of organized society, from the Prime Minister to the humblest policeman on his beat.

Although everybody in the scientific world disliked him, very few dared to attack him, because of his unscrupulous skill in controversy, which succeeded almost always in making his adversary look foolish. There was only one thing in all the world that he loved, and that was his private laboratory. Unfortunately, its equipment had run him into enormous expense and he was in imminent danger of having to dispose of it to settle his debts. It was while this danger hung over him that he was approached by Sir Theophilus, who offered to save him from disaster in return for his help as the fourth member of the secret syndicate.

At the first meeting of the syndicate, Sir Theophilus explained what he had in mind, and asked for suggestions as to the realization of his hopes. It should be possible, he said, for the four of them in collaboration to achieve complete domination of the world—not only of this or that part of the world, not only of Western Europe, or of Western Europe and America, but equally of the world on the other side of the Iron Curtain. If they used their skill and their opportunities wisely, nothing should be able to resist them.

"All that is wanted," so he said in his opening address, "is a really fruitful idea. The supplying of ideas shall be the business of Markle. Given a good idea, I will finance it, Carper will advertise it, and Frutiger will rouse to frenzy the passions of the public against those who oppose it. It is possible that Markle may require a little time to invent the sort of idea which the rest of us would think it worth while to promote. I therefore propose that this meeting do adjourn for a week, at the end of which time, I am convinced, science will be prepared to vindicate its position as one of the four forces dominating our society."

With this, after a bow to Mr. Markle, he dismissed the meeting.

When the syndicate met again a week later, Sir Theophilus, smiling at Mr. Markle, remarked: "Well, Markle, and what has science to say?" Markle cleared his throat and entered upon a speech:

"Sir Theophilus, Sir Bulbus and Sir Publius," he began, "throughout the past week I have given my best thought—and my best thought, I assure you, is very good—to the concoction of such a scheme as was adumbrated at our last meeting. Various notions occurred to me, only to be rejected. The public has been inundated with horrors connected with nuclear energy, and I decided very quickly that this whole subject has now become hackneyed. Moreover, it is a matter as to which Governments are on the alert, and anything that we might attempt in this direction would probably meet with official opposition. I thought next of what could be done by means of bacteriology. It might be possible, so I thought, to give hydrophobia to all the Heads of State. But it was not quite clear how we should profit by this, and there was always a risk that one of them might bite one of us before his disease was diagnosed. Then, of course, there was the scheme for creating a satellite of the earth which should complete its revolution once every three days, with a clockwork mechanism timed to fire at the Kremlin every time it passed that way. This, however, is a project for Governments. We should be above the battle. It is not for us to take sides in the controversies between East and West. It is for us to ensure that, whatever happens, we shall be supreme. I therefore rejected all schemes which involve an abandonment of neutrality.

"I have a scheme to propose to you which I think is not open to any of the objections to the other schemes. The public has heard much in recent years about infra-red photography. It is as ignorant on this subject as on every other, and I see no reason why we should not exploit its ignorance. I propose that we invent a machine to be called the 'infra-redioscope,' which (so we shall assure the public) will photograph by means of infra-red rays objects not otherwise perceptible. It shall be a very delicate machine, capable of getting out of order if carelessly handled. We shall see to it that this happens whenever the machine is in the possession of persons whom we cannot control. What it is to see we shall determine, and I think that, by our united efforts, we can persuade the world that it really sees whatever we shall decide that it makes visible. If you adopt my scheme, I will undertake to devise the machine, but as to how it is to be utilized, that, I think, is a matter for Sir Bulbus and Sir Publius."

Both these gentlemen had listened with attention to the suggestion of Pendrake Markle. Both of them seized upon his ideas with enthusiasm, seeing great opportunities for the exploitation of their respective skills.

"I know," said Sir Bulbus, "what it is that the machine should reveal. It shall reveal a secret invasion from Mars, an invasion of horrible creatures, whose invisible army, but for our machine, would be certain of victory. I shall, in all my newspapers, rouse the public to a consciousness of their peril. Millions of them will buy the machine. Sir Theophilus will make the greatest fortune ever possessed by a single man. My newspapers will outsell all others and will be, before long, the only newspapers of the world. Nor will my friend Publius be less important in this campaign. He will cover every hoarding with pictures of the dreadful creatures and a caption beneath—"Do you wish to be dispossessed by THIS?" And in vast letters he will put notices along all the main roads, in all stations of the country, and wherever the public has leisure to see such things, and the notices will say: 'Men of earth, now is the hour of decision. Rise in your millions. Be not appalled by the cosmic danger. Courage shall yet triumph, as it has done ever since the days of Adam. Buy an infra-redioscope and be prepared!'"

At this point Sir Theophilus intervened.

"The scheme is good," he said. "It requires only one thing, and that is that the picture of the Martian should be sufficiently horrible and terrifying. You all know Lady Millicent, but you know her perhaps only in her gentler aspects. I, as her husband, have been privileged to become aware of regions in her imagination which are concealed from most people. She is, as you know, skilled in water colors. Let her make a water-color picture of the Martian, and let photographs of her picture form the basis of our campaign."

The others at first looked a little doubtful. Lady Millicent as they had seen her was soft, perhaps a trifle silly, not the sort of person whom they had imagined as taking part in so grim a campaign. After some debate it was decided to allow her to make the attempt, and if her picture was sufficiently dreadful to satisfy Mr. Markle, Sir Bulbus should then be informed that all was in readiness for the launching of the campaign.

Sir Theophilus, on returning home from his momentous meeting, set to work to explain to the lovely Millicent what it was that he wanted. He did not enlarge upon the general aspects of his campaign, for it was a principle with him that one should not take women into one's confidence. He told her merely that he wished for pictures of terrifying imaginary creatures, for which he had a business use which she would find it difficult to understand.

Lady Millicent, who was very much younger than Sir Theophilus, belonged to a good county family now fallen upon evil days. Her father, an impoverished earl, was the owner of an exquisite Elizabethan mansion, which he loved with a devotion inherited from all the generations that had inhabited it. It had seemed inevitable that he should sell this ancestral mansion to some rich Argentinian, and the prospect was slowly breaking his heart. His daughter adored him and decided to use her staggering beauty to enable him to end his days in peace. Almost all men adored her at sight. Sir Theophilus was the richest of her adorers and so she chose him, exacting as her price a sufficient settlement upon her father to free him from all financial anxiety. She did not dislike Sir Theophilus, who adored her and gratified her every whim, but she did not love him—indeed, no one, up to this moment, had ever touched her heart. She felt it her duty, in return for all he gave her, to obey him whenever possible.

His request for a water color of a monster seemed to her a little odd, but she was accustomed to actions on his part to which she had no clue, nor had she ever any desire to understand his business schemes. She therefore duly set to work. He did go so far as to tell her that the picture was wanted for the purpose of showing what could be seen by means of a new instrument to be called the "infra-redioscope." After several attempts which did not satisfy her, she produced a picture of a creature with a body somewhat resembling that of a beetle, but six feet long, with seven hairy legs, with a human face, completely bald head, staring eyes, and a fixed grin. She made indeed two pictures. In the first, a man is looking through an infra-redioscope and seeing this creature. In the second, the man, in terror, has dropped the instrument. The monster, seeing that it is observed, has stood upright on its seventh leg and is entwining the other six in hairy embrace round the asphyxiated man. These two pictures, at the orders of Sir Theophilus, she showed to Mr. Markle. Mr. Markle accepted them as adequate, and it was after his departure that she telephoned the fateful words to Sir Bulbus.

III

As soon as Sir Bulbus received this message, the vast apparatus controlled by the syndicate was set in motion. Sir Theophilus caused innumerable workshops throughout the world to manufacture the infra-redioscope, a simple machine, containing a lot of wheels that made whirring noises, but not in fact enabling anyone to see anything. Sir Bulbus filled his newspapers with articles on the wonders of science, all of them with a "slant" towards the infra-red. Some of these contained genuine information by reputable men of science; others were more imaginative. Sir Publius had bills posted everywhere: "The infra-redioscope is coming! See the world's invisible marvels!" or "What is the infra-redioscope? The Frutiger newspapers will tell you. Do not miss this chance of strange knowledge!"

As soon as sufficient numbers of infra-redioscopes had been manufactured, Lady Millicent let is be known that by means of one of these instruments she had observed the horror crawling upon her bedroom floor. She was interviewed naturally by all the newspapers under the control of Sir Bulbus, but the matter was of such dramatic interest that other newspapers were compelled to follow suit. Under her husband's instructions, she uttered in broken and apparently terrified sentences exactly the sentiments that were required by the scheme of the syndicate. At the same time infra-redioscopes were given to various leaders of opinion whom Sir Theophilus, by means of his secret service, knew to be in financial difficulties. Each of them was offered a thousand pounds if he would say that he had seen one of the awful creatures. Lady Millicent's two pictures were reproduced everywhere through the advertising agency of Sir Publius, with the legend: "Do not drop your infra-redioscope. It protects as well as reveals."

There was, of course, an instant sale of many thousands of infra-redioscopes and a world-wide wave of horror. Pendrake Markle invented a new instrument to be found only in his private laboratory. This new instrument proved that the creatures came from Mars. Other men of science grew envious of the enormous fame which accrued to Markle, and one of the more venturesome of these would-be rivals invented a machine that read the thoughts of the creatures. By means of this machine he professed to have discovered that they were the advance guard of a Martian campaign to exterminate the human race.

Just at first the earlier purchasers of infra-redioscopes had complained that they saw nothing through these instruments, but naturally their remarks were not printed in any of the newspapers controlled by Sir Bulbus, and very soon the universal panic reached such dimensions that any person claiming to have failed to detect the presence of Martians was assumed to be a traitor and pro-Martian. After some thousands of persons had been lynched, the rest found it prudent to hold their tongues, except for a very few who were interned. There was now such a wave of horror that many people who had hitherto been considered harmless incurred the gravest suspicion. Any person who unguardedly praised the appearance of the planet Mars in the night sky was instantly suspect. All astronomers who had made a special study of Mars were interned. Those among them who had maintained that there is no life on Mars were sentenced to long terms of imprisonment.

There were, however, some groups who, throughout the early stages of the panic, remained friends of Mars. The Emperor of Abyssinia announced that a careful study of the picture showed the Martian to resemble closely the Lion of Judah, and to be therefore obviously good and not bad. The Tibetans said that from a study of ancient books they had concluded that the Martian was a Bodhisattva, come to liberate them from the yoke of the infidel Chinese. Peruvian Indians revived sun worship, and pointed out that since Mars shines by reflected sunlight, Mars too is to be adored. When it was remarked that the Martians might cause carnage, they replied that sun worship had always involved human sacrifice, and that therefore the truly devout would not repine. The anarchists argued that Martians would dissolve all government and would therefore bring the millennium. The pacifists said that they should be met with love, and that if the love were sufficiently great, it would take the grin off their faces.

For a short time these various groups, wherever they existed in sufficient numbers, remained unmolested. But their respite ceased when the Communist world was brought into the anti-Martian campaign. This was achieved by the syndicate with some skill. They approached first certain Western men of science known to be friendly to the Soviet Government. They told these men frankly how the campaign had been engineered. They pointed out that fear of the Martians could be made the basis of reconciliation between East and West. They also succeeded in persuading the fellow-travelling scientists that an East-West war could well result in the defeat of the East, and that therefore whatever would prevent a third world war should be favored by the Communists. They pointed out further that if terror of the Martians was to effect a reconciliation between East and West, it was necessary that all the governments, Eastern as well as Western, should believe in the Martian invasion. The fellow-travelling scientists, after listening to these arguments, found themselves reluctantly compelled to agree. For were they not realists? And was not this realism, as stark as realism could be? And was not this perhaps the very synthesis that dialectical materialism demanded? They therefore agreed that they would not reveal to the Soviet Government the fact that the whole thing was a hoax. For its own sake they would allow it to believe this plot, inaugurated by vile capitalists for vile capitalist ends, but incidentally and accidentally furthering the interests of mankind, and giving a chance that when, in due course, the deception was unmasked a general reaction would sweep the whole world into the arms of Moscow. Convinced by this reasoning, they represented to Moscow the imminent danger of the destruction of the human race, and pointed out that there was no reason to believe the Martians to be Communists. On the basis of their representations, Moscow, after some hesitation, decided to join with the West in the anti-Martian campaign.

From this moment the Abyssinians, the Tibetans, the Peruvians, the anarchists, and the pacifists received short shrift. Some were killed, some were set to forced labor, some recanted, and in a very short time there was no longer any explicit opposition anywhere in the world to the great anti-Martian campaign.

Fear, however, could not be confined to fear of the Martians. There was still fear of traitors in their midst. A great meeting of the United Nations was summoned to organize propaganda and publicity. It was felt that a word was needed to represent the inhabitants of earth as opposed to the inhabitants of other planets. "Earthy" obviously would not do. "Earthly" was inadequate because of the usual alternative was "heavenly." "Terrestrial" would not do because the usual alternative was "celestial." At last, after much eloquence, in which the South Americans especially distinguished themselves, the world "Tellurian" was adopted. The United Nations then appointed a committee against un-Tellurian activities, which established a political reign of terror throughout the whole world. It was also decided that the United Nations should be in permanent session, so long as the crisis lasted, under a permanent head. A President was chosen from among the elder statesmen, a man of immense dignity and vast experience, no longer embroiled in party warfare, and prepared by two world wars for the even more terrible war that now seemed imminent. He rose to the occasion, and in his opening address said:

"Friends, Fellow Inhabitants of Earth, Tellurians, united as never before, I address you on this solemn occasion, not as heretofore in the cause of world peace, but in an even greater cause—an even greater cause—the cause of the preservation of this our human existence with all its human values, with all its joys and sorrows, all its hopes and all its fears, the preservation, I say, of this our human life from a foul assault wafted across the ether by we know not what foul and dreadful means, revealed to us, I am happy to say, by the amazing skill of our men of science, who have shown us what by infra-rediation can be discovered, and have made visible to us the strange, repellent and horrible beasts which crawl upon our floors unseen save by these marvelous instruments, which crawl, I say, nay, which infect us, which pollute our very thoughts, which would destroy within us the very fiber of our moral being, which would reduce us, I say, not to the level of beasts—for beasts are, after all, Tellurians—nay, to the level of Martians—and can I say anything worse? No lower term, no greater word of infamy exists in the languages of this Earth that we all love. I call upon you, I call upon you, my brethren, to stand shoulder to shoulder in the great fight, the fight to preserve our earthly values against this insidious and degrading invasion of monsters, alien monsters, monsters who, we can only say, should go back where they came from."

With this he sat down. And the applause was such that for five several minutes nothing else could be heard. The next speaker was the Representative of the United States.

"Fellow Citizens of Earth," he began, "those who have had the misfortune to be compelled by their public duties to study that abominable planet against whose evil machinations we are here embattled, are aware that its surface is scarred by strange straight marks, known among astronomers as canals. These marks, as must be evident to every student of economic activity, can only be the product of totalitarianism. We have therefore a right, the right of the highest scientific authority, to believe that these invaders threaten not only us in our personal and private being, but also that way of life which was established by our ancestors nearly two hundred years ago, and which, until the present danger, produced unity— unity apparently threatened by a certain Power, which, at the present moment, it would be injudicious to name. It may be that man represents but a passing phase in the evolution of the life of the cosmos, but there is one law which the cosmos will always obey, one divine law, the law of eternal progress. This law, Fellow Citizens of Earth, this law is safeguarded by free enterprise, the immortal heritage which the West has brought to man. Free enterprise must have long since ceased in that red planet which now menaces us, for the canals which we see are not a thing of yesterday. Not only in the name of Man, but in the name of free enterprise, I call upon this Assembly to give of its best, to give till it hurts, without stint, without thought of self. It is with confident hope that I make this appeal to all the other nations here assembled."

It was not to be left to the West alone to sound the note of unity. No sooner had the Representative of the United States sat down than he was succeeded by Mr. Growlovsky, the Representative of the Soviet Union.

"The hour is come," he said, "to fight, not to speak. Were I to speak, there are things which I could controvert in the speech which we have just heard. Astronomy is Russian. Some few sparse students of the subject have existed in other countries, but Soviet erudition has shown how shallow and imitative their theories have been. Of these we have had an example in what has just been said about the canals in that infamous planet which I disdain to name. The great astronomer Lukupsky has shown conclusively that it was private enterprise that produced the canals, and that it was competition that stimulated their duplication. But this is not the hour for such reflections. This is the hour for action, and when the assault has been repelled, it will be found that the world has become one, and that in the throes of battle, totalitarianism has become, willy-nilly, universal."

Some fears were felt at this point that the new-found unity of the Great Powers might not survive the strain of public debate. India, Paraguay, and Iceland poured oil upon the troubled waters, and at last the soothing words of the Republic of Andorra enabled the delegates to separate with that glow of harmony that resulted from ignorance of each other's sentiments. Before separating, the Assembly decreed world peace and an amalgamation of the armed forces of the planet. It was hoped that the main assault of the Martians might be delayed until this amalgamation was complete. But meanwhile, in spite of all preparations, in spite of harmony, in spite of pretended confidence, fear lurked in every heart— except those of the syndicate and its coadjutors.

IV

Throughout this period of excited panic, however, there were some who, though prudence kept them silent, had their doubts about the whole matter. Members of Governments knew that they themselves had never seen the Martian monster, and their private secretaries knew that *they* had never seen them, but while the terror was at its height, neither dared to confess this, since avowed scepticism involved a fall from power and perhaps even a lynching. The business rivals of Sir Theophilus, Sir Bulbus, and Sir Publius naturally were envious of the immense success which these men were achieving, and wished, if it were in any way possible, to find some means of bringing them down. The *Daily Thunder* had been almost as great a power as the *Daily Lightning*, but while the campaign was at its height, the *Daily Thunder* was inaudible. Its editor gnashed his teeth, but, as a prudent man, he bided his time, knowing that a popular frenzy, while it lasts, cannot be opposed with profit. The scientists, who had always disliked and distrusted Pendrake Markle, were naturally indignant to see him treated as though he were the greatest scientist of all time. Many of them had taken the infra-redioscope to pieces and had seen that it was a fraud, but since they valued their own skins, they thought it wise to be silent.

Among them all, only one young man was indifferent to the claims of prudence. This young man was Thomas Shovelpenny, who was still viewed in many English quarters with suspicion because his grandfather had been a German named Schimmelpfennig and had changed his name during the first world war. Thomas Shovelpenny was a quiet student, totally unaccustomed to great affairs, ignorant of politics and economics alike, and skilled only in physics. He was too poor to buy an infra-redioscope and therefore was unable to make for himself the discovery of its fraudulent character. Those who had made this discovery kept their knowledge secret and did not whisper it even in moments of vinous conviviality. But Thomas Shovelpenny could not but observe strange discrepancies in the reported observations, and these discrepancies bred in him purely scientific doubts, though in his innocence he was totally at a loss to imagine what purpose could be served by inventing such myths.

Though himself a man of exemplary and abstemious conduct, he had a friend whom he valued for his penetration and his insight, in spite of habits by no means such as a well-behaved student could approve of. This friend, whose name was Verity Hogg-Paucus, was almost always intoxicated, and scarcely to be met with except in public houses. It was supposed that he must sleep somewhere, but he did not allow anyone to know the truth, which was that he had a single bedroom in one of the worst slums of London. He had brilliant talents as a journalist, and when his money gave out, the enforced sobriety would lead him to write articles of such mordant wit that the journals which liked that sort of thing could not refuse to publish them. The better-class journals, of course, were closed to him, since he would make no concessions to humbug. He knew all the underworld of politics, but did not know how to make his knowledge advantageous to himself. He had had many jobs, but had lost them all through allowing his chiefs to know that he had discovered shady secrets which the chiefs wished to keep concealed. Whether from imprudence or from a remnant of moral feeling, he had never made a penny by blackmailing the objects of his unpleasant knowledge. Instead of using his knowledge to his own advantage, he would let it trickle out of him in bibulous loquacity while drinking with any casual acquaintance in some unfashionable bar.

Shovelpenny consulted him in his perplexity.

"It seems to me," he said, "that this whole business must be fraudulent, and yet I cannot imagine either how the fraud is worked or what purpose it can serve. Perhaps you, with your great knowledge of what men wish to keep secret, will be able to help me to understand what is happening."

Hogg-Paucus, who had watched cynically the growth of public hysteria and Sir Theophilus's fortune, was delighted.

"You," he said, "are the very man I want. I have no doubt that the whole thing is bogus, but remember that it is dangerous to say so. Perhaps together, you, with your knowledge of science, and I, with my knowledge of politics, we shall be able to unravel the mystery. But since it is dangerous to talk, and since I am garrulous in my cups, it will be necessary for you to keep me locked up in your rooms, and if you supply me with sufficient liquor, I shall be able to endure the temporary imprisonment without excessive discomfort."

Shovelpenny liked the proposal, but his purse was limited, and he did not see how he could hope to keep Hogg-Paucus in drink throughout a period which might not be short. Hogg-Paucus, however, who had not always been so low in the social scale, had known Lady Millicent when both were children, and wrote a flamboyant article about her virtues and charms at the age of ten, which he sold for a large sum to a fashion magazine. This, it was thought, together with Shovelpenny's salary as a school teacher, would, with care and economy, supply the necessary amount of drink for the necessary period of time.

Hogg-Paucus thereupon set to work on a systematic investigation. It was obvious that the campaign had begun from the *Daily Lightning*. Hogg-Paucus, who knew everything in the way of personal gossip, was aware that the *Daily Lightning* was intimately connected with Sir Theophilus. It was common knowledge that Lady Millicent had been the first to see a Martian, and that Markle was mainly instrumental in the scientific part of the proceedings. A vague outline of what must have happened formed itself in the fertile mind of Hogg-Paucus, but it seemed impossible to arrive at anything more definite unless some one of those who knew could

be induced to speak. Hogg-Paucus advised Shovelpenny to request
an interview with Lady Millicent, as being the originator of the first
photograph, and therefore clearly concerned in the very beginning
of the whole matter. Shovelpenny only half believed the various
cynical hypotheses that his friend produced, but his scientific mind
showed him that the best way to begin an investigation would be
an interview with Lady Millicent, as Hogg-Paucus advised. He
therefore wrote her a careful letter, saying that he wished to see
her on a matter of importance. Somewhat to his surprise, she agreed,
and made an appointment. He brushed his hair and his clothes,
and made himself much tidier than usual. Thus prepared, he went
to a momentous interview.

V

The maid showed him into Lady Millicent's boudoir, where, as
before, she reclined in her armchair, with the doll-telephone on
the little table beside her.

"Well, Mr. Shovelpenny," she said, "your letter caused me to
wonder what it can be that you wish to discuss with me. You, so I
have always understood, are a brilliant man of science; I am a poor
scatter-brained lady, with nothing to recommend me except a rich
husband. But since I got your letter, I have taken pains to acquaint
myself with your circumstances and career, and I cannot imagine
that it is money you wish to see me about."

So saying, she smiled charmingly. Shovelpenny had never before
met a woman who was both rich and lovely, and he found himself
somewhat disconcerted by the unexpected emotions which she
roused in him. "Come, come," he said to himself, "you are not here
to feel emotions. You are here to conduct a grave investigation."
He pulled himself together with an effort, and replied:

"Lady Millicent, in common with the rest of mankind you must
be aware of the strange commotion which has taken place throughout the human race, owing to the fear of a Martian invasion. If my
information is correct, you were the first to see one of these Martians. I find it difficult to say what I have to say, but it is my duty.
Careful investigation has made me doubt whether you or anybody
else has seen any of these horrible creatures, and whether anything
whatever is to be seen by means of the infra-redioscope. If my
investigations have not misled me, I am painfully forced to the

conclusion that you have been a prime mover in a gigantic fraud. I shall not be surprised if, after hearing me utter these words, you have me removed by force from your presence, and give orders to your domestics that I am not to be admitted again to your house. Such a reaction would be natural if you were innocent, and even more natural if you were guilty. But if there is any possibility that I have not thought of, if there is any way by which I can avoid condemning one so lovely as you, and one so apparently gentle as your smile proclaims you to be, if I might, throwing science to the winds, trust my instincts in your favor, then I beseech you, I implore you, for the sake of my peace of mind, let me know the whole truth!"

His obvious sincerity and his unwillingness to flatter in spite of his instinct in her favor, affected Lady Millicent as none of her usual acquaintances had ever affected her. For the first time since she had left her father to marry Sir Theophilus, she came in contact with simple sincerity. The attempt to live artificially which she had been making ever since she entered the mansion of Sir Theophilus became intolerable to her. The world of lies and schemes and intrigues and heartless power she found that she could no longer endure.

"Oh, Mr. Shovelpenny," she said, "how can I answer you? I have a duty to my husband, I have a duty to mankind, and I have a duty to truth. To one at least of these I must be false. How can I decide to which of them my paramount duty is owing?"

"Lady Millicent," he replied, "you kindle my hope and my curiosity in equal measure. You live, as I perceive from your surroundings, an artificial life, and yet, if I am not mistaken, there is within you something that is not artificial, something sincere and simple by which you might yet be saved from the pollution that surrounds you. Speak, I implore you. Let the cleansing fire of truth purge your soul of dross!"

For a moment she was silent. Then in a firm voice she answered:

"Yes, I will speak. I have kept silence too long. I have given myself to unimaginable evil, little knowing what I was doing until, as I thought, it was too late. But you give me new hope; perhaps it is not too late; perhaps something can yet be saved—and whether anything be saved or not, I can recover that integrity which I sold to save my father from misery. Little did I know, when Sir Theophilus, in honeyed tones, and with even more than his usual conjugal blandishments, invited me to use my pictorial talents in the creation of a monster, little did I know, I repeat, in that fateful moment, for what frightful purpose the picture was required. I did as I was bid. I made the monster. I allowed myself to be quoted as having seen it, but I did not then know the fell purpose for which my husband—oh, that I must still call him such—desired me to do this deed. Step by step, as his strange campaign has unfolded itself, my conscience has troubled me more and more. Every night on my knees I have besought God to forgive me, but I know He will not do so while I am yet lapped in the luxury with which Sir Theophilus delights to surround me. Until I am willing to abandon all this, my soul cannot be purged. Your coming has been the last straw. Your coming and your simple invocation of truth has shown me at last what I must do. I will tell you all. You shall know how base is the woman to whom you are speaking. No tiniest portion of my vast turpitude will I conceal from you. And when I have stripped myself bare, perhaps I can once more feel cleansed of the foul impurity that has invaded me."

Having so said, she told him all. As she spoke, instead of the revulsion of horror which she had expected to witness, she saw in his eyes a growing admiration, and he felt in his heart a love to which he had hitherto been a stranger. When she had told all, he took her in his arms, and she yielded to his embrace.

"Ah, Millicent," he said, "how tangled and how dreadful is human life. All that Hogg-Paucus told me is true, and yet, at the very fount of this evil wickedness I find you, you, who are still capable of feeling the pure flame of truth, you in whom, now that to your own ruin you have confessed all, I find a comrade, a spiritual comrade such as I did not believe the world to contain. But what to do in this strange tangle, I cannot yet decide. For twenty-four hours I must meditate. When that time has elapsed, I will come back and tell you my decision."

When Shovelpenny returned to his apartment, he returned in a state of intellectual and emotional bewilderment, knowing neither what he felt nor what he thought. Hogg-Paucus lay on his bed, snoring in a drunken stupor. He had no wish for this man's cynicism, which he could not bring into harmony with his feelings about Millicent, whose beauty made it impossible for him to condemn her. He placed a large bottle of whisky and a glass beside Hogg-Paucus's bed, knowing that if, during the coming twenty-four hours, that worthy man should have a moment of wakefulness, the sight of the liquor would quickly overcome him, and he would return to oblivion. Having thus secured twenty-four hours without interruption, he sat down in his chair before his gas fire, and set to work to bring some kind of order into his mind.

Public and private duty alike were difficult to determine. The men who had made the plot were wicked men; their motives were vile, and they cared nothing whether mankind was the better or the worse for their activities. Private gain and private power were their sole aims. Lies, deception, and terror were their means. Could he, by his silence, make himself a party to such an infamy? And if he did not, if he persuaded Millicent to confess, as he well knew that he could, what would become of her? What would her husband do to her? What would her dupes throughout the world do to her? In imagination he saw her loveliness trampled in the dust and savage mobs tearing her to pieces. The vision was scarcely bearable, but yet, he thought, if that spark of nobility which was awakened in her while they spoke was not to be quenched anew, she must not go on living in the soft bed of profitable lies.

And so his thoughts turned to the other alternative. Should he allow Sir Theophilus and his accomplices to triumph? There were powerful arguments in favor of this course. Before the hatching of the plot, East and West had been on the verge of war, and it was thought by many that the human race would exterminate itself in futile fury. Now, from fear of a wholly imaginary danger, the real danger existed no longer. The Kremlin and the White House, united in hatred of the imaginary Martians, had become the best of friends. The armies of the world might still be mustered, but they were mustered against a foe that did not exist, and their ineffectual armaments could not do the damage for which they were intended. "Perhaps," so ran his meditations, "perhaps it is only through lies that men can be induced to live sensibly. Perhaps human passions are such that to the end of time truth will be dangerous. Perhaps I have erred in giving my allegiance to truth. Perhaps Sir Theophilus is wiser than I. Perhaps it is folly in me to lead my beloved Millicent towards her ruin."

And then his thoughts took another turn. "Sooner or later," so he said to himself, "the deception will be discovered. If it is not discovered by those who, like myself, are actuated by love of truth, it will be discovered by those who have rival interests every bit as sinister as those of Sir Theophilus. What use will these men make of their discovery? They will use it only to exacerbate the revulsion against the Tellurian harmony that the lies of Sir Theophilus have engendered. Is it not better, since, sooner or later, the whole plot must be unmasked, is it not better that it should be unmasked in the name of a noble ideal, the ideal of truth, rather than in the ignoble pursuit of competition and envy? But who am I to judge such matters? I am not God. I cannot read the future. It is all dark. Wherever I look, horror stares me in the face. I know not whether to support wicked men to good ends, or good men to the destruction of the world. For that is the dreadful dilemma with which I am confronted. It is too difficult for me."

For twenty-four hours he sat immovable in his chair, neither eating nor drinking, swayed by the to-and-fro of conflicting arguments. At the end of that time his appointment with Lady Millicent called him. He rose wearily and stiffly, sighed deeply, and with heavy steps went on foot towards her mansion.

He found Lady Millicent as shattered as he was himself. She also had been torn by perplexity. But the world played less part in her thoughts than her husband and her now dearly loved Thomas. She had not the habit of political thinking. Her world was composed of persons, persons whose activities, she knew, had various effects outside the periphery of her consciousness; but these effects she could not hope to understand. What she could understand was the human passions of the men and women who made up her private world. Throughout the twenty-four hours she had meditated on the shining qualities of Thomas's disinterestedness, with a futile and desperate wish that it had been her good fortune to come across some person possessing this character before the coils of Sir Theophilus's machinations had inextricably entwined her. She had found one thing to do which had made the suspense of those hours just bearable. She had painted from memory a miniature of Thomas, and this miniature she had placed in a locket that in more frivolous times had contained the likeness of her husband. The locket she hung on a chain round her neck, and when the suspense became unendurable she sought relief in gazing upon the likeness of him whom she yearned to call her lover.

At last he was with her, but there was no buoyancy in his step, no brightness in his eye, no resonance in his voice. Dejected and slow, he took her hand in his. With his other hand he extracted from his pocket a pill which he quickly swallowed.

"Millicent," he said, "this pill which I have swallowed will in a few minutes cause me to breathe no more. The choice before me is too difficult. When I was a younger man I had hopes, high hopes. I thought that I should be able to dedicate my life to the twin gods of truth and humanity. Alas! it was not to be. Shall I serve truth and cause humanity to perish, or shall I serve humanity and let truth lie trampled in the dust? O dreadful alternative! How with such a choice before me can I bear to live? How can I draw my breath beneath the sun which must either look upon carnage or be darkened by a cloud of lies? Nay, it is impossible. You, Millicent, you, you are dear to me, you believe in me, you know how true my love is...and yet...and yet....What can you do for a tortured soul in such a dilemma as mine? Alas, alas, not your gentle arms, not your lovely eyes, not anything that you can offer can console me for this sorrow. No. I must die. But as I die I leave to my successors this dreadful choice—the choice between truth and life. Which to choose I know not. Goodbye, goodbye dear Millicent. I go where riddles no longer torture the guilty soul. Goodbye...."

For a moment he embraced her in a last delirium of passion. She felt his heart cease to beat, and fell prostrate in momentary immobility. When she came to, she snatched the locket from her slim neck. Opening it with delicate fingers she extracted the miniature from its nest. Embracing it passionately upon the lips she exclaimed:

"O thou great spirit, thou noble mind, though thou be dead, though these lips that I vainly kiss can speak no more, yet something of thee still lives. It lives in my breast. Through me, through poor little me, the message that thou wouldst give to man shall yet be given."

Having spoken these words she lifted the receiver of the telephone and called the *Daily Thunder*.

VI

After a few days, during which Lady Millicent was protected by the *Daily Thunder* from the fury of her husband and his minions, her story won universal belief. Everybody suddenly plucked up courage and confessed to having seen nothing whatever through the infra-redioscope. The Martian terror subsided as quickly as it had arisen. As it subsided, the East-West dissension revived, and soon developed into open war.

The embattled nations met on the great central plain. Airplanes darkened the sky. Atomic explosions to right and to left scattered destruction. Vast guns of new make let loose strange missiles that sought their targets unguided by human agency. Suddenly the din stilled. The planes sank to earth. The artillery ceased to fire. On the furthest outskirts of the battle, the journalists, who had been watching with that eagerness which belongs to their strange profession, noticed the sudden silence. They could not imagine to what this silence was due. But, taking their courage in their hands, they advanced towards what had been the battle. They found the troops dead where they had fought—dead, not by wounds inflicted by the enemy, but by some strange, new, and unknown death. They rushed to the telephones. They telephoned to their several capitals. In the capitals most widely removed from the field of battle, the stop-press got so far as to say, "The battle has been stopped by..." They got no farther. When they reached this point, the compositors fell dead. The machines fell silent. Universal death spread throughout the world. The Martians *had* come.

EPILOGUE

By the Professor of Indoctrination
in the Central Martian University

I have been commissioned by that great hero whom we all revere—I allude, of course, to Martin the Conqueror—to compose the above history of the last days of the human race. That great Martian, having observed here and there among his subjects a somewhat weak-kneed sentimentality as regards those mendacious bipeds whom his hosts so gallantly and so deservedly exterminated, decided in his wisdom that all the resources of erudition should be employed to portray with exact faithfulness the circumstances preceding his victorious campaign. For he is of opinion—and I am sure that every reader of the foregoing pages will agree with him— that it could not be a good thing to allow such creatures to continue to pollute our fair cosmos.

Could anyone imagine a more foul slander than to accuse us of heptapody? And how could the Tellurians be pardoned for describing that sweet smile with which we greet changing events as a fixed grin? And what are we to think of governments which tolerate such creatures as Sir Theophilus? That love of power which led him to his enterprise is, with us, justly confined within the breast of King Martin. And what could anyone say in defense of that freedom of discussion which was shown in the debate of the United Nations? How much nobler is life on this our planet, where what is to be thought is determined by the word of the heroic Martin, and lesser men have only to obey!

The record which is here given is an authentic one. It has been pieced together with enormous labor from such fragments of newspapers and gramophone records as have survived the last Tellurian battle and the assault of our brave boys. Some may be surprised at the intimacy of some of the details that are here revealed, but it appeared that Sir Theophilus, without the knowledge of his wife, had installed a dictaphone in her boudoir, and it is from this that the last words of Mr. Shovelpenny have been derived.

Every true Martian heart must breathe more freely now in the knowledge that these creatures are no more. And in that exultant thought we shall go on to wish deserved victory to our beloved King Martin in his projected expedition against the equally degraded inhabitants of Venus.

LONG LIVE KING MARTIN!

Ernest Hemingway

THE SHORT HAPPY LIFE OF FRANCIS MACOMBER

NOBEL PRIZE 1954

The fourth American to win the literature prize, Ernest Hemingway (1899–1961) was born in Oak Park, Illinois. Tragedy and adventure shaped his attitude toward his life and his fiction—he was wounded on the western front in the First World War and witnessed much suffering and at least some heroism. Like many other writers in this book, he was a newspaper reporter for a number of years, covering wars and political upheavals. In 1921 he joined the legendary group of American writers and artists in Paris, returning to America in 1928, one year after becoming a full-time writer. He won the Pulitzer Prize the year before receiving the Nobel.

Ernest Hemingway was in many ways a twentieth century heir to a tradition in American literature that extolled things individualistic, masculine, and especially, heroic. Although he wrote of love, it was almost always in the context of violence, a fascinating combination apparent in such works as The Sun Also Rises *(1926),* A Farewell to Arms *(1929),* To Have and Have Not *(1937), and* For Whom the Bell Tolls *(1940). The great Hemingway values include facing death without fear and understanding that courage is more important than life; qualities found in perhaps his greatest work,* The Old Man and the Sea *(1952).*

IT WAS NOW LUNCH time and they were all sitting under the double green fly of the dining tent pretending that nothing had happened.

"Will you have lime juice or lemon squash?" Macomber asked.

"I'll have a gimlet," Robert Wilson told him.

"I'll have a gimlet too. I need something," Macomber's wife said.

"I suppose it's the thing to do," Macomber agreed. "Tell him to make three gimlets."

The mess boy had started them already, lifting the bottles out of the canvas cooling bags that sweated wet in the wind that blew through the trees that shaded the tents.

"What had I ought to give them?" Macomber asked.

"A quid would be plenty," Wilson told him. "You don't want to spoil them."

"Will the headman distribute it?"

"Absolutely."

Francis Macomber had, half an hour before, been carried to his tent from the edge of the camp in triumph on the arms and shoulders of the cook, the personal boys, the skinner and the porters. The gun-bearers had taken no part in the demonstration. When the native boys put him down at the door of his tent, he had shaken all their hands, received their congratulations, and then gone into the tent and sat on the bed until his wife came in. She did not speak to him when she came in and he left the tent at once to wash his face and hands in the portable wash basin outside and go over to the dining tent to sit in a comfortable canvas chair in the breeze and the shade.

"You've got your lion," Robert Wilson said to him, "and a damned fine one too."

Mrs. Macomber looked at Wilson quickly. She was an extremely handsome and well-kept woman of the beauty and social position which had, five years before, commanded five thousand dollars as the price of endorsing, with photographs, a beauty product which she had never used. She had been married to Francis Macomber for eleven years.

"He is a good lion, isn't he?" Macomber said. His wife looked at him now. She looked at both these men as though she had never seen them before.

One, Wilson, the white hunter, she knew she had never truly seen before. He was about middle height with sandy hair, a stubby

mustache, a very red face and extremely cold blue eyes with faint
white wrinkles at the corners that grooved merrily when he smiled.
He smiled at her now and she looked away from his face at the
way his shoulders sloped in the loose tunic he wore with the four
big cartridges held in loops where the left breast pocket should
have been, at his big brown hands, his old slacks, his very dirty
boots and back to his red face again. She noticed where the baked
red of his face stopped in a white line that marked the circle left
by his Stetson hat that hung now from one of the pegs of the tent
pole.

"Well, here's to the lion," Robert Wilson said. He smiled at her
again and, not smiling, she looked curiously at her husband.

Francis Macomber was very tall, very well built if you did not
mind that length of bone, dark, his hair cropped like an oarsman,
rather thin-lipped, and was considered handsome. He was dressed
in the same sort of safari clothes that Wilson wore except that his
were new, he was thirty-five years old, kept himself very fit, was
good at court games, had a number of big-game fishing records,
and had just shown himself, very publicly, to be a coward.

"Here's to the lion," he said. "I can't ever thank you for what
you did."

Margaret, his wife, looked away from him and back to Wilson.

"Let's not talk about the lion," she said.

Wilson looked over at her without smiling and now she smiled
at him.

"It's been a very strange day," she said. "Hadn't you ought to
put your hat on even under the canvas at noon? You told me that,
you know."

"Might put it on," said Wilson.

"You know you have a very red face, Mr. Wilson," she told him
and smiled again.

"Drink," said Wilson.

"I don't think so," she said. "Francis drinks a great deal, but his
face is never red."

"It's red today," Macomber tried a joke.

"No," said Margaret. "It's mine that's red today. But Mr. Wilson's
is always red."

"Must be racial," said Wilson. "I say, you wouldn't like to drop
my beauty as a topic, would you?"

"I've just started on it."

"Let's chuck it," said Wilson.

"Conversation is going to be so difficult," Margaret said.

"Don't be silly, Margot," her husband said.

"No difficulty," Wilson said. "Got a damn fine lion."

Margot looked at them both and they both saw that she was going to cry. Wilson had seen it coming for a long time and he dreaded it. Macomber was past dreading it.

"I wish it hadn't happened. Oh, I wish it hadn't happened," she said and started for her tent. She made no noise of crying but they could see that her shoulders were shaking under the rose-colored, sun-proofed shirt she wore.

"Women upset," said Wilson to the tall man. "Amounts to nothing. Strain on the nerves and one thing'n another."

"No," said Macomber. "I suppose that I rate that for the rest of my life now."

"Nonsense. Let's have a spot of the giant killer," said Wilson. "Forget the whole thing. Nothing to it anyway."

"We might try," said Macomber. "I won't forget what you did for me though."

"Nothing," said Wilson. "All nonsense."

So they sat there in the shade where the camp was pitched under some wide-topped acacia trees with a boulder-strewn cliff behind them, and a stretch of grass that ran to the bank of a boulder-filled stream in front with forest beyond it, and drank their just-cool lime drinks and avoided one another's eyes while the boys set the table for lunch. Wilson could tell that the boys all knew about it now and when he saw Macomber's personal boy looking curiously at his master while he was putting dishes on the table he snapped at him in Swahili. The boy turned away with his face blank.

"What were you telling him?" Macomber asked.

"Nothing. Told him to look alive or I'd see he got about fifteen of the best."

"What's that? Lashes?"

"It's quite illegal," Wilson said. "You're supposed to fine them."

"Do you still have them whipped?"

"Oh, yes. They could raise a row if they chose to complain. But they don't. They prefer it to the fines."

"How strange!" said Macomber.

"Not strange, really," Wilson said. "Which would you rather do? Take a good birching or lose your pay?"

Then he felt embarrassed at asking it and before Macomber could answer he went on, "We all take a beating every day, you know, one way or another."

This was no better. "Good God," he thought. "I am a diplomat, aren't I?"

"Yes, we take a beating," said Macomber, still not looking at him. "I'm awfully sorry about that lion business. It doesn't have to go any further, does it? I mean no one will hear about it, will they?"

"You mean will I tell it at the Mathaiga Club?" Wilson looked at him now coldly. He had not expected this. So he's a bloody four-letter man as well as a bloody coward, he thought. I rather liked him too until today. But how is one to know about an American?

"No," said Wilson. "I'm a professional hunter. We never talk about our clients. You can be quite easy on that. It's supposed to be bad form to ask us not to talk though."

He had decided now that to break would be much easier. He would eat, then, by himself and could read a book with his meals. They would eat by themselves. He would see them through the safari on a very formal basis—what was it the French called it? Distinguished consideration—and it would be a damn sight easier than having to go through his emotional trash. He'd insult him and make a good clean break. Then he could read a book with his meals and he'd still be drinking their whisky. That was the phrase for it when a safari went bad. You ran into another white hunter and you asked, "How is everything going?" and he answered, "Oh, I'm still drinking their whisky," and you knew everything had gone to pot.

"I'm sorry," Macomber said and looked at him with his American face that would stay adolescent until it became middle-aged, and Wilson noted his crew-cropped hair, fine eyes only faintly shifty, good nose, thin lips and handsome jaw. "I'm sorry I didn't realize that. There are lots of things I don't know."

So what could he do, Wilson thought. He was all ready to break if off quickly and neatly and here the beggar was apologizing after he had just insulted him. He made one more attempt. "Don't worry about me talking," he said. "I have a living to make. You know in Africa no woman ever misses her lion and no white man ever bolts."

"I bolted like a rabbit," Macomber said.

Now what in hell were you going to do about a man who talked like that, Wilson wondered.

Wilson looked at Macomber with his flat, blue, machine-gunner's eyes and the other smiled back at him. He had a pleasant smile if you did not notice how his eyes showed when he was hurt.

"Maybe I can fix it up on buffalo," he said. "We're after them next, aren't we?"

"In the morning if you like," Wilson told him. Perhaps he had been wrong. This was certainly the way to take it. You most certainly could not tell a damned thing about an American. He was all for Macomber again. If you could forget the morning. But, of course, you couldn't. The morning had been about as bad as they come.

"Here comes the Memsahib," he said. She was walking over from her tent looking refreshed and cheerful and quite lovely. She had a very perfect oval face, so perfect that you expected her to be stupid. But she wasn't stupid, Wilson thought, no, not stupid.

"How is the beautiful red-faced Mr. Wilson? Are you feeling better, Francis, my pearl?"

"Oh, much," said Macomber.

"I've dropped the whole thing," she said, sitting down at the table. "What importance is there to whether Francis is any good at killing lions? That's not his trade. That's Mr. Wilson's trade. Mr. Wilson is really very impressive killing anything. You do kill anything, don't you?"

"Oh, anything," said Wilson. "Simply anything." They are, he thought, the hardest in the world; the hardest, the cruelest, the most predatory and the most attractive and their men have softened or gone to pieces nervously as they have hardened. Or is it that they pick men they can handle? They can't know that much at the age they marry, he thought. He was grateful that he had gone through his education on American women before now because this was a very attractive one.

"We're going after buff in the morning," he told her.

"I'm coming," she said.

"No, you're not."

"Oh, yes, I am. Mayn't I, Francis?"

"Why not stay in camp?"

"Not for anything," she said, "I wouldn't miss something like today for anything."

When she left, Wilson was thinking, when she went off to cry, she seemed a hell of a fine woman. She seemed to understand, to realize, to be hurt for him and for herself and to know how things really stood. She is away for twenty minutes and now she is back, simply enamelled in that American female cruelty. They are the damnedest women. Really the damnedest.

"We'll put on another show for you tomorrow," Francis Macomber said.

"You're not coming," Wilson said.

"You're very mistaken," she told him. "And I want *so* to see you perform again. You were lovely this morning. That is if blowing things' heads off is lovely."

"Here's the lunch," said Wilson. "You're very merry, aren't you?"

"Why not? I didn't come out here to be dull."

"Well, it hasn't been dull," Wilson said. He could see the boulders in the river and the high bank beyond with the trees and he remembered the morning.

"Oh, no," she said. "It's been charming. And tomorrow. You don't know how I look forward to tomorrow."

"That's eland he's offering you," Wilson said.

"They're the big cowy things that jump like hares, aren't they?"

"I suppose that describes them," Wilson said.

"It's very good meat," Macomber said.

"Did you shoot it, Francis?" she asked.

"Yes."

"They're not dangerous, are they?"

"Only if they fall on you," Wilson told her.

"I'm so glad."

"Why not let up on the bitchery just a little, Margot," Macomber said, cutting the eland steak and putting some mashed potato, gravy and carrot on the down-turned fork that tined through the piece of meat.

"I suppose I could," she said, "since you put it so prettily."

"Tonight we'll have champagne for the lion," Wilson said. "It's a bit too hot at noon."

"Oh, the lion," Margot said. "I'd forgotten the lion!"

So, Robert Wilson thought to himself, she *is* giving him a ride, isn't she? Or do you suppose that's her idea of putting up a good show? How should a woman act when she discovers her husband is a bloody coward? She's damn cruel but they're all cruel. They govern, of course, and to govern one has to be cruel sometimes. Still, I've seen enough of their damn terrorism.

"Have some more eland," he said to her politely.

That afternoon, late, Wilson and Macomber went out in the motor car with the native driver and the two gun-bearers. Mrs. Macomber stayed in the camp. It was too hot to go out, she said, and she was going with them in the early morning. As they drove off Wilson saw her standing under the big tree, looking pretty rather than beautiful in her faintly rosy khaki, her dark hair drawn back off her forehead and gathered in a knot low on her neck, her face as fresh, he thought, as though she were in England. She waved to them as the car went off through the swale of high grass and curved around through the trees into the small hills of orchard bush.

In the orchard bush they found a herd of impala, and leaving the car they stalked one old ram with long, wide-spread horns and Macomber killed it with a very creditable shot that knocked the buck down at a good two hundred yards and sent the herd off bounding wildly and leaping over one another's backs in long, leg-drawn-up leaps as unbelievable and as floating as those one makes sometimes in dreams.

"That was a good shot," Wilson said. "They're a small target."

"Is it a worth-while head?" Macomber asked.

"It's excellent," Wilson told him. "You shoot like that and you'll have no trouble."

"Do you think we'll find buffalo tomorrow?"

"There's a good chance of it. They feed out early in the morning and with luck we may catch them in the open."

"I'd like to clear away that lion business," Macomber said. "It's not very pleasant to have your wife see you do something like that."

I should think it would be even more unpleasant to do it, Wilson thought, wife or no wife, or to talk about it having done it. But he said, "I wouldn't think about that any more. Any one could be upset by his first lion. That's all over."

But that night after dinner and a whisky and soda by the fire before going to bed, as Francis Macomber lay on his cot with the mosquito bar over him and listened to the night noises it was not all over. It was neither all over nor was it beginning. It was there exactly as it happened with some parts of it indelibly emphasized and he was miserably ashamed at it. But more than shame he felt cold, hollow fear in him. The fear was still there like a cold slimy hollow in all the emptiness where once his confidence had been and it made him feel sick. It was still there with him now.

It had started the night before when he had wakened and heard the lion roaring somewhere up along the river. It was a deep sound and at the end there were sort of coughing grunts that made him seem just outside the tent, and when Francis Macomber woke in the night to hear it he was afraid. He could hear his wife breathing quietly, asleep. There was no one to tell he was afraid, nor to be afraid with him, and, lying alone, he did not know the Somali proverb that says a brave man is always frightened three times by a lion; when he first sees his track, when he first hears him roar and when he first confronts him. Then while they were eating breakfast by lantern light out in the dining tent, before the sun was up, the lion roared again and Francis thought he was just at the edge of camp.

"Sounds like an old-timer," Robert Wilson said, looking up from his kippers and coffee. "Listen to him cough."

"Is he very close?"

"A mile or so up the stream."

"Will we see him?"

"We'll have a look."

"Does his roaring carry that far? It sounds as though he were right in camp."

"Carries a hell of a long way," said Robert Wilson. "It's strange the way it carries. Hope he's a shootable cat. The boys said there was a very big one about here."

"If I get a shot, where should I hit him," Macomber asked, "to stop him?"

"In the shoulders," Wilson said. "In the neck if you can make it. Shoot for bone. Break him down."

"I hope I can place it properly," Macomber said.

"You shoot very well," Wilson told him. "Take your time. Make sure of him. The first one in is the one that counts."

"What range will it be?"

"Can't tell. Lion has something to say about that. Won't shoot unless it's close enough so you can make sure."

"At under a hundred yards?" Macomber asked.

Wilson looked at him quickly.

"Hundred's about right. Might have to take him a bit under. Shouldn't chance a shot at much over that. A hundred's a decent range. You can hit him wherever you want at that. Here comes the Memsahib."

"Good morning," she said. "Are we going after that lion?"

"As soon as you deal with your breakfast," Wilson said. "How are you feeling?"

"Marvellous," she said. "I'm very excited."

"I'll just go and see that everything is ready," Wilson went off. As he left the lion roared again.

"Noisy beggar," Wilson said. "We'll put a stop to that."

"What's the matter, Francis?" his wife asked him.

"Nothing," Macomber said.

"Yes, there is," she said. "What are you upset about?"

"Nothing," he said.

"Tell me," she looked at him. "Don't you feel well?"

"It's that damned roaring," he said. "It's been going on all night, you know."

"Why didn't you wake me," she said. "I'd love to have heard it."

"I've got to kill the damned thing," Macomber said, miserably.

"Well, that's what you're out here for, isn't it?"

"Yes. But I'm nervous. Hearing the thing roar gets on my nerves."

"Well then, as Wilson said, kill him and stop his roaring."

"Yes, darling," said Francis Macomber. "It sounds easy, doesn't it?"

"You're not afraid, are you?"

"Of course not. But I'm nervous from hearing him roar all night."

"You'll kill him marvellously," she said. "I know you will. I'm awfully anxious to see it."

"Finish your breakfast and we'll be starting."

"It's not light yet," she said. "This is a ridiculous hour."

Just then the lion roared in a deep-chested moaning, suddenly guttural, ascending vibration that seemed to shake the air and ended in a sigh and a heavy, deep-chested grunt.

"He sounds almost here," Macomber's wife said.

"My God," said Macomber. "I hate that damned noise."

"It's very impressive."

"Impressive. It's frightful."

Robert Wilson came up then carrying his short, ugly, shockingly big-bored .505 Gibbs and grinning.

"Come on," he said. "Your gun-bearer has your Springfield and the big gun. Everything's in the car. Have you solids?"

"Yes."

"I'm ready," Mrs. Macomber said.

"Must make him stop that racket," Wilson said. "You get in front. The Memsahib can sit back here with me."

They climbed into the motor car and, in the gray first daylight, moved off up the river through the trees. Macomber opened the breech of his rifle and saw he had metal-cased bullets, shut the bolt and put the rifle on safety. He saw his hand was trembling. He felt in his pocket for more cartridges and moved his fingers over the cartridges in the loops of his tunic front. He turned back to where Wilson sat in the rear seat of the doorless, box-bodied motor car beside his wife, them both grinning with excitement, and Wilson leaned forward and whispered,

"See the birds dropping. Means the old boy has left his kill."

On the far bank of the stream Macomber could see, above the trees, vultures circling and plummeting down.

"Chances are he'll come to drink along here," Wilson whispered. "Before he goes to lay up. Keep an eye out."

They were driving slowly along the high bank of the stream which here cut deeply to its boulder-filled bed, and they wound in and out through big trees as they drove. Macomber was watching the opposite bank when he felt Wilson take hold of his arm. The car stopped.

"There he is," he heard the whisper. "Ahead and to the right. Get out and take him. He's a marvellous lion."

Macomber saw the lion now. He was standing almost broadside, his great head up and turned toward them. The early morning breeze that blew toward them was just stirring his dark mane, and the lion looked huge, silhouetted on the rise of bank in the gray morning light, his shoulders heavy, his barrel of a body bulking smoothly.

"How far is he?" asked Macomber, raising his rifle.

"About seventy-five. Get out and take him."

"Why not shoot from where I am?"

"You don't shoot them from cars," he heard Wilson saying in his ear. "Get out. He's not going to stay there all day."

Macomber stepped out of the curved opening at the side of the front seat, onto the step and down onto the ground. The lion still stood looking majestically and coolly toward this object that his eyes only showed in silhouette, bulking like some super-rhino. There was no man smell carried toward him and he watched the object, moving his great head a little from side to side. Then watching the object, not afraid, but hesitating before going down the bank to drink with such a thing opposite him, he saw a man figure detach itself from it and he turned his heavy head and swung away toward the cover of the trees as he heard a cracking crash and felt the slam of a .30–06 220-grain solid bullet that bit his flank and ripped in sudden hot scalding nausea through his stomach. He trotted, heavy, big-footed, swinging wounded full-bellied, through the trees toward the tall grass and cover, and the crash came again to go past him ripping the air apart. Then it crashed again and he felt the blow as it hit his lower ribs and ripped on through, blood sudden hot and frothy in his mouth, and he galloped toward the high grass where he could crouch and not be seen and make them bring the crashing thing close enough so he could make a rush and get the man that held it.

Macomber had not thought how the lion felt as he got out of the car. He only knew his hands were shaking and as he walked away from the car it was almost impossible for him to make his legs move. They were stiff in the thighs, but he could feel the muscles fluttering. He raised the rifle, sighted on the junction of the lion's head and shoulders and pulled the trigger. Nothing happened though he pulled until he thought his finger would break. Then he knew he had the safety on and as he lowered the rifle to move the safety over he moved another frozen pace forward, and the lion seeing his silhouette now clear of the silhouette of the car, turned and started off at a trot, and, as Macomber fired, he heard a whunk that meant that the bullet was home; but the lion kept on going. Macomber shot again and every one saw the bullet throw a spout of dirt beyond the trotting lion. He shot again, remembering to lower his aim, and they all heard the bullet hit, and the lion went into a gallop and was in the tall grass before he had the bolt pushed forward.

Macomber stood there feeling sick at his stomach, his hands that held the Springfield still cocked, shaking, and his wife and Robert Wilson were standing by him. Beside him too were the two gun-bearers chattering in Wakamba.

"I hit him," Macomber said. "I hit him twice."

"You gut-shot him and you hit him somewhere forward," Wilson said without enthusiasm. The gun-bearers looked very grave. They were silent now.

"You may have killed him," Wilson went on. "We'll have to wait a while before we go in to find out."

"What do you mean?"

"Let him get sick before we follow him up."

"Oh," said Macomber.

"He's a hell of a fine lion," Wilson said cheerfully. "He's gotten into a bad place though."

"Why is it bad?"

"Can't see him until you're on him."

"Oh," said Macomber.

"Come on," said Wilson. "The Memsahib can stay here in the car. We'll go to have a look at the blood spoor."

"Stay here, Margot," Macomber said to his wife. His mouth was very dry and it was hard for him to talk.

"Why?" she asked.

"Wilson says to."

"We're going to have a look," Wilson said. "You stay here. You can see even better from here."

"All right."

Wilson spoke in Swahili to the driver. He nodded and said. "Yes, Bwana."

Then they went down the steep bank and across the stream, climbing over and around the boulders and up the other bank, pulling up by some projecting roots, and along it until they found where the lion had been trotting when Macomber first shot. There was dark blood on the short grass that the gun-bearers pointed out with grass stems, and that ran away behind the river bank trees.

"What do we do?" asked Macomber.

"Not much choice," said Wilson. "We can't bring the car over. Bank's too steep. We'll let him stiffen up a bit and then you and I'll go in and have a look for him."

"Can't we set the grass on fire?" Macomber asked.

"Too green."

"Can't we send bearers?"

Wilson looked at him appraisingly. "Of course we can," he said. "But it's just a touch murderous. You see we know the lion's wounded. You can drive an unwounded lion—he'll move on ahead of a noise—but a wounded lion's going to charge. You can't see him until you're right on him. He'll make himself perfectly flat in cover you wouldn't think would hide a hare. You can't very well send boys in there to that sort of a show. Somebody bound to get mauled."

"What about the gun-bearers?"

"Oh, they'll go with us. It's their *shauri*. You see, they signed on for it. They don't look too happy though, do they?"

"I don't want to go in there," said Macomber. It was out before he knew he'd said it.

"Neither do I," said Wilson very cheerily. "Really no choice though." Then, as an afterthought, he glanced at Macomber and saw suddenly how he was trembling and the pitiful look on his face.

"You don't have to go in, of course," he said. "That's what I'm hired for, you know. That's why I'm so expensive."

"You mean you'd go in by yourself? Why not leave him there?"

Robert Wilson, whose entire occupation had been with the lion and the problem he presented, and who had not been thinking about Macomber except to note that he was rather windy, suddenly felt as though he had opened the wrong door in a hotel and seen something shameful.

"What do you mean?"

"Why not just leave him?"

"You mean pretend to ourselves he hasn't been hit?"

"No. Just drop it."

"It isn't done."

"Why not?"

"For one thing, he's certain to be suffering. For another, some one else might run onto him."

"I see."

"But you don't have to have anything to do with it."

"I'd like to," Macomber said. "I'm just scared, you know."

"I'll go ahead when we go in," Wilson said, "with Kongoni tracking. You keep behind me and a little to one side. Chances are we'll hear him growl. If we see him we'll both shoot. Don't worry about anything. I'll keep you backed up. As a matter of fact, you know, perhaps you'd better not go. It might be much better. Why don't you go over and join the Memsahib while I just get it over with?"

"No, I want to go."

"All right," said Wilson. "But don't go in if you don't want to. This is my *shauri* now, you know."

"I want to go," said Macomber.

They sat under a tree and smoked.

"Want to go back and speak to the Memsahib while we're waiting?" Wilson asked.

"No."

"I'll just step back and tell her to be patient."

"Good," said Macomber. He sat there, sweating under his arms, his mouth dry, his stomach hollow feeling, wanting to find the courage to tell Wilson to go on and finish off the lion without him. He could not know that Wilson was furious because he had not noticed the state he was in earlier and sent him back to his wife. While he sat there Wilson came up. "I have your big gun," he said. "Take it. We've given him time, I think. Come on."

Macomber took the big gun and Wilson said:

"Keep behind me and about five yards to the right and do exactly as I tell you." Then he spoke in Swahili to the two gun-bearers who looked the picture of gloom.

"Let's go," he said.

"Could I have a drink of water?" Macomber asked. Wilson spoke to the older gun-bearer, who wore a canteen on his belt, and the man unbuckled it, unscrewed the top and handed it to Macomber, who took it noticing how heavy it seemed and how hairy and shoddy the felt covering was in his hand. He raised it to drink and looked ahead at the high grass with the flat-topped trees behind it. A breeze was blowing toward them and the grass rippled gently in the wind. He looked at the gun-bearer and he could see the gun-bearer was suffering too with fear.

Thirty-five yards into the grass the big lion lay flattened out along the ground. His ears were back and his only movement was a slight twitching up and down of his long, black-tufted tail. He had turned at bay as soon as he had reached this cover and he was sick with the wound through his full belly, and weakening with the wound through his lungs that brought a thin foamy red to his mouth each time he breathed. His flanks were wet and hot and flies were on the little openings the solid bullets had made in his tawny hide, and his big yellow eyes, narrowed with hate, looked straight ahead, only blinking when the pain came as he breathed, and his claws dug in the soft baked earth. All of him, pain, sickness, hatred and all of his remaining strength, was tightening into an absolute concentration for a rush. He could hear the men talking and he waited, gathering all of himself into this preparation for a charge as soon as the men would come into the grass. As he heard their voices his tail stiffened to twitch up and down, and, as they came into the edge of the grass, he made a coughing grunt and charged.

Kongoni, the old gun-bearer, in the lead watching the blood

spoor, Wilson watching the grass for any movement, his big gun ready, the second gun-bearer looking ahead and listening, Macomber close to Wilson, his rifle cocked, they had just moved into the grass when Macomber heard the blood-choked coughing grunt, and saw the swishing rush in the grass. The next thing he knew he was running; running wildly, in panic in the open, running toward the stream.

He heard the *ca-ra-wong!* of Wilson's big rifle, and again in a second crashing *carawong!* and turning saw the lion, horrible-looking now, with half of his head seeming to be gone, crawling toward Wilson in the edge of the tall grass while the red-faced man worked the bolt on the short ugly rifle and aimed carefully as another blasting *carawong!* came from the muzzle, and the crawling, heavy, yellow bulk of the lion stiffened and the huge, mutilated head slid forward and Macomber, standing by himself in the clearing where he had run, holding a loaded rifle, while two black men and a white man looked back at him in contempt, knew the lion was dead. He came toward Wilson, his tallness all seeming a naked reproach, and Wilson looked at him and said:

"Want to take pictures?"

"No," he said.

That was all any one had said until they reached the motor car. Then Wilson had said:

"Hell of a fine lion. Boys will skin him out. We might as well stay here in the shade."

Macomber's wife had not looked at him nor he at her and he had sat by her in the back seat with Wilson sitting in the front seat. Once he had reached over and taken his wife's hand without looking at her and she had removed her hand from his. Looking across the stream to where the gun-bearers were skinning out the lion he could see that she had been able to see the whole thing. While they sat there his wife had reached forward and put her hand on Wilson's shoulder. He turned and she had leaned forward over the low seat and kissed him on the mouth.

"Oh, I say," said Wilson, going redder than his natural baked color.

"Mr. Robert Wilson," she said. "The beautiful red-faced Mr. Robert Wilson."

Then she sat down beside Macomber again and looked away across the stream to where the lion lay, with uplifted, white-muscled, tendon-marked naked forearms, and white bloating belly, as the black men fleshed away the skin. Finally the gun-bearers brought the skin over, wet and heavy, and climbed in behind with it, rolling it up before they got in, and the motor car started. No one had said anything more until they were back in camp.

That was the story of the lion. Macomber did not know how the lion had felt before he started his rush, nor during it when the unbelievable smash of the .505 with a muzzle velocity of two tons had hit him in the mouth, nor what kept him coming after that, when the second ripping crash had smashed his hind quarters and he had come crawling on toward the crashing, blasting thing that had destroyed him. Wilson knew something about it and only expressed it by saying, "Damned fine lion," but Macomber did not know how Wilson felt about things either. He did not know how his wife felt except that she was through with him.

His wife had been through with him before but it never lasted. He was very wealthy, and would be much wealthier, and he knew she would not leave him ever now. That was one of the few things that he really knew. He knew about that, about motor cycles—that was earliest—about motor cars, about duck-shooting, about fishing, trout, salmon and big-sea, about sex in books, many books, too many books, about all court games, about dogs, not much about horses, about hanging on to his money, about most of the other things his world dealt in, and about his wife not leaving him. His wife had been a great beauty and she was still a great beauty in Africa, but she was not a great enough beauty any more at home to be able to leave him and better herself and she knew it and he knew it. She had missed the chance to leave him and he knew it. If he had been better with women she would probably have started to worry about him getting another new, beautiful wife; but she knew too much about him to worry about him either. Also, he had always had a great tolerance which seemed the nicest thing about him if it were not the most sinister.

All in all they were known as a comparatively happily married couple, one of those whose disruption is often rumored but never occurs, and as the society columnist put it, they were adding more than a spice of *adventure* to their much envied and ever-enduring *Romance* by a *Safari* in what was known as *Darkest Africa* until the Martin Johnsons lighted it on so many silver screens where they were pursuing *Old Simba* the lion, the buffalo, *Tembo* the elephant and as well collecting specimens for the Museum of Natural History. This same columnist had reported them *on the verge* at least three times in the past and they had been. But they always made it up. They had a sound basis of union. Margot was too beautiful for Macomber to divorce her and Macomber had too much money for Margot ever to leave him.

It was now about three o'clock in the morning and Francis Macomber, who had been asleep a little while after he had stopped thinking about the lion, wakened and then slept again, woke suddenly, frightened in a dream of the bloody-headed lion standing over him, and listening while his heart pounded, he realized that his wife was not in the other cot in the tent. He lay awake with that knowledge for two hours.

At the end of that time his wife came into the tent, lifted her mosquito bar and crawled cozily into bed.

"Where have you been?" Macomber asked in the darkness.

"Hello," she said. "Are you awake?"

"Where have you been?"

"I just went out to get a breath of air."

"You did, like hell."

"What do you want me to say, darling?"

"Where have you been?"

"Out to get a breath of air."

"That's a new name for it. You *are* a bitch."

"Well, you're a coward."

"All right," he said. "What of it?"

"Nothing as far as I'm concerned. But please let's not talk, darling, because I'm very sleepy."

"You think that I'll take anything."

"I know you will, sweet."

"Well, I won't."

"Please, darling, let's not talk. I'm so very sleepy."

"There wasn't going to be any of that. You promised there wouldn't be."

"Well, there is now," she said sweetly.

"You said if we made this trip that there would be none of that. You promised."

"Yes, darling. That's the way I meant it to be. But the trip was spoiled yesterday. We don't have to talk about it, do we?"

"You don't wait long when you have an advantage, do you?"

"Please let's not talk. I'm so sleepy, darling."

"I'm going to talk."

"Don't mind me then, because I'm going to sleep." And she did.

At breakfast they were all three at the table before daylight and Francis Macomber found that, of all the many men that he had hated, he hated Robert Wilson the most.

"Sleep well?" Wilson asked in his throaty voice, filling a pipe.

"Did you?"

"Topping," the white hunter told him.

You bastard, thought Macomber, you insolent bastard.

So she woke him when she came in, Wilson thought, looking at them both with his flat, cold eyes. Well, why doesn't he keep his wife where she belongs? What does he think I am, a bloody plaster saint? Let him keep her where she belongs. It's his own fault.

"Do you think we'll find buffalo?" Margot asked, pushing away a dish of apricots.

"Chance of it," Wilson said and smiled at her. "Why don't you stay in camp?"

"Not for anything," she told him.

"Why not order her to stay in camp?" Wilson said to Macomber.

"You order her," said Macomber coldly.

"Let's not have any ordering, nor," turning to Macomber, "any silliness, Francis," Margot said quite pleasantly.

"Are you ready to start?" Macomber asked.

"Any time," Wilson told him. "Do you want the Memsahib to go?"

"Does it make any difference whether I do or not?"

The hell with it, thought Robert Wilson. The utter complete hell with it. So this is what it's going to be like. Well, this is what it's going to be like, then.

"Makes no difference," he said.

"You're sure you wouldn't like to stay in camp with her yourself and let me go out and hunt the buffalo?" Macomber asked.

"Can't do that," said Wilson. "Wouldn't talk rot if I were you."

"I'm not talking rot. I'm disgusted."

"Bad word, disgusted."

"Francis, will you please try to speak sensibly?" his wife said.

"I speak too damned sensibly," Macomber said. "Did you ever eat such filthy food?"

"Something wrong with the food?" asked Wilson quietly.

"No more than with everything else."

"I'd pull yourself together, laddybuck," Wilson said very quietly. "There's a boy waits at table that understands a little English."

"The hell with him."

Wilson stood up and puffing on his pipe strolled away, speaking a few words in Swahili to one of the gun-bearers who was standing waiting for him. Macomber and his wife sat on at the table. He was staring at his coffee cup.

"If you make a scene I'll leave you, darling," Margot said quietly.

"No, you won't."

"You can try it and see."

"You won't leave me."

"No," she said. "I won't leave you and you'll behave yourself."

"Behave myself? That's a way to talk. Behave myself."

"Yes. Behave yourself."

"Why don't *you* try behaving?"

"I've tried it so long. So very long."

"I hate that red-faced swine," Macomber said. "I loathe the sight of him."

"He's really *very* nice."

"Oh, *shut up*," Macomber almost shouted. Just then the car came up and stopped in front of the dining tent and the driver and the two gun-bearers got out. Wilson walked over and looked at the husband and wife sitting there at the table.

"Going shooting?" he asked.

"Yes," said Macomber, standing up. "Yes."

"Better bring a woolly. It will be cool in the car," Wilson said.

"I'll get my leather jacket," Margot said.

"The boy has it," Wilson told her. He climbed into the front with the driver and Francis Macomber and his wife sat, not speaking, in the back seat.

Hope the silly beggar doesn't take a notion to blow the back of my head off, Wilson thought to himself. Women *are* a nuisance on safari.

The car was grinding down to cross the river at a pebbly ford in the gray daylight and then climbed, angling up the steep bank, where Wilson had ordered a way shovelled out the day before so they could reach the parklike wooded rolling country on the far side.

It was a good morning, Wilson thought. There was a heavy dew and as the wheels went through the grass and low bushes he could smell the odor of the crushed fronds. It was an odor like verbena and he liked this early morning smell of the dew, the crushed bracken and the look of the tree trunks showing black through the early morning mist, as the car made its way through the untracked, parklike country. He had put the two in the back seat out of his mind now and was thinking about buffalo. The buffalo that he was after stayed in the daytime in a thick swamp where it was impossible to get a shot, but in the night they fed out into an open stretch of country and if he could come between them and their swamp with the car, Macomber would have a good chance at them in the open. He did not want to hunt buff with Macomber in thick cover. He did not want to hunt buff or anything else with Macomber at all, but he was a professional hunter and he had hunted with some rare ones in his time. If they got buff today there would only be rhino to come and the poor man would have gone through his dangerous game and things might pick up. He'd have nothing more to do with the woman and Macomber would get over that too. He must have gone through plenty of that before by the look of things. Poor beggar. He must have a way of getting over it. Well, it was the poor sod's own bloody fault.

He, Robert Wilson, carried a double size cot on safari to accommodate any windfalls he might receive. He had hunted for a certain clientele, the international, fast, sporting set, where the women did not feel they were getting their money's worth unless they had shared that cot with the white hunter. He despised them when he was away from them although he liked some of them well enough at the time, but he made his living by them; and their standards were his standards as long as they were hiring him.

They were his standards in all except the shooting. He had his own standards about the killing and they could live up to them or get some one else to hunt them. He knew, too, that they all respected him for this. This Macomber was an odd one though. Damned if he wasn't. Now the wife. Well, the wife, Yes, the wife. Hm, the wife. Well he'd dropped all that. He looked around at them. Macomber sat grim and furious. Margot smiled at him. She looked younger today, more innocent and fresher and not so professionally beautiful. What's in her heart God knows, Wilson thought. She hadn't talked much last night. At that it was a pleasure to see her.

The motor car climbed up a slight rise and went on through the trees and then out into a grassy prairie-like opening and kept in the shelter of the trees along the edge, the driver going slowly and Wilson looking carefully out across the prairie and all along its far side. He stopped the car and studied the opening with his field glasses. Then he motioned to the driver to go on and the car moved slowly along, the driver avoiding wart-hog holes and driving around the mud castles ants had built. Then, looking across the opening, Wilson suddenly turned and said,

"By God, there they are!"

And looking where he pointed, while the car jumped forward and Wilson spoke in rapid Swahili to the driver, Macomber saw three huge, black animals looking almost cylindrical in their long heaviness, like big black tank cars, moving at a gallop across the far edge of the open prairie. They moved at a stiff-necked, stiff bodied gallop and he could see the upswept wide black horns on their heads as they galloped heads out; the heads not moving.

"They're three old bulls," Wilson said. "We'll cut them off before they get to the swamp."

The car was going a wild forty-five miles an hour across the open and as Macomber watched, the buffalo got bigger and bigger until he could see the gray, hairless, scabby look of one huge bull and how his neck was a part of his shoulders and the shiny black of his horns as he galloped a little behind the others that were strung out in that steady plunging gait; and then, the car swaying as though it had just jumped a road, they drew up close and he could see the plunging hugeness of the bull, and the dust in his sparsely haired hide, the wide boss of horn and his outstretched, wide-nostrilled muzzle, and he was raising his rifle when Wilson shouted, "Not from the car, you fool!" and he had no fear, only hatred of Wilson, while the brakes clamped on and the car skidded, plowing sideways to an almost stop and Wilson was out on one side and he on the other, stumbling as his feet hit the still speeding-by of the earth, and then he was shooting at the bull as he moved away, hearing the bullets whunk into him, emptying his rifle at him as he moved steadily away, finally remembering to get his shots forward into the shoulder, and as he fumbled to re-load, he saw the bull was down. Down on his knees, his big head tossing, and seeing the other two still galloping he shot at the leader and hit him. He shot again and missed and he heard the *carawonging* roar as Wilson shot and saw the leading bull slide forward onto his nose.

"Get that other," Wilson said. "Now you're shooting!"

But the other bull was moving steadily at the same gallop and he missed, throwing a spout of dirt, and Wilson missed and the dust rose in a cloud and Wilson shouted, "Come on. He's too far!" and grabbed his arm and they were in the car again, Macomber and Wilson hanging on the sides and rocketing swayingly over the uneven ground, drawing up on the steady, plunging, heavy-necked, straight-moving gallop of the bull.

They were behind him and Macomber was filling his rifle, dropping shells onto the ground, jamming it, clearing the jam, then they were almost up with the bull when Wilson yelled "Stop," and the car skidded so that it almost swung over and Macomber fell forward onto his feet, slammed his bolt forward and fired as far forward as he could aim into the galloping, rounded black back, aimed and shot again, then again, then again, and the bullets, all of them hitting, had no effect on the buffalo that he could see. Then Wilson shot, the roar deafening him, and he could see the bull stagger. Macomber shot again, aiming carefully, and down he came, onto his knees.

"All right," Wilson said. "Nice work. That's the three."

Macomber felt a drunken elation.

"How many times did you shoot?" he asked.

"Just three," Wilson said. "You killed the first bull. The biggest one. I helped you finish the other two. Afraid they might have got into cover. You had them killed. I was just mopping up a little. You shot damn well."

"Let's go to the car," said Macomber. "I want a drink."

"Got to finish off that buff first," Wilson told him. The buffalo was on his knees and he jerked his head furiously and bellowed in pig-eyed, roaring rage as they came toward him.

"Watch he doesn't get up," Wilson said. Then, "Get a little broadside and take him in the neck just behind the ear."

Macomber aimed carefully at the center of the huge, jerking, rage-driven neck and shot. At the shot the head dropped forward.

"That does it," said Wilson. "Got the spine. They're a hell of a looking thing, aren't they?"

"Let's get the drink," said Macomber. In his life he had never felt so good.

In the car Macomber's wife sat very white faced. "You were marvellous, darling," she said to Macomber. "What a ride."

"Was it rough?" Wilson asked.

"It was frightful. I've never been more frightened in my life."

"Let's all have a drink," Macomber said.

"By all means," said Wilson. "Give it to the Memsahib." She drank the neat whisky from the flask and shuddered a little when she swallowed. She handed the flask to Macomber who handed it to Wilson.

"It was frightfully exciting," she said. "It's given me a dreadful headache. I didn't know you were allowed to shoot them from cars though."

"No one shot from cars," said Wilson coldly.

"I mean chase them from cars."

"Wouldn't ordinarily," Wilson said. "Seemed sporting enough to me though while we were doing it. Taking more chance driving that way across the plain full of holes and one thing and another than hunting on foot. Buffalo could have charged us each time we shot if he liked. Gave him every chance. Wouldn't mention it to anyone though. It's illegal if that's what you mean."

"It seemed very unfair to me," Margot said, "chasing those big helpless things in a motor car."

"Did it?" said Wilson.

"What would happen if they heard about it in Nairobi?"

"I'd lose my licence for one thing. Other unpleasantnesses," Wilson said, taking a drink from the flask. "I'd be out of business."

"Really?"

"Yes, really."

"Well," said Macomber, and he smiled for the first time all day. "Now she has something on you."

"You have such a pretty way of putting things, Francis," Margot Macomber said. Wilson looked at them both. If a four-letter man marries a five-letter woman, he was thinking, what number of letters would their children be? What he said was, "We lost a gun-bearer. Did you notice it?"

"My God, no," Macomber said.

"Here he comes," Wilson said. "He's all right. He must have fallen off when we left the first bull."

Approaching them was the middle-aged gun-bearer, limping along in his knitted cap, khaki tunic, shorts and rubber sandals, gloomy-faced and disgusted looking. As he came up he called out to Wilson in Swahili and they all saw the change in the white hunter's face.

"What does he say?" asked Margot.

"He says the first bull got up and went into the bush," Wilson said with no expression in his voice.

"Oh," said Macomber blankly.

"Then it's going to be just like the lion," said Margot, full of anticipation.

"It's not going to be a damned bit like the lion," Wilson told her. "Did you want another drink, Macomber?"

"Thanks, yes," Macomber said. He expected the feeling he had had about the lion to come back but it did not. For the first time in his life he really felt wholly without fear. Instead of fear he had a feeling of definite elation.

"We'll go and have a look at the second bull," Wilson said. "I'll tell the driver to put the car in the shade."

"What are you going to do?" asked Margaret Macomber.

"Take a look at the buff," Wilson said.

"I'll come."

"Come along."

The three of them walked over to where the second buffalo bulked blackly in the open, head forward on the grass, the massive horns swung wide.

"He's a very good head," Wilson said. "That's close to a fifty-inch spread."

Macomber was looking at him with delight.

"He's hateful looking," said Margot. "Can't we go into the shade?"

"Of course," Wilson said. "Look," he said to Macomber, and pointed. "See that patch of bush?"

"Yes."

"That's where the first bull went in. The gun-bearer said when he fell off the bull was down. He was watching us helling along and the other two buff galloping. When he looked up there was the bull up and looking at him. Gun-bearer ran like hell and the bull went off slowly into that bush."

"Can we go in after him now?" asked Macomber eagerly.

Wilson looked at him appraisingly. Damned if this isn't a strange one, he thought. Yesterday he's scared sick and today he's a ruddy fire eater.

"No, we'll give him a while."

"Let's please go into the shade," Margot said. Her face was white and she looked ill.

They made their way to the car where it stood under a single, wide-spreading tree and all climbed in.

"Chances are he's dead in there," Wilson remarked. "After a little we'll have a look."

Macomber felt a wild unreasonable happiness that he had never known before.

"By God, that was a chase," he said. "I've never felt any such feeling. Wasn't it marvellous, Margot?"

"I hated it."

"Why?"

"I hated it," she said bitterly. "I loathed it."

"You know I don't think I'd ever be afraid of anything again," Macomber said to Wilson. "Something happened in me after we first saw the buff and started after him. Like a dam bursting. It was pure excitement."

"Cleans out your liver," said Wilson. "Damn funny things happen to people."

Macomber's face was shining. "You know something did happen to me," he said. "I feel absolutely different."

His wife said nothing and eyed him strangely. She was sitting far back in the seat and Macomber was sitting forward talking to Wilson who turned sideways talking over the back of the front seat.

"You know, I'd like to try another lion," Macomber said. "I'm really not afraid of them now. After all, what can they do to you?"

"That's it," said Wilson. "Worst one can do is kill you. How does it go? Shakespeare. Damned good. See if I can remember. Oh, damned good. Used to quote it to myself at one time. Let's see. 'By my troth, I care not; a man can die but once; we owe God a death and let it go which way it will he that dies this year is quit for the next.' Damned fine, eh?"

He was very embarrassed, having brought out this thing he had lived by, but he had seen men come of age before and it always moved him. It was not a matter of their twenty-first birthday.

It had taken a strange chance of hunting, a sudden precipitation into action without opportunity for worrying beforehand, to bring this about with Macomber, but regardless of how it had happened it had most certainly happened. Look at the beggar now, Wilson thought. It's that some of them stay little boys so long, Wilson thought. Sometimes all their lives. Their figures stay boyish when they're fifty. The great American boy-men. Damned strange people. But he liked this Macomber now. Damned strange fellow. Probably meant the end of cuckoldry too. Well, that would be a damned good thing. Damned good thing. Beggar had probably been afraid all his life. Don't know what started it. But over now. Hadn't had time to be afraid with the buff. That and being angry too. Motor car too. Motor cars made it familiar. Be a damn fire eater now. He'd seen it in the war work the same way. More of a change than any loss of virginity. Fear gone like an operation. Something else grew in its place. Main thing a man had. Made him into a man. Women knew it too. No bloody fear.

From the far corner of the seat Margot Macomber looked at the two of them. There was no change in Wilson. She saw Wilson as she had seen him the day before when she had first realized what his great talent was. But she saw the change in Francis Macomber now.

"Do you have that feeling of happiness about what's going to happen?" Macomber asked, still exploring his new wealth.

"You're not supposed to mention it," Wilson said, looking in the other's face. "Much more fashionable to say you're scared. Mind you, you'll be scared too, plenty of times."

"But you *have* a feeling of happiness about action to come?"

"Yes," said Wilson. "There's that. Doesn't do to talk too much about all this. Talk the whole thing away. No pleasure in anything if you mouth it up too much."

"You're both talking rot," said Margot. "Just because you've chased some helpless animals in a motor car you talk like heroes."

"Sorry," said Wilson. "I have been gassing too much." She's worried about it already, he thought.

"If you don't know what we're talking about why not keep out of it?" Macomber asked his wife.

"You've gotten awfully brave, awfully suddenly," his wife said contemptuously, but her contempt was not secure. She was very afraid of something.

Macomber laughed, a very natural hearty laugh. "You know I *have*," he said. "I really have."

"Isn't it sort of late?" Margot said bitterly. Because she had done the best she could for many years back and the way they were together now was no one person's fault.

"Not for me," said Macomber.

Margot said nothing but sat back in the corner of the seat.

"Do you think we've given him time enough?" Macomber asked Wilson cheerfully.

"We might have a look," Wilson said. "Have you any solids left?"

"The gun-bearer has some."

Wilson called in Swahili and the older gun-bearer, who was skinning out one of the heads, straightened up, pulled a box of solids out of his pocket and brought them over to Macomber, who filled his magazine and put the remaining shells in his pocket.

"You might as well shoot the Springfield," Wilson said. "You're used to it. We'll leave the Mannlicher in the car with the Memsahib. Your gun-bearer can carry your heavy gun. I've this damned cannon. Now let me tell you about them." He had saved this until the last because he did not want to worry Macomber. "When a buff comes he comes with his head high and thrust straight out. The boss of the horns covers any sort of a brain shot. The only shot is straight into the nose. The only other shot is into his chest or, if you're to one side, into the neck or the shoulders. After they've been hit once they take a hell of a lot of killing. Don't try anything fancy. Take the easiest shot there is. They've finished skinning out that head now. Should we get started?"

He called to the gun-bearers, who came up wiping their hands, and the older one got into the back.

"I'll only take Kongoni," Wilson said. "The other can watch to keep the birds away."

As the car moved slowly across the open space toward the island of brushy trees that ran in a tongue of foliage along a dry water course that cut the open swale, Macomber felt his heart pounding and his mouth was dry again, but it was excitement, not fear.

"Here's where he went in," Wilson said. Then to the gun-bearer in Swahili, "Take the blood spoor."

The car was parallel to the patch of bush. Macomber, Wilson and the gun-bearer got down. Macomber, looking back, saw his wife, with the rifle by her side, looking at him. He waved to her and she did not wave back.

The brush was very thick ahead and the ground was dry. The middle-aged gun-bearer was sweating heavily and Wilson had his hat down over his eyes and his red neck showed just ahead of Macomber. Suddenly the gun-bearer said something in Swahili to Wilson and ran forward.

"He's dead in there," Wilson said. "Good work," and he turned to grip Macomber's hand and as they shook hands, grinning at each other, the gun-bearer shouted wildly and they saw him coming out of the bush sideways, fast as a crab, and the bull coming, nose out, mouth tight closed, blood dripping, massive head straight out, coming in a charge, his little pig eyes bloodshot as he looked at them. Wilson, who was ahead was kneeling shooting, and Macomber, as he fired, unhearing his shot in the roaring of Wilson's gun, saw fragments like slate burst from the huge boss of the horns, and the head jerked, he shot again at the side nostrils and saw the horns jolt again and fragments fly, and he did not see Wilson now and, aiming carefully, shot again with the buffalo's huge bulk almost on him and his rifle almost level with the on-coming head, nose out, and he could see the little wicked eyes and the head started to lower and he felt a sudden white-hot, blinding flash explode inside his head and that was all he ever felt.

Wilson had ducked to one side to get in a shoulder shot. Macomber had stood solid and shot for the nose, shooting a touch high each time and hitting the heavy horns, splintering and chipping them like hitting a slate roof, and Mrs. Macomber, in the car, had shot at the buffalo with the 6.5 Mannlicher as it seemed about to gore Macomber and had hit her husband about two inches up and a little to one side of the base of his skull.

Francis Macomber lay now, face down, not two yards from where the buffalo lay on his side and his wife knelt over him with Wilson beside her.

"I wouldn't turn him over," Wilson said.

The woman was crying hysterically.

"I'd get back in the car," Wilson said. "Where's the rifle?"

She shook her head, her face contorted. The gun-bearer picked up the rifle.

"Leave it as it is," said Wilson. Then, "Go get Abdulla so that he may witness the manner of the accident."

He knelt down, took a handkerchief from his pocket, and spread it over Francis Macomber's crew-cropped head where it lay. The blood sank into the dry, loose earth.

Wilson stood up and saw the buffalo on his side, his legs out, his thinly-haired belly crawling with ticks. "Hell of a good bull," his brain registered automatically. "A good fifty inches, or better. Better." He called to the driver and told him to spread a blanket over the body and stay by it. Then he walked over to the motor car where the woman sat crying in the corner.

"That was a pretty thing to do," he said in a toneless voice. "He *would* have left you too."

"Stop it," she said.

"Of course it's an accident," he said. "I know that."

"Stop it," she said.

"Don't worry," he said. "There will be a certain amount of unpleasantness but I will have some photographs taken that will be very useful at the inquest. There's the testimony of the gun-bearers and the driver too. You're perfectly all right."

"Stop it," she said.

"There's a hell of a lot to be done," he said. "And I'll have to send a truck off to the lake to wireless for a plane to take the three of us into Nairobi. Why didn't you poison him? That's what they do in England."

"Stop it. Stop it. Stop it," the woman cried.

Wilson looked at her with his flat blue eyes.

"I'm through now," he said. "I was a little angry. I'd begun to like your husband."

"Oh, please stop it," she said. "Please, please stop it."

"That's better," Wilson said. "Please is much better. Now I'll stop."

John Steinbeck

THE LEADER OF
THE PEOPLE

Nobel Prize 1962

The fifth American to win the Nobel Prize for literature, John Steinbeck (1902–1968) was born in Salinas, California, and attended local schools there. He held a wide variety of jobs from 1925 to 1935, including that of fruit picker, before becoming a full-time writer. And write he did, winning the New York Drama Critics Circle Award and the Pulitzer Prize before the Nobel. Steinbeck also worked as a screenwriter after the success of his novels, scripting such films as Lifeboat *(1944, with Jo Swerling) and* Viva Zapata! *(1952).*

One of the leading writers of the 1930s, he captured the flavor of working Americans in hard times better than anyone else, with an ironic style and a flair for naturalism that catapulated him to fame, which was reinforced by the films made from his books. His strong social concerns are well expressed in such landmark books as Tortilla Flat *(1935),* Of Mice and Men *(1937),* The Grapes of Wrath *(1938), and* Cannery Row *(1945). His work after the end of World War II never approached the power of his earlier masterpieces, but this is a common enough occurrence among writers generally, and does not detract in the least from his greatness and influence.*

213

ON SATURDAY AFTERNOON BILLY Buck, the ranch-hand, raked together the last of the old year's haystack and pitched small forkfuls over the wire fence to a few mildly interested cattle. High in the air small clouds like puffs of cannon smoke were driven eastward by the March wind. The wind could be heard whishing in the brush on the ridge crests, but no breath of it penetrated down into the ranch-cup.

The little boy, Jody, emerged from the house eating a thick piece of buttered bread. He saw Billy working on the last of the haystack. Jody tramped down scuffing his shoes in a way he had been told was destructive to good shoe-leather. A flock of white pigeons flew out of the black cypress tree as Jody passed, and circled the tree and landed again. A half-grown tortoise-shell cat leaped from the bunkhouse porch, galloped on stiff legs across the road, whirled and galloped back again. Jody picked up a stone to help the game along, but he was too late, for the cat was under the porch before the stone could be discharged. He threw the stone into the cypress tree and started the white pigeons on another whirling flight.

Arriving at the used-up hay-stack, the boy leaned against the barbed wire fence. "Will that be all of it, do you think?" he asked.

The middle-aged ranch-hand stopped his careful raking and stuck his fork into the ground. He took off his black hat and smoothed down his hair. "Nothing left of it that isn't soggy from ground moisture," he said. He replaced his hat and rubbed his dry leathery hands together.

"Ought to be plenty mice," Jody suggested.

"Lousy with them," said Billy. "Just crawling with mice."

"Well, maybe, when you get all through, I could call the dogs and hunt the mice."

"Sure, I guess you could," said Billy Buck. He lifted a forkful of the damp ground-hay and threw it into the air. Instantly three mice leaped out and burrowed frantically under the hay again.

Jody sighed with satisfaction. Those plump, sleek, arrogant mice were doomed. For eight months they had lived and multiplied in the haystack. They had been immune from cats, from traps, from poison and from Jody. They had grown smug in their security, overbearing and fat. Now the time of disaster had come; they would not survive another day.

Billy looked up at the top of the hills that surrounded the ranch.

"Maybe you better ask your father before you do it," he suggested.

"Well, where is he? I'll ask him now."

"He rode up to the ridge ranch after dinner. He'll be back pretty soon."

Jody slumped against the fence post. "I don't think he'd care."

As Billy went back to his work he said ominously, "You'd better ask him anyway. You know how he is."

Jody did know. His father, Carl Tiflin, insisted upon giving permission for anything that was done on the ranch, whether it was important or not. Jody sagged farther against the post until he was sitting on the ground. He looked up at the little puffs of wind-driven cloud. "Is it like to rain, Billy?"

"It might. The wind's good for it, but not strong enough."

"Well, I hope it don't rain until after I kill those damn mice." He looked over his shoulder to see whether Billy had noticed the mature profanity. Billy worked on without comment.

Jody turned back and looked at the side-hill where the road from the outside world came down. The hill was washed with lean March sunshine. Silver thistles, blue lupins and a few poppies bloomed among the sage bushes. Halfway up the hill Jody could see Doubletree Mutt, the black dog, digging in a squirrel hole. He paddled for a while and then paused to kick bursts of dirt out between his hind legs, and he dug with an earnestness which belied the knowledge he must have had that no dog had ever caught a squirrel by digging a hole.

Suddenly, while Jody watched, the black dog stiffened, and backed out of the hole and looked up the hill toward the cleft in the ridge where the road came through. Jody looked up too. For a moment Carl Tiflin on horseback stood out against the pale sky and then he moved down the road toward the house. He carried something white in his hand.

The boy started to his feet. "He's got a letter," Jody cried. He trotted away toward the ranch house, for the letter would probably be read aloud and he wanted to be there. He reached the house before his father did, and ran in. He heard Carl dismount from his creaking saddle and slap the horse on the side to send it to the barn where Billy would unsaddle it and turn it out.

Jody ran into the kitchen. "We got a letter!" he cried.

His mother looked up from a pan of beans. "Who has?"

"Father has. I saw it in his hand."

Carl strode into the kitchen then, and Jody's mother asked, "Who's the letter from, Carl?"

He frowned quickly. "How did you know there was a letter?"

She nodded her head in the boy's direction. "Big-Britches Jody told me."

Jody was embarrassed.

His father looked down at him contemptuously. "He *is* getting to be a Big-Britches," Carl said. "He's minding everybody's business but his own. Got his big nose into everything."

Mrs. Tiflin relented a little. "Well, he hasn't enough to keep him busy. Who's the letter from?"

Carl still frowned on Jody. "I'll keep him busy if he isn't careful." He held out a sealed letter. "I guess it's from your father."

Mrs. Tiflin took a hairpin from her head and slit open the flap. Her lips pursed judiciously. Jody saw her eyes snap back and forth over the lines. "He says," she translated, "he says he's going to drive out Saturday to stay for a little while. Why, this is Saturday. The letter must have been delayed." She looked at the postmark. "This was mailed day before yesterday. It should have been here yesterday." She looked up questioningly at her husband, and then her face darkened angrily. "Now what have you got that look on you for? He doesn't come often."

Carl turned his eyes away from her anger. He could be stern with her most of the time, but when occasionally her temper arose, he could not combat it.

"What's the matter with you?" she demanded again.

In his explanation there was a tone of apology Jody himself might have used. "It's just that he talks," Carl said lamely. "Just talks."

"Well, what of it? You talk yourself."

"Sure I do. But your father only talks about one thing."

"Indians!" Jody broke in excitedly. "Indians and crossing the plains!"

Carl turned fiercely on him. "You get out, Mr. Big-Britches! Go on, now! Get out!"

Jody went miserably out the back door and closed the screen with elaborate quietness. Under the kitchen window his shamed, downcast eyes fell upon a curiously shaped stone, a stone of such fascination that he squatted down and picked it up and turned it over in his hands.

The voices came clearly to him through the open kitchen window. "Jody's damn well right," he heard his father say. "Just Indians and crossing the plains. I've heard that story about how the horses got driven off about a thousand times. He just goes on and on, and he never changes a word in the things he tells."

When Mrs. Tiflin answered her tone was so changed that Jody, outside the window, looked up from his study of the stone. Her voice had become soft and explanatory. Jody knew how her face would have changed to match the tone. She said quietly, "Look at it this way, Carl. That was the big thing in my father's life. He led a wagon train clear across the plains to the coast, and when it was finished, his life was done. It was a big thing to do, but it didn't last long enough. Look!" she continued, "it's as though he was born to do that, and after he finished it, there wasn't anything more for him to do but think about it and talk about it. If there'd been any farther west to go, he'd have gone. He's told me so himself. But at last there was the ocean. He lives right by the ocean where he had to stop."

She had caught Carl, caught him and entangled him in her soft tone.

"I've seen him," he agreed quietly. "He goes down and stares off west over the ocean." His voice sharpened a little. "And then he goes up to the Horseshoe Club in Pacific Grove, and he tells people how the Indians drove off the horses."

She tried to catch him again. "Well, it's everything to him. You might be patient with him and pretend to listen."

Carl turned impatiently away. "Well, if it gets too bad, I can always go down to the bunkhouse and sit with Billy," he said irritably. He walked through the house and slammed the front door after him.

Jody ran to his chores. He dumped the grain to the chickens without chasing any of them. He gathered the eggs from the nests. He trotted into the house with the wood and interlaced it so carefully in the wood-box that two armloads seemed to fill it to overflowing.

His mother had finished the beans by now. She stirred up the fire and brushed off the stove-top with a turkey wing. Jody peered cautiously at her to see whether any rancor toward him remained. "Is he coming today?" Jody asked.

"That's what his letter said."

"Maybe I better walk up the road to meet him."

Mrs. Tiflin clanged the stove-lid shut. "That would be nice," she said. "He'd probably like to be met."

"I guess I'll just do it then."

Outside, Jody whistled shrilly to the dogs. "Come on up the hill," he commanded. The two dogs waved their tails and ran ahead. Along the roadside the sage had tender new tips. Jody tore off some pieces and rubbed then on his hands until the air was filled with the sharp wild smell. With a rush the dogs leaped from the road and yapped into the brush after a rabbit. That was the last Jody saw of them, for when they failed to catch the rabbit, they went back home.

Jody plodded on up the hill toward the ridge top. When he reached the little cleft where the road came through, the afternoon wind struck him and blew up his hair and ruffled his shirt. He looked down on the little hills and ridges below and then out at the huge green Salinas Valley. He could see the white town of Salinas far out in the flat and the flash of its windows under the waning sun. Directly below him, in an oak tree, a crow congress had convened. The tree was black with crows all cawing at once.

Then Jody's eyes followed the wagon road down from the ridge where he stood, and lost it behind a hill, and picked it up again on the other side. On that distant stretch he saw a cart slowly pulled by a bay horse. It disappeared behind the hill. Jody sat down on the ground and watched the place where the cart would reappear again. The wind sang on the hilltops and the puff-ball clouds hurried eastward.

Then the cart came into sight and stopped. A man dressed in black dismounted from the seat and walked to the horse's head. Although it was so far away, Jody knew he had unhooked the check-rein, for the horse's head dropped forward. The horse moved on, and the man walked slowly up the hill beside it. Jody gave a glad cry and ran down the road toward them. The squirrels bumped along off the road, and a road-runner flirted its tail and raced over the edge of the hill and sailed out like a glider.

Jody tried to leap into the middle of his shadow at every step. A stone rolled under his foot and he went down. Around a little bend he raced, and there, a short distance ahead, were his grandfather and the cart. The boy dropped from his unseemly running and approached at a dignified walk.

The horse plodded stumble-footedly up the hill and the old man walked beside it. In the lowering sun their giant shadows flickered darkly behind them. The grandfather was dressed in a black broadcloth suit and he wore kid congress gaiters and a black tie on a short, hard collar. He carried his black slouch hat in his hand. His white beard was cropped close and his white eyebrows overhung his eyes like moustaches. The blue eyes were sternly merry. About the whole face and figure there was a granite dignity, so that every motion seemed an impossible thing. Once at rest, it seemed the old man would be stone, would never move again. His steps were slow and certain. Once made, no step could ever be retraced; once headed in a direction, the path would never bend nor the pace increase nor slow.

When Jody appeared around the bend, Grandfather waved his hat slowly in welcome, and he called, "Why, Jody! Come down to meet me, have you?"

Jody sidled near and turned and matched his step to the old man's step and stiffened his body and dragged his heels a little. "Yes, sir," he said. "We got your letter only today."

"Should have been here yesterday," said Grandfather. "It certainly should. How are all the folks?"

"They're fine, sir." He hesitated and then suggested shyly, "Would you like to come on a mouse hunt tomorrow, sir?"

"Mouse hunt, Jody?" Grandfather chuckled. "Have the people of this generation come down to hunting mice? They aren't very strong, the new people, but I hardly thought mice would be game for them."

"No, sir. It's just play. The haystack's gone. I'm going to drive out the mice to the dogs. And you can watch, or even beat the hay a little."

The stern, merry eyes turned down on him. "I see. You don't eat them, then. You haven't come to that yet."

Jody explained, "The dogs eat them, sir. It wouldn't be much like hunting Indians, I guess."

"No, not much—but then later, when the troops were hunting Indians and shooting children and burning teepees, it wasn't much different from your mouse hunt."

They topped the rise and started down into the ranch cup, and they lost the sun from their shoulders. "You've grown," Grandfather said. "Nearly an inch, I should say."

"More," Jody boasted. "Where they mark me on the door, I'm up more than an inch since Thanksgiving even."

Grandfather's rich throaty voice said, "Maybe you're getting too much water and turning to pith and stalk. Wait until you head out, and then we'll see."

Jody looked quickly into the old man's face to see whether his feelings should be hurt, but there was no will to injure, no punishing nor putting-in-your-place light in the keen blue eyes. "We might kill a pig," Jody suggested.

"Oh, no! I couldn't let you do that. You're just humoring me. It isn't the time and you know it."

"You know Riley, the big boar, sir?"

"Yes. I remember Riley well."

"Well, Riley ate a hole into that same haystack, and it fell down on him and smothered him."

"Pigs do that when they can," said Grandfather.

"Riley was a nice pig, for a boar, sir. I rode him sometimes, and he didn't mind."

A door slammed at the house below them, and they saw Jody's mother standing on the porch waving her apron in welcome. And they saw Carl Tiflin walking up from the barn to be at the house for the arrival.

The sun had disappeared from the hills by now. The blue smoke from the house chimney hung in flat layers in the purpling ranch-cup. The puff-ball clouds, dropped by the falling wind, hung list-lessly in the sky.

Billy Buck came out of the bunkhouse and flung a wash basin of soapy water on the ground. He had been shaving in mid-week, for Billy held Grandfather in reverence, and Grandfather said that Billy was one of the few men of the new generation who had not gone soft. Although Billy was in middle age, Grandfather considered him a boy. Now Billy was hurrying toward the house too.

When Jody and Grandfather arrived, the three were waiting for them in front of the yard gate.

Carl said, "Hello, sir. We've been looking for you."

Mrs. Tiflin kissed Grandfather on the side of his beard, and stood still while his big hand patted her shoulder. Billy shook hands solemnly, grinning under his straw moustache. "I'll put up your horse," said Billy, and he led the rig away.

Grandfather watched him go, and then, turning back to the

group, he said as he had said a hundred times before, "There's a good boy. I knew his father, old Mule-tail Buck. I never knew why they called him Mule-tail except he packed mules."

Mrs. Tiflin turned and led the way into the house. "How long are you going to stay, Father? Your letter didn't say."

"Well, I don't know. I thought I'd stay about two weeks. But I never stay as long as I think I'm going to."

In a short while they were sitting at the white oilcloth table eating their supper. The lamp with the tin reflector hung over the table. Outside the dining-room windows the big moths battered softly against the glass.

Grandfather cut his steak into tiny pieces and chewed slowly. "I'm hungry," he said. "Driving out here got my appetite up. It's like when we were crossing. We all got so hungry every night we could hardly wait to let the meat get done, I could eat about five pounds of buffalo meat every night."

"It's moving around does it," said Billy. "My father was a government packer. I helped him when I was a kid. Just the two of us could about clean up a deer's ham."

"I knew your father, Billy," said Grandfather. "A fine man he was. They called him Mule-tail Buck. I don't know why except he packed mules."

"That was it," Billy agreed. "He packed mules."

Grandfather put down his knife and fork and looked around the table. "I remember one time we ran out of meat—" His voice dropped to a curious low sing-song, dropped into a tonal groove the story had worn for itself. "There was no buffalo, no antelope, not even rabbits. The hunters couldn't even shoot a coyote. That was the time for the leader to be on the watch. I was the leader, and I kept my eyes open. Know why? Well, just the minute the people began to get hungry they'd start slaughtering the team oxen. Do you believe that? I've heard of parties that just ate up their draft cattle. Started from the middle and worked toward the ends. Finally they'd eat the lead pair, and then the wheelers. The leader of a party had to keep them from doing that."

In some manner a big moth got into the room and circled the hanging kerosene lamp. Billy got up and tried to clap it between his hands. Carl struck with a cupped palm and caught the moth and broke it. He walked to the window and dropped it out.

"As I was saying," Grandfather began again, but Carl interrupted him. "You'd better eat some more meat. All the rest of us are ready for our pudding."

Jody saw a flash of anger in his mother's eyes. Grandfather picked up his knife and fork. "I'm pretty hungry, all right," he said. "I'll tell you about that later."

When supper was over, when the family and Billy Buck sat in front of the fireplace in the other room, Jody anxiously watched Grandfather. He saw the signs he knew. The bearded head leaned forward; the eyes lost their sternness and looked wonderingly into the fire; the big lean fingers laced themselves on the black knees. "I wonder," he began, "I just wonder whether I ever told you how those thieving Piutes drove off thirty-five of our horses."

"I think you did," Carl interrupted. "Wasn't it just before you went up into the Tahoe country?"

Grandfather turned quickly toward his son-in-law. "That's right. I guess I must have told you that story."

"Lots of times," Carl said cruelly, and he avoided his wife's eyes. But he felt the angry eyes on him, and he said, "'Course I'd like to hear it again."

Grandfather looked back at the fire. His fingers unlaced and laced again. Jody knew how he felt, how his insides were collapsed and empty. Hadn't Jody been called a Big-Britches that very afternoon? He arose to heroism and opened himself to the term Big-Britches again. "Tell about Indians," he said softly.

Grandfather's eyes grew stern again. "Boys always want to hear about Indians. It was a job for men, but boys want to hear about it. Well, let's see. Did I ever tell you how I wanted each wagon to carry a long iron plate?"

Everyone but Jody remained silent. Jody said, "No. You didn't."

"Well, when the Indians attacked, we always put the wagons in a circle and fought from between the wheels. I thought that if every wagon carried a long plate with rifle holes, the men could stand the plates on the outside of the wheels when the wagons were in the circle and they would be protected. It would save lives and that would make up for the extra weight of the iron. But of course the party wouldn't do it. No party had done it before and they couldn't see why they should go to the expense. They lived to regret it, too."

Jody looked at his mother, and knew from her expression that she was not listening at all. Carl picked at a callus on his thumb and Billy Buck watched a spider crawling up the wall.

Grandfather's tone dropped into its narrative groove again. Jody knew in advance exactly what words would fall. The story droned on, speeded up for the attack, grew sad over the wounds, struck a dirge at the burials on the great plains. Jody sat quietly watching Grandfather. The stern blue eyes were detached. He looked as though he were not very interested in the story himself.

When it was finished, when the pause had been politely respected as the frontier of the story, Billy Buck stood up and stretched and hitched his trousers. "I guess I'll turn in," he said. Then he faced Grandfather. "I've got an old powder horn and a cap and ball pistol down to the bunkhouse. Did I ever show them to you?"

Grandfather nodded slowly. "Yes, I think you did, Billy. Reminds me of a pistol I had when I was leading the people across." Billy stood politely until the little story was done, and then he said, "Goodnight," and went out of the house.

Carl Tiflin tried to turn the conversation then. "How's the country between here and Monterey? I've heard it's pretty dry."

"It is dry," said Grandfather. "There's not a drop of water in the Laguna Seca. But it's a long pull from '87. The whole country was powder then, and in '61 I believe all the coyotes starved to death. We had fifteen inches of rain this year."

"Yes, but it all came too early. We could do with some now." Carl's eye fell on Jody. "Hadn't you better be getting to bed?"

Jody stood up obediently. "Can I kill the mice in the old haystack, sir?"

"Mice? Oh! Sure, kill them all off. Billy said there isn't any good hay left."

Jody exchanged a secret and satisfying look with Grandfather. "I'll kill every one tomorrow," he promised.

Jody lay in his bed and thought of the impossible world of Indians and buffaloes, a world that had ceased to be forever. He wished he could have been living in the heroic time, but he knew he was not of heroic timber. No one living now, save possibly Billy Buck, was worthy to do the things that had been done. A race of giants had lived then, fearless men, men of a staunchness unknown in this day. Jody thought of the wide plains and of the wagons moving across like centipedes. He thought of Grandfather on a huge white horse, marshaling the people. Across his mind marched the great phantoms, and they marched off the earth and they were gone.

He came back to the ranch for a moment, then. He heard the

dull rushing sound that space and silence make. He heard one of the dogs, out in the doghouse, scratching a flea and bumping his elbow against the floor with every stroke. Then the wind arose again and the black cypress groaned and Jody went to sleep.

He was up half an hour before the triangle sounded for breakfast. His mother was rattling the stove to make the flames roar when Jody went through the kitchen. "You're up early," she said. "Where are you going?"

"Out to get a good stick. We're going to kill the mice today."

"Who is 'we'?"

"Why, Grandfather and I."

"So you've got him in it. You always like to have someone in with you in case there's blame to share."

"I'll be right back," said Jody. "I just want to have a good stick ready for after breakfast."

He closed the screen door after him and went out into the cool blue morning. The birds were noisy in the dawn and the ranch cats came down from the hill like blunt snakes. They had been hunting gophers in the dark, and although the four cats were full of gopher meat, they sat in a semi-circle at the back door and mewed piteously for milk. Doubletree Mutt and Smasher moved sniffing along the edge of the brush, performing the duty with rigid ceremony, but when Jody whistled, their heads jerked up and their tails waved. They plunged down to him, wriggling their skins and yawning. Jody patted their heads seriously, and moved on to the weathered scrap pile. He selected an old broom handle and a short piece of inch-square scrap wood. From his pocket he took a shoelace and tied the ends of the sticks loosely together to make a flail. He whistled his new weapon through the air and struck the ground experimentally, while the dogs leaped aside and whined with apprehension.

Jody turned and started down past the house toward the old haystack ground to look over the field of slaughter, but Billy Buck, sitting patiently on the back steps, called to him, "You better come back. It's only a couple of minutes till breakfast."

Jody changed his course and moved toward the house. He leaned his flail against the steps. "That's to drive the mice out," he said. "I'll bet they're fat. I'll bet they don't know what's going to happen to them today."

"No, nor you either," Billy remarked philosophically, "nor me, nor anyone."

Jody was staggered by this thought. He knew it was true. His imagination twitched away from the mouse hunt. Then his mother came out on the back porch and struck the triangle, and all thoughts fell in a heap.

Grandfather hadn't appeared at the table when they sat down. Billy nodded at his empty chair. "He's all right? He isn't sick?"

"He takes a long time to dress," said Mrs. Tiflin. "He combs his whiskers and rubs up his shoes and brushes his clothes."

Carl scattered sugar on his mush. "A man that's led a wagon train across the plains has got to be pretty careful how he dresses."

Mrs. Tiflin turned on him. "Don't do that, Carl! Please don't!" There was more of threat than of request in her tone. And the threat irritated Carl.

"Well, how many times do I have to listen to the story of the iron plates, and the thirty-five horses? That time's done. Why can't he forget it, now it's done?" He grew angrier while he talked, and his voice rose. "Why does he have to tell them over and over? He came across the plains. All right! Now it's finished. Nobody wants to hear about it over and over."

The door into the kitchen closed softly. The four at the table sat frozen. Carl laid his mush spoon on the table and touched his chin with his fingers.

Then the kitchen door opened and Grandfather walked in. His mouth smiled tightly and his eyes were squinted. "Good morning," he said, and he sat down and looked at his mush dish.

Carl could not leave it there. "Did—did you hear what I said?"

Grandfather jerked a little nod.

"I don't know what got into me, sir. I didn't mean it. I was just being funny."

Jody glanced in shame at his mother, and he saw that she was looking at Carl, and that she wasn't breathing. It was an awful thing that he was doing. He was tearing himself to pieces to talk like that. It was a terrible thing to him to retract a word, but to retract it in shame was infinitely worse.

Grandfather looked sidewise. "I'm trying to get right side up," he said gently. "I'm not being mad. I don't mind what you said, but it might be true, and I would mind that."

"It isn't true," said Carl. "I'm not feeling well this morning. I'm sorry I said it."

"Don't be sorry, Carl. An old man doesn't see things sometimes. Maybe you're right. The crossing is finished. Maybe it should be forgotten, now it's done."

Carl got up from the table. "I've had enough to eat. I'm going to work. Take your time, Billy!" He walked quickly out of the dining-room. Billy gulped the rest of his food and followed soon after. But Jody could not leave his chair.

"Won't you tell any more stories?" Jody asked.

"Why, sure I'll tell them, but only when—I'm sure people want to hear them."

"I like to hear them, sir."

"Oh! Of course you do, but you're a little boy. It was a job for men, but only little boys like to hear about it."

Jody got up from his place. "I'll wait outside for you, sir. I've got a good stick for those mice."

He waited by the gate until the old man came out on the porch. "Let's go down and kill the mice now," Jody called.

"I think I'll just sit in the sun, Jody. You go kill the mice."

"You can use my stick if you like."

"No, I'll just sit here a while."

Jody turned disconsolately away, and walked down toward the old haystack. He tried to whip up his enthusiasm with thoughts of the fat juicy mice. He beat the ground with his flail. The dogs coaxed and whined about him, but he could not go. Back at the house he could see Grandfather sitting on the porch, looking small and thin and black.

Jody gave up and went to sit on the steps at the old man's feet.

"Back already? Did you kill the mice?"

"No, sir. I'll kill them some other day."

The morning flies buzzed close to the ground and the ants dashed about in front of the steps. The heavy smell of sage slipped down the hill. The porch boards grew warm in the sunshine.

Jody hardly knew when Grandfather started to talk. "I shouldn't stay here, feeling the way I do." He examined his strong old hands. "I feel as though the crossing wasn't worth doing." His eyes moved up the side-hill and stopped on a motionless hawk perched on a dead limb. "I tell those old stories, but they're not what I want to tell. I only know how I want people to feel when I tell them.

"It wasn't Indians that were important, nor adventures, nor even getting out here. It was a whole bunch of people made into one big crawling beast. And I was the head. It was westering and westering. Every man wanted something for himself, but the big beast that was all of them wanted only westering. I was the leader, but if I hadn't been there, someone else would have been the head. The thing had to have a head.

"Under the little bushes the shadows were black at white noonday. When we saw the mountains at last, we cried—all of us. But it wasn't getting here that mattered, it was movement and westering.

"We carried life out here and set it down the way those ants carry eggs. And I was the leader. The westering was as big as God, and the slow steps that made the movement piled up and piled up until the continent was crossed.

"Then we came down to the sea, and it was done." He stopped and wiped his eyes until the rims were red. "That's what I should be telling instead of stories."

When Jody spoke, Grandfather started and looked down at him. "Maybe I could lead the people some day," Jody said.

The old man smiled. "There's no place to go. There's the ocean to stop you. There's a line of old men along the shore hating the ocean because it stopped them."

"In boats I might, sir."

"No place to go, Jody. Every place is taken. But that's not the worst—no, not the worst. Westering has died out of the people. Westering isn't a hunger any more. It's all done. Your father is right. It is finished." He laced his fingers on his knees and looked at them.

Jody felt very sad. "If you'd like a glass of lemonade I could make it for you."

Grandfather was about to refuse, and then he saw Jody's face. "That would be nice," he said. "Yes, it would be nice to drink a lemonade."

Jody ran into the kitchen where his mother was wiping the last of the breakfast dishes. "Can I have a lemon to make a lemonade for Grandfather?"

His mother mimicked—"And another lemon to make a lemonade for you."

"No, ma'am. I don't want one."

"Jody! You're sick!" Then she stopped suddenly. "Take a lemon out of the cooler," she said softly. "Here, I'll reach the squeezer down to you."

PATRICK WHITE

THE COCKATOOS

NOBEL PRIZE 1973

Novelist, poet, and playwright, Patrick White is a fourth generation Australian who was, ironically, born in London while his parents were traveling there. He spent his childhood on sheep and cattle ranches, but returned to England for advanced schooling and obtained a degree in modern languages from Cambridge in 1935. He traveled in Europe and the United States for several years, then returned home to write the first of his great Australian novels, Happy Valley *(1939). After interrupting his career to serve as an RAF intelligence officer in Greece and the Middle East during WW II, he resumed writing and eventually produced complex works, such as* Voss *(1957),* Riders in the Chariot *(1961) and* The Eye of the Storm *(1973). In 1973, he became the first Australian to be awarded the Nobel Prize in literature, being cited for his "epic and psychological narrative art which ...introduced a new continent into literature."*

DRESSED CASUAL FOR SUNDAY and his mission, Mr. Goodenough ran at the path.

As soon as she opened, he started trying to freshen up his patter, which by now was on the stale side, "...the old door-knock for the

229

Heart Foundation. Care to make a contribution?" He touched the heart pinned to his shirt.

Half expecting Jehovah she frowned at first at the paper heart, then smiled, it was almost dreamy, for remembering the smell of raspberry tartlets aligned on greaseproof in one of the safe kitchens of childhood.

"Oh yes," she said and sighed and went down a passage to fetch her purse.

She was a tall, thin, yellow-skinned woman. Like most people in the neighbourhood, Mrs. Davoren and Mr. Goodenough had lived there many years without addressing each other more than ritually and in the street; though nobody held anything against anybody else, excepting Figgis, who had been an undertaker, and was still a nark.

"There," she said, handing the two-dollar bill, which was as much as you had reckoned Mrs. Davoren would part with. "What with the price of things! Never seems to stop, does it?"

If his smile was more like a tightening of the skin, it was because he was writing a receipt on his knee. "What initial have we?" he asked.

"O", she said. "Mrs. O. Davoren."

"What about your old man? Think he's good for a coupler bucks?"

"I don't really know. He mightn't be here."

"Seen 'im come in. Went around the back."

"Oh, well, he could be here—at the back."

"Wouldn't like to ask 'im, would you?"

Clyde Goodenough turned on the smile which made ladies overlook his lack of stature and his varicose veins. He liked to play the charmer with strangers; it was all above board, of course.

Something must have worked with Mrs. Davoren: if not charm, an autumn sunlight, or the paper heart pinned to his shirt or, most likely, her own munificence.

She suddenly said, and it was the heart she was staring at, "Mr. Davoren and I haven't spoken for six—no, it must be seven years."

You could have knocked Mr. Goodenough over.

"But there must be things you gotter say—on and off—like putting out the garbage or paying the milk."

"There are things—yes—and then we write them on a pad—which we keep for that purpose."

In spite of it all, Mr. Goodenough turned on the smile again.

"What about pushing the pad at 'im for the Heart Foundation's Door-Knock?"

"Oh, I couldn't!" she said, her feet shifting on the gritty step. "No, I just couldn't!" Then, although everything seemed to show how she regretted her impulsiveness, Mrs. Davoren confided still more rashly, "It began on account of the boodgie. He didn't bother. When I went down to Kiama for Essie's funeral—he let my boodgie—die."

Gawd strewth! "Anyway, you've got a cockie now," Mr. Goodenough consoled, as he handed the receipt and returned the ballpoint to his shirt pocket. "Looks pretty tame, too."

"A cockie?" She couldn't have looked more alarmed if he had mentioned a tiger.

"That cockatoo in front—walking around in front of the tree."

Mrs. Davoren's thin legs and long feet carried her by quick steps along the concrete as far as the corner.

"A cocka*too*!" she breathed.

Under a gumtree, a fairly large one for a front yard in those parts, a cockatoo was striding and stamping. He looked angry, Mr. Goodenough thought. The sulphur crest flicked open like a many-bladed pocketknife. Then he screeched, and opened his wings, and flew away across the park. It was an ugly, clumsy-looking action.

"Ohhh!" Mrs. Davoren was moaning. "D'you think he'll come back?"

"Must have forgot to latch the cage door, did you?"

"Oh, no! He's wild. I never set eyes on him before. Though he could have belonged to someone, of course. How they'll suffer when they find they've lost their cockatoo!"

Mr. Goodenough made his getaway.

"Do you think if I put out seed?" Mrs. Davoren was desperately calling for advice. "I read somewhere that sunflower seed..."

"P'raps." Clyde Goodenough had reached the gate; one thing about the Door-Knock, it was giving him plenty to tell the wife.

Mrs. Davoren went back along the concrete and was swallowed up inside her house.

•

Olive Davoren found consolation moving around through her dark house, unless she happened to hear Him moving around at

the same time, in a different part; this was liable to give her heart-
burn. Dadda had left her comfortable: the house in a respectable
street, and the interest in Friendly Loans, which Mr. Armstrong
the partner managed. The house was in liver brick, not so large as
to attract thieves, but large enough to impress those who officially
weren't. The tuck-pointing was falling out. She must have it fixed.
And woodwork painted, inside and out. But not yet. For the trials
she would have to bear, at any rate in the interior, and perhaps
for having to face Mick at moments when she least wanted to.

Dadda had been right, she wished she had listened. *That man is
you can't say no good but a no-hoper you can't blame him you can't blame
a man for the Irish in him.* Hard to believe she had been so headstrong
as a girl. Whether it was marriage or music, she was the one that
knew. And ended up not scarcely daring to hold an opinion. Except
on the one subject.

This evening she could hear Him *(your Irishman)* stalking through
the rear part of the house. She heard the wire door twang as he
stepped out into the back yard. He liked to pick the grubs off the
fuchsias growing alongside the palings.

As for music, her violin had lain untouched these many years
on the top shelf of her silky-oak-veneer wardrobe. Whenever she
remembered she buried it deeper under the overflow of linen from
the press.

She was artistic. Mumma took her to the Eisteddfods, fluffed
out her skirt, prinked her hair before the performance. When they
found it was the violin rather than recitation, Dadda sent her to
the Con. Although she knew that she should love Bach, and did,
she decided she would play the Bruch at her first concert with
orchestra.

(None of it ever meant a thing to Mick, who liked to listen—in
the early days—to his own silky Irish tenor, over the sink, or in
front of friends.)

But she, she had her vocation, till Professor Mumberson took
her through the baize door, not into the office, but outside in the
tiled corridor, to tell her confidentially *I have had to fail you Olive
in the circumstances...* What those circumstances were she hadn't
asked, because she couldn't believe. It was Dadda who asked and
got the answer, but never told, because he was a kind man. If he
had a belief in money and what it would buy he didn't succeed in

buying Professor Mumberson. Dadda couldn't believe in his own failure, just as she would never (till she married Mick) let herself believe in hers.

She took a few pupils at first, kids from the neighbourhood who acquired an accomplishment of sorts and got it cheap. Most of them hated it: sawing away, all elbows and fingers, in a front room overlooking the park. Her own demonstration of a theme often seemed to sound as deadly thin, its tone as yellow, as the grass around the araucarias.

Not that it mattered: those were war years, and everything could be blamed on the War. (Mrs. Dulhunty fell downstairs and broke a hip the night of the Jap sub in the harbour.) It was only when the War was over that you realized the great excuse it had been.

Once while they were still speaking, after they became man and wife, He told her how the War had given him the best years of his life. A sergeant-pilot in the Middle East, he kept his medals in a tin box. He told her he would always hope to take part in another war.

She had just put the food in front of him. "It doesn't say much for me, does it? I'm to blame, I suppose. Because somebody is always to blame." She would truly have liked to accept it, not out of spite either, if not from what you would call love; it was as simple as that.

He cocked his head to one side, and laughed at the plateful of overdone steak (it was how he liked it) and she couldn't see his light-coloured eyes for the angle at which he was holding himself. She had wanted to catch sight of the eyes, of a slate blue, or more sort of periwinkle, as she worked out while they were still what people call "courting," and herself still craving for love or hurt. At that time he was driving the interstate passenger buses. They met at Mildura, or it could have been Wagga, where he took over. She forgot what she ought to remember.

He was always telling her, still friendly, "What sort of head have you got? To forget!" She never forgot the chill thrill of the slate—or periwinkle—eyes; she could remember whole sonatas she would never have the ability to play.

Olive Davoren sopped up her nose with a mauve Kleenex she found down her front. On account of the cockie—she remembered that—she tiptoed past the glass doors. Perhaps because of the brown Holland the light the blinds allowed from under them sat on the lino as solid as bars of yellow soap.

She twitched aside the blind from a bow-window, to see whether the cockatoo. There were two of them. Stamping and striding around the tree. Her heart was beating. Sometimes the birds got so angry, she could hear them screeching through the glass. She wouldn't have dared open the window: she might have frightened the cockatoos. Who tore at the lawn with furious beaks, or calming down, composed their crests along their heads, eyes tender with a wisdom which, like most wisdom, threatened to become obscure or irrelevant.

Oh dear, Olive Davoren moaned beneath her breath, *the sunflower seed is what I must remember...*

And what would He have to say when he found she was coaxing cockatoos? *Mick!* Her scorn rose above her pallid hair; she had rinsed it Thursday, though to what purpose?

She had told him, "You let it die on purpose. Because I was gone. You knew I loved the bird. You was jealous—that was it!" Her grief made her forget the grammar she had always been respectful of.

"It was sick," he said. "Anyone could see. A person only had to look at its toenails."

"I should have cut his claws," she admitted. "But was afraid. He was too frail and small."

"Sick to anyone else."

(She had asked to see what they had taken from her—you couldn't have called it a child. She had even touched it. And wouldn't ever let herself remember. He certainly wouldn't be one to remind her of it.)

She must have cried at that point. She had called her boodgie Perk, but the bird hadn't lived up to it. And died.

So they seemed agreed not to speak. At any rate, for the time being, for a few days after the burial. It probably surprised them both that their decision should have hardened into permanence. In her case, there was a wound left over, from which all the blood hadn't flowed; some remained to suppurate. When at the secret burial—she would have died if anyone had seen—she had cried everything out of her, she thought, at the roots of Mrs. Herbert Stevens.

It was seven years since Perk died; before that they had it—more or less what people call "good." Dadda took *this Irishman* into the business, but he couldn't stick it. Had to lead an outdoor life. He was happiest on the buses, she guessed, meeting people and leaving it at that. Girls offered him lollies, girls he had never set eyes on. They called him "Mick" soon as ever they found out. He had black hair and a strong neck, yarning into the mike about the historical places they were passing through. Yes, the buses suited Mick.

As soon as they were seated at the café table he complimented her on her hands. Well, she knew her hands were fine from seeing them at the violin, but it hurt rather than flattered hearing it from the Irishman; her throat tightened, and she could not look at him for some time. It didn't seem to worry him: he was telling her about his boyhood at Lucan, how he used to sit, legs dangling, on a stone parapet, watching the water flow beneath the bridge of a Sunday.

"Why?" she asked. "Was there nothing better to do?"

"That's what you do in Ireland." She couldn't help noticing his teeth when he laughed. "Waitin' for somethun to turn up!"

Beyond the window, under the tree, the two cockatoos had raised their crests, not the violent flicking of knives, but gentle almost as ladies' fans. Their currants of eyes looked sweet and moist.

Somebody was coming from around the corner. It was Him, she saw. She made to open the window, by instinct, against her principle, to call out and warn Mick not to frighten the cockies.

But he was walking down the path, not exactly tiptoe, keeling over on the edges of his soles, looking in the opposite direction, as though he hadn't seen, or didn't want to let on that he had.

He passed by, and the cockatoos held their expression of sweet, black-eyed wisdom.

He had reached the gate, his blue suit shiny around the shoulders and the seat, that he must have been wearing for best ever since he left off being the sergeant-pilot. His body was that of a younger man, his hair greyish, such of it as you could see. For he was wearing the hat which made it look as though he was going farther than a few doors along, to Her.

Olive Davoren got so cranky she jerked the Holland blind to shut herself off from her thoughts. She must have frightened the cockatoos. She could no longer see, but heard them as they gathered themselves, wings creaking at first, then beating the air, steadily, till faint.

Probably they would never come back however much sunflower

seed she put. She snivelled a bit, before cooking the tea He would not be there to eat.

•

"Six years—no, seven, she told me. Without exchanging a bloody word! If they have to, they write it on a pad."

"Waddayerknow!" Gwen Goodenough stirred the pan. "That's a way, Clyde, it'll never take you an' me."

The boy had come in with some kind of old bottle he kept on stroking and looking at.

"Who didn't speak for seven years?"

"Somebody," the father said.

He had unpinned the paper heart. His legs, his varicose veins, ached. He was tired by now, and ready for a beer or two.

"Lots of people don't speak," said the boy, still stroking what looked like an old medicine bottle.

"I never heard of anybody, Tim. Not when they live together." The mother was more concerned about the contents of her pan.

"Lots," said Tim. "They speak, but don't say."

"Mr. Clever, eh?" Clyde Goodenough had taken offence, though he could hardly have explained why.

"I don't know anything, of course," the boy answered, too quick for parents.

"Here," said the mother, "don't you cheek your dad!"

For the moment Tim hated his dad. An old man in shorts! He hated his father for showing his varicose veins from door to door the day of the Heart Appeal.

After Dad had knocked back his first beer, and Mum only a sip of sherry, and they were all eating the gristly old stew, Tim Good-enough continued fingering the bottle he had stood on the table beside his plate.

"What's this?" the father asked. "I'm blowed—a dirty old bottle at table!"

"It's an antique liniment bottle. Found it in Figgis's incinerator." He held it to the light. "Look at the lovely colours in it."

If you looked hard, you could see a faint tinge of amethyst, even a burnish of incinerated green.

It troubled the father: what if the boy turned out a nut? or worse, a poof—or artist?

"That's not anything to keep," he advised. "You oughter throw the filthy thing away. Carrying home useless junk out of Figgis's back yard!"

"I'm going to put it in my museum."

"Museum?" the mother asked, in a voice which would have sounded severe if she hadn't remembered to make it chummy. "You never told us you have a museum."

"I don't tell everything," said Tim.

The father sucked his teeth; he looked as though he might have been going to throw up, till he got the better of his disgust. "D'you know what? There's a wild cockatoo in Davorens' garden."

"Someone must have left the cage open," Mrs. Goodenough said because it was her turn.

"That's what I told 'er. But she said it was wild."

"How could she possibly know?" Mrs. Goodenough wasn't all that interested in cockatoos.

Tim said, "There's mobs of wild cockatoos in the park."

This was something the parents couldn't contradict: they couldn't remember when they had last been in the park. Mr. Goodenough sighed; he wondered why his charm never worked at home. Mrs. Goodenough sighed too: she suspected her monthly was coming on.

When he had finished the IXL peaches, Tim Goodenough got down from the table, taking his antique bottle with him.

"You're in a hurry tonight, my lad."

"I'm going to Davorens' to see the cockie." It sounded younger than he was, and sickly, because that way he often pacified them.

Mum said, "I'm not a naturalist, but know that cockatoos don't take root. It's more than likely flown off."

It was true, he knew, but also as stupid as truth can often be. The cockatoo's presence in Davorens' garden was only the half of looking for it.

He went out humming, first to the garage, to put his bottle in the museum.

It did exist, in a disused bathroom cupboard, stashed away behind a roll of Feltex and several of wire-netting. In it he kept the skull of a small animal, probably a rat, found in a storm-water drain which emptied itself into the park. He also had—still a matter for surprise—a silver Maria Theresa dollar.

"Zis is from Ethiopia," said Mr. Lipski, the old gentleman from whom he had got it.

"Will you give it to me—please?"

Mr. Lipski laughed because caught off his guard. "Sure," he said, "vhy shouldn't you keep it? May be ze start of somsink."

"Ooh, Tim, d'you think you ought? Something so valuable!" Mum pretended to be shocked, or was; greedy herself, he had noticed she suspected others of greed.

But in this case you couldn't honestly say it was that. He had never owned what he recognized as a talisman—well, there was the rat's skull perhaps. But he badly needed this coin as well.

Now in the dusk of the garage and the stink of damp Feltex, he could only explore the shapes of the silver dollar and the rat's skull by touch. In their mystic company, he left the liniment bottle he had churned up out of Figgis's incinerator.

There were several mobs of kids with mongrel dogs playing in the dusk after tea on the pavement and in the road. A lot of the owners of the houses which made an island between the parks were old and childless, but several large families had migrated to the neighbourhood so that their children could benefit from the parks. Tim Goodenough didn't often play with the mobs of other kids. Being an only child made him superior, or shy. You couldn't say the others disliked, but they didn't like him. Nor did he encourage them to. Not that he despised them for being stupid (several of them never stopped doing well at exams and already thought of becoming doctors and lawyers). It was just that they didn't know what he knew though what he knew he didn't altogether know— but knew.

Sometimes the mongrel dogs belonging to the large, consolidated families followed him wagging their tails, licking the backs of his hands as they never did to their owners. He liked that.

This evening one of the boys shouted, "What are you up to, Tim-the-Snoop?"

"I'm sauntering," he called back.

Because it was unexpected and peculiar, the girls giggled, several of the boys jeered, and somebody threw a seed-pod at his head.

When he reached the Davorens' the house was dark; the brown blinds were down, making it look deserted, though the old girl was probably inside or round at the back. There was no sign of a cockatoo. But he climbed the fence and lay for a while under the spread of a hibiscus bush. Some of the white flowers had grown immense with the gathering dusk; their red pistils glittered with a stickiness which looked like dew. In the west, above the liver-coloured house, the sky still dripped red where it wasn't streaked with green and gold.

Of course any cockatoo would have flown to roost by now, but he didn't need one. He could make the whole mob spread their wings, exposing that faint shadow of yellow, claws clenched tight and black as they veered against the netted sky, then flew screeching past the solid holm-oaks and skeleton-pines, into space.

He lay awhile longer under the hibiscus, gathering one of the white flowers to taste the stickiness on its feathered pistil. It tasted of nothing to explain its attraction for bird and bee, but he felt content.

•

Miss Le Cornu was leaning on her gate. She was wearing the jeans she always wore, and a pair of sloppy old moccasins. Her shirt white against the dusk. It made Mr. Figgis snort: a mature woman dressing like a teenage girl; bursting out of the jeans besides.

Did she know, he asked, that wild cockatoos were around? He had seen two of them under Davorens' big sugar-gum.

Miss Le Cornu didn't know, but now she came to think, she might have heard.

Figgis said, "If there's anything I hate it's a cockatoo. Dirty, screeching, destructive brutes! I'm prepared to poison any cockatoo and be rid of a public nuisance."

Miss Le Cornu had never considered whether she was for or against cockatoos. "Don't you think they might look pretty in a garden? Climbing through that big magnolia, for instance." She stopped short, and sniggered, because for the moment she was feeling high.

Figgis found himself looking into the gap between Miss Le Cornu's breasts. The breasts themselves, though draped with shirt, looked peculiarly naked in the dusk.

Figgis opened and closed his mouth. Having delivered himself on cockatoos, he would have liked to offer a few remarks on Miss Le Cornu's bursting jeans, but as he couldn't very well, he left her. There was an awful lot he would have wished dead, perhaps because he had spent life as an undertaker.

Dur-dur-dur dur-durr, Miss Le Cornu hummed against her teeth.

She couldn't think why she felt so good, except she had taken a handful—anyway, up to five. And He would probably come; it was his time. More often than not he did, so this was hardly reason for exhilaration. Nothing more than habit. Which was why it had begun, and continued. She had needed a habit.

That first occasion, a sleep-walker, he mightn't have been addressing her, "...told me I'd let 'er bally boodgie die..."

Miss Le Cornu had never kept a bird, but was moved spontaneously to sympathize. "Well, it's sad, isn't it? to lose something you're fond of. And getting back from her sister's funeral." When she realized it wasn't Mrs. Davoren at whom she was aiming her sympathy; and a bird is a detached, uncommunicative creature.

He leant on her gate, the hair already grey at the nape of his neck. Although he had glanced at her out of social obligation, it was his own predicament he was looking at.

"Why don't you come inside?" she suggested. "I've got a nice T-bone steak I'll grill."

That was seven years ago. She had never thought about a man before, or to be truthful, she had, and most men were distasteful to her. After Mother died, she had invited a girl called Marnie Prosser to share her life; but it hadn't worked: Marnie picked her nose rather too ostentatiously, and smeared honey on things: there was honey on all the door-knobs.

While he sat eating the steak in the sun-room which opened off the kitchen, it occurred to her: this is more than a neighbour's face I've seen a hundred times in the street, it's Mick Davoren, and an Irishman into the bargain. It was too fantastical to contemplate for long.

"Is it good?" she asked in a voice louder than necessary.

He half laughed and some red juice trickled down from a corner of his mouth. "A bit raw, isn't ut?"

At least she could admire his teeth.

"That's how my father liked it," she said. "Very rare. He was most particular—in everything. He was a colonel, you know. Came here on leave from India. And married Mother. And settled. Not that I remember Father at all distinctly. I was too young when he died. They used to have to press his trousers, always before he put them on. He was hot tempered. That was what made his pants wrinkle." She couldn't think when she had said so much at one go.

After he had wiped his mouth and pushed away the plate with almost the whole of the rare steak—delicately enough, she observed—Mr. Davoren asked her, "Was it your mother had the money then?"

"Yes. She was a Busby."

It did not occur to her to explain who the Busbys were. Nor him to ask. He looked gloomier, though. Like when he told her about the boodgie.

"Mother died—August last. You may have heard."

He had heard something about it, he admitted, but continued sitting, looking, not at her, but inward, above the unfinished steak.

Miss Le Cornu thought she had never heard the house more silent.

That it was *her* house appalled her. First her parents', then her mother's—still a normal situation. But not *hers*! She had never felt the need for possessions. What she needed was a habit. Father died too soon to become one. And Mother, her great, her consuming habit, had left her without warning, over a cup of hot milk, the milk-skin hanging from her lower lip.

She had tried to figure out what consolation she would find in living. Certainly not freedom—if that exists. But was relieved to realize that, if she took care, no one would again address her by her first name. (They had christened her Busby for her mother's family, and she had grown up big and rather furry.)

Now to her own surprise, Busby Le Cornu was asking this Mr. Davoren, again in a voice far too loud for the silence of the house, "What do you like best? If it isn't raw steak!" Anyone else might have giggled, but she was too serious for that.

He too, evidently; although it became obvious he had misunderstood her intention. "What I liked best—ever—was the days when I did a bit of prospectun on me own. I was hard up, you see, Miss Le Cornu. And I got this idea in me head. To look for gold. But never washed more than a few specks—that I kept in a bloom-un bottle. I must have throwed ut away in the end. After I took the job drivun the interstate buses. But the skies, I remember, of a mornun, and the smell of wood-ash, when I was prospectun down south."

That was where she began to blubber. She was heaving—and glugging, it sounded. He must have got a fright. He stood up, and put an arm around her, then thought better, and removed it.

"Are you okay?"

"Yes," she said.

But it increased her sense of loss, and not knowing what to do next, she took his hand and looked at it. The strangeness of her own behaviour, in which she could never afterwards believe, turned the hand into a thing lying in hers: an object rough enough as to palm, but in its veins and structure singularly elegant. She would have liked to put it somewhere and keep it.

Instead she said in a voice she made as much as possible like a man's, "All right, Mr. Davoren, we're not going to eat each other, are we?"

They both laughed then, and she saw that his eyes were of a light colour.

Busby Le Cornu had only once slept with a man, and that was equally unexpected: he had come to mend the dishwasher. It had not given her great pleasure. There had been another occasion, earlier, but she preferred not to think about, or had forgotten, it.

Now, out of deference to Mr. Davoren as well as herself, she did not switch lights on, but lay waiting on her mother's bed. Her body looked long, strong, and white, her breasts spread white and cushiony in glimmers from the street lighting. The fuzz of hair between her thighs—her "bush" the dishwasher man had called it—looked by this same light fathomlessly black. She hoped the Irishman would not become unnerved. As for herself, she was by now nerveless, or indifferent.

Neither of them much enjoyed it, she imagined. He had taken off his shoes, but not his clothes. His buttons grazed her only briefly.

But when he was sitting in the dark, getting back into his shoes, she said out of need rather than politeness, "Next time it will be better. I'll frizzle it up. I only did it rare because that was the way Father liked it."

That old chair never stopped creaking, which Father brought from India, which meant that Mother couldn't throw it out, although she laddered her stockings on it.

Mr. Davoren stamped his foot to help with a shoe, and the chair creaked enough to give up the ghost. "That time I was tellun you of—when I was prospectun for gold down along the Murrumbidgee—things got so bad I had to look for work at last. I presented meself to the manager of a station down that way. It was harvest time. They put me an' one or two other young fellers stookun up the oats behind the harvester. And as fast as we built the stooks, the cockatoos would pull um down." He laughed; the chair had quietened: he must have finished his shoes. "Have you ever seen a mob of wild cockatoos? A bit what you'd call slapdash in flight. But real dazzlers of birds! I'd say heartless, from the way they slash at one another. Kind too, when they want to be. They have a kind eye. And still. You see um settun in a tree, and the tree isn't stiller than the cockatoos."

"Oh?" She yawned; she wished he would go; if Figgis wouldn't have rung the police, she would have liked to play a record to herself.

"See you later, then," he said. "For the frizzled steak!"

See you later was an expression she disliked, because half the time it didn't mean what it was supposed to.

But He had meant it. He had become her habit. Here she was leaning on the gate, after so many years, waiting for him to approach. Neighbours had stopped seeing an "immoral relationship," even Mr. Figgis and Mrs. Dulhunty no longer hinted at it aloud. And anyway, what was there immoral in cooking tea for a man you didn't love and who didn't love you? If you had done it together a few times—no more than three or four, or five, or perhaps six—it was only as if you were making a bow to convention. Neither of you referred to it. Had he ever enjoyed it, she wondered? She had read that Irishmen, conditioned by the priests, had little taste for sexual indulgence, which made it difficult for the women, and turned many of them into nuns.

If Miss Le Cornu ever felt immoral it was in thinking of that yellow woman down the street, to whom she had never spoken, not even before taking the weight of her husband.

Miss Le Cornu felt less high. If it hadn't been for expecting Him, she would have gone and put on a record. This was the longest established of any of her habits, and might have sustained her, if you didn't also need the touch of skin. She preferred sopranos, or best of all, a velvety mezzo, and through such materializations of her inner self, would pursue the curlicues and almost reach the pinnacle, that golden cupola, or bubble of sound.

If she had never tried out a record on her friend Mick Davoren, who was just now approaching up the street, hat cocked against the dusk, it was because they said his wife had been a music teacher in her youth. Miss Le Cornu sometimes wondered which of all music Mrs. Davoren favoured.

"Thought you'd given it away this evening." Something had roused her anger; she might even have owned to a slight twinge of jealousy.

"It's late," he admitted from under the hat he wore for propriety's sake, but which made him look less respectable.

He was staring straight at her too, out of his light-coloured eyes, which blended with the bluish dusk to the extent that he was, once again, not looking.

"A button come off," he said, "and I had to sew ut on."

She grunted leading the way along the path, under the magnolia tree which was rooted on Figgis's side of the fence.

"You should have brought it and let me sew it." She knew she sounded half hearted: sewing and mending, occupations she didn't care for, had not become woven into the habit they had cultivated. "The food's in the warmer," she said more kindly, if not kind; whatever was making her angry, unpunctuality couldn't enter into it, not when somebody liked things frizzled up.

While he was eating the spoiled steak, she sat with her back half turned, rocking, in the kitchen where she served the food, never in the sun-room after they became used to each other.

Would it be the rates that had caused her anger? "I can't remember whether I paid them—the rates," she explained, and rocked.

He couldn't help her. If they had received their notice, Mrs. O. Davoren would have attended to it.

When he had finished his meat, and laid his knife and fork together, unneccessarily precise, it seemed, he cleared his throat, and told, "This evenun as I was comun out there was two cockatoos strollun around at the foot of the big tree. I didn't see a wild cockatoo in years. The white ones. Yeller topknots."

She was rocking furiously by now, and laughed too loud. "So I heard. Figgis is out to poison any pests of cockatoos."

"He hadn't better!" She was surprised at such vehemence. "Not mine—he better not."

"How do you know these tramps of birds would want to belong to anybody?"

"I wouldn't want um to *belong*! Not more than to be fed."

She stopped rocking. "What would you feed them on?"

"Sunflower seed. Accordun to packuts I've seen in the shops."

As though her friend's eye were a mirror to her own mind, she saw a cockatoo groping after, then balancing on, a chimney-pot; she saw a second, circling overhead; a whole strung-out flight was labouring against the wind. But those which clambered through magnolia branches, themselves like big white drunken flowers in motion, were the most desirable of all.

She sighed, and said, rubbing a cheek on its neighbouring shoulder, "Yes. It would look lovely. I could use a few of those cockatoos." When they were accustomed to her, she would try out some music on them: the mezzo voice most likely to have been hers.

He had got up. "Not any of mine you can't—Busby," he said.

Then her anger rose again and, cresting over, rocked the chair she was clinging to. "How did you know to call me by my bloody name? Nobody knows—since Father and Mother."

"I heard as somebody saw the electoral roll, and well, ut's your name, Busby." He was Irish enough to sound tender when it served his purpose, not for her, pleading of course for his birds.

"I wouldn't want to coax away anybody's bloody cockatoo," she shouted.

Soon after, he left. Perhaps he would tell Her—at any rate write it on the pad—let her know he was sold on cockatoos.

Miss Le Cornu had to restore herself. She opened the bottle, and poured several into the palm of her hand. And would not sleep.

In fact, all around her there was this flashing and slashing of wings, white except where yellow-tinged. She could have shrieked.

In the end she took a sedative.

•

Olive Davoren had continued cooking tea for Him. She kept it in the warmer. When he didn't come, she might eat a little of it herself, but mostly she had no appetite. She shot the rest in with the garbage. She could afford it, couldn't she? Then she would go to bed.

Tonight she waited up longer, thinking about the wild cockatoos. She had gone back once to have a look—in any case she had to lock up—and for a moment imagined she saw something stirring in the white hibiscus. It could not have been a cockatoo; it was too late for any bird.

She went to bed, early though it was, because there seemed nothing left to do, and heard Him, when he came in, bumping around across the passage.

She had forgotten how fine her hands were. Or thin? She thought of the violin lying buried under linen on the upper shelf of her silky-oak-veneer wardrobe.

And slept.

She woke sweating. The big clam-shell continued shining, under the tree on the lawn, as in her dream. Dry, unless for rainwater reduced to a little slime. She must clean out the slime in the morning with her long fine hands. Her birds would need water as well as seed.

Olive Davoren fell asleep, a pillow-end between shoulder and cheek, like a violin.

She had noticed seed at Woolworths and Coles; it was only a matter of choosing.

One of the birds was pecking at her womb. He rejected it as though finding a husk.

Her hollow pillow was reverberating horribly.

She woke, and flew down at such speed, she could have forgotten something. She had. She returned, and put in her teeth, and began again.

The light was growing transparent around her as she filled the watering-can. Then she noticed that someone else had already poured water in the shell. More, they had cleaned it out first. The clam-shell shone like new teeth.

He used to eat the breakfast she cooked and left for him in the warmer, then go out about his Business. That, she had heard, was how he liked to refer to it. One of his mates from the bus days had invented a patent tin-opener. Mick would go from door to door "marketing the Miracle Opener." How successfully she had never been told. All this had happened since they introduced the pad, and she could hardly have written, "How is your Business doing, Mick?"

He seldom held down a job for long: said it was the War had unsettled him. More likely he considered himself exempt from ordinary human activity. Or dedicated to the open air. When Dadda took him into Friendly Loans, he sat at the desk not above a few weeks. He took to gardening, but tired of digging weeds in. Green-keeping was more in his line: the unobstructed sweep of the links. He kept at that for several years, and became less fidgety, she could hear. "Deep-breathing is the secret," she once found written on the pad, but came to the conclusion it was an observation not intended for herself or any second person.

Now here he was, descending the path in his business suit, carrying the case with the samples in it. Breathing deep, she could see from the action of his shoulders. Hatless (he never wore one unless on his way to Her). The nape of his neck might have made you cry if you hadn't remembered the hat he wasn't wearing.

So Mrs. Davoren no more than wiped her nose on the Kleenex she kept down her front. And Mr. Davoren continued down the path, looking sideways at the base of the tree where cockatoos had landed the evening before. He had stopped breathing. But there weren't any cockatoos this morning. He went on, still what Mrs. Dulhunty called "a fine figure of an Irishman."

As soon as the gate squealed, Mrs. Davoren couldn't smear the powder quick enough, get herself ready for the supermarket. Or was it a Holiday? The possibility made her heart toll cold for several instants. It wasn't a holiday, though. She bought her seed, both plain and mixed, with a pottery dish to put it in and, loaded with her purchases, she made for home.

Where someone else had already put out sunflower seed. In a pottery dish. Olive Davoren could have kicked it. The tears shot out and she didn't bother to wipe them with the Kleenex.

The cockatoos came at evening, the pair, stamping round the dish at the foot of the tree. Clumsy, beautiful creatures! On seeing them, her mouth fell open: their crests flicked like knives threatening intruders; then when the first seeds were cracked, the feathers so gently laid in a yellow wisp along the head. She loved her birds.

They *were* hers, surely? whoever had put out the seed. They were given to her as compensation.

In her anxiety, Olive Davoren twitched the blind behind which she was hiding in one of the front rooms, and the cockatoos took fright; they flew up into a tree. She was miserable, but could do nothing beyond wait and look.

She was sitting watching the empty garden, when there in the opposite bay of the other room, who was it half hidden behind the opposite brown blind? She had never accepted herself before as a woman of anger.

Pretending not to see her as he watched her birds!

She might not have felt mollified when they resettled on the grass around the gum, if they hadn't become three—no, five cock-atoos!

The two watchers were almost for glancing at each other from behind their blinds in opposite bays.

They were saved by the birds starting to menace one another like human beings. Perhaps it was the original pair who couldn't tolerate the newcomers. Crests whipped open in flashes of sulphur; beaks clashed; breast was thrust at ruffled breast, as they stomped and thumped around the dish on callused claws, rolling as though they were riding a swell instead of flat lawn.

She was so entranced she forgot Him.

And soon it was time to cook tea. When it was done, she put it in the warmer. He hadn't gone out; she could hear him moving in remote parts of the darkening house.

After giving adequate thought to a proposition she would like to make, Olive Davoren wrote on the pad, "Be considerate for once..." She crossed it out and substituted, "I hope you will allow me the pleasure of putting out the morning seed."

In the morning the sheet was gone from the pad, and she found written, "Don't forget water, v. important."

So it was arranged, anonymously.

Mornings became hers, when she removed the husks, filled the dish with striped seed, and the clam-shell with water, She shared his sentiments over the water: it *was* important.

In the evenings, which were his, they sat in their opposite bays, watching the cockatoos feed after he had done his duty by them.

For some time she had not caught sight of him strolling down the path, then along the street, hat cocked for Her. Instead she heard him moving through distant rooms, or sitting the other side of a wall, at least thinking, she hoped, but sighing.

•

Once as he sat looking out through his window at his birds feed-ing in the gathering dusk, Mick Davoren realized they had multiplied: he could count eleven cockatoos. All docile for the moment, kindness and wisdom in the currant-eyes. Or if the crests rose, it was like ladies delicately opening fans.

While himself no longer sat looking out: he was the boy outside, who stood looking in through this great window to where the company was seated, in knots on gilded chairs, as well as a wider circle round a curved settee, the meeker, sleeker girls all of them in docile white, their harsher elders ablaze with a white fire of diamonds, as they picked at the words they chose to offer in conversation. When a certain elderly lady shrieked, for some secret perhaps, that she was making public. And all the ladies and meek girls were joining in the general screech. Whirling as they changed position. Diamonds bounding. Some disagreement, but with a fine display of polite temper. Then the gentlemen were coming in, laughing too, some of them stumbling, some arguing, others full of ostentatious consideration for their neighbours. While he, the boy standing in the dark the wrong side of this stately window, retreated backwards into the drizzle, all but tumbling over a giant hound that was lying on the lawn pointing her nose at a watery moon.

Mick Davoren hawked the phlegm up out of his throat.

It must have frightened the cockatoos: they rose in a wave, white to greenish by present light, and broke on the shores of holm-oak and araucaria in the park opposite.

He dared glance at the window in the other bay, where Olive, the woman he had married, sat glaring into nothing.

•

Mrs. Dulhunty had read that birds bring lice. Starlings do for a fact: the lice drop off of them down the chimneys.

Cockatoos! Figgis was becoming ropeable.

Most of the kids in the neighbourhood had been and seen the birds, and *oo-arrr*'d, and shouted, and thrown stones, preferably to hit, or if that failed, to frighten the cockies. If Tim Goodenough hadn't yet seen them in the flesh, it was because he got home from school before the cockatoos had landed, and by the time his mum and dad let him up from his blasted tea, the birds had flown. All he found was Mr. and Mrs. Davoren looking out from opposite windows.

Once in passing her gate, he asked Miss Le Cornu whether she had seen the cockatoos, and she answered, "Ye-ehss," about to share a secret with him, it seemed.

But he didn't need it. As though he had stared at them as deeply as he stared at the people in buses, he knew what would be going on behind cockatoo eyes; he knew about the wisps of yellow feather the books showed cockatoos as wearing, as good as if he had touched these tufts, like people he brushed up against, simply to find out about them, and discovered he already knew.

•

The cockatoos were coming less often, then only three or four of them. Occasionally none. Or one elderly creature who hobbled, and at times trailed a wing. It was the children who had frightened the birds, and probably stoned the loner. Mrs. Davoren almost suggested it to her husband, not in writing, but in spoken words, then was saved by her principles.

She felt sorry for Mick, however, seeing from the corner of an eye that their birds' defection was making him suffer. She heard her husband fart softly in the dark, the other side of the separating wall, and forgave him for it.

She herself was taking the bicarbonate, you couldn't say by handfuls, but always increasing the quantity.

•

When Mick Davoren put on his hat and went up the street to Miss Le Cornu, it was still broad daylight, or broad enough for neighbours to revive their interpretation of motives. This evening she wasn't leaning on the gate in accordance with custom. A cockatoo was perched on one of her chimneys, a wing outstretched straight and stiff as he picked beneath the coverts. A second bird, feathers ruffled as he sat clutching a terracotta fireman's helmet, screeched at the intruder. Or was it a former love?

Davoren took the brick path which led towards the back, under the Figgis magnolia tree.

"What—who is it?" she called.

Her shirt was open, which she buttoned quickly.

Several cockatoos, heads bobbing, were cracking seed in a circle at her feet.

Davoren roared with a laughter which wasn't.

The cockatoos flew off. That much he had achieved. (He could even imagine telling his wife.)

When Busby Le Cornu started laughing. "You bugger!" she cried. "You bloody—*Irish* bugger!"

He was so enraged, he snatched at her shirt, and again it was open on her. He continued roaring, red with pseudo-joviality.

"Coming," she was now giggling, while stifling it in her nostrils, "too early," she shrieked, "for the frizzling! If I've got any," she added in the throes of her convulsions.

All this time she was leading him into the house, away from neighbours' ears and the scene of her deception.

Neither of them was any longer much deceived.

"Those are my cockatoos," he shouted on the stairs.

"They're free to make their choice, aren't they?" As if anybody ever more than imagined they were.

When they reached the room to which they were being conducted, he did not wait for her to take her shirt off, but ripped it away. She seemed to hear the last of her buttons hit the wainscot.

Davoren was caressing her large but flat breasts, as she had never experienced, or if she had, it was so long ago she could barely remember. He was mumbling on them, about the blessed cockatoos. Then, because he had begun pulling off his clothes (it hadn't occurred to him to make such a move on their other occasions), she took her jeans off, and lay waiting for him on the bed.

In the light just before dark, her own body surprised her. Till Davoren was straddling it. She had never allowed herself to look at a man's cock, though she had seen it celebrated on walls, graphically, as well as in writing. Now she looked and the sight was splendid.

"See here, Busby," he was hectoring from above, knees planted on either side, "the violation of a confidence is what I'm objectun to. I didn't tell you about me birds to have you seduce um away from me."

He became so congested he couldn't contain himself. It spurted on her stomach, burning her.

She sighed from within the crook of her arm, "I don't see why we can't share what doesn't belong to either of us."

He was already getting back into his clothes. "The wife would be disappointed," he said.

For some time after he had gone, she was left without the power to move. The light was failing. She tried to think which solution she should choose: should it be the sedative? or whether to let the fireworks off. In the end she opened neither bottle, but went down as she was, flat-footed, into the garden. There was moss between the bricks in the path, which at least her feet were able to enjoy. She looked down and wiped away a drop from what the dishwasher man had referred to as her "bush."

Of course the cockatoos had not returned, except that in the magnolia tree she thought for a moment she could see one of them moving amongst the giant flowers. Or flowers stirring.

•

Whatever influenced the cockatoos' movements, Olive Davoren was overjoyed whenever they honoured her with their presence. One morning, when He had gone out early, she counted fourteen of them. They would stand still for moments, wondering whether to be afraid, looking like china ornaments. Then, it seemed, they became reassured, and the kindness in their eyes was directed at her as she stood in the window.

It was on this particular morning that she conceived her idea. She in turn wondered whether she ought to feel frightened as she went upstairs and groped around in the wardrobe, under the linen on the upper shelf.

By the time she opened the glass doors within sight and hearing of the cockatoos she was as brittle as the violin she had not touched in years. Which she began to tinker with, and tune. Fearfully. What if some human being caught sight of her from the street? Her skin grew glossy with anxiety.

She was playing, though: what she remembered of what she had found most difficult. It issued thin and angular out of the disused violin. It sounded yellow. But grave and honest. The composer was collaborating with her. And cockatoos. Whatever penetrated the down, their eyes were engaged, as they continued bobbling, cracking seed, hobbling, and occasionally jumping.

If the composer and the cockatoos had joined with her in the Sarabande, she entered on the Chaconne with deeper misgiving, and alone. But drove herself at her arduous climb. One of the birds flew off. He sat looking back at the scene through a window in one of the holm-oaks opposite. The rest of the flock stayed listening to her music. If they accepted her, it must have been from recognizing something of their own awkwardness.

When a string snapped, her breath tore.

Ballooning upward, the birds spread out, and flew clattering across the park, shrieking back at her, it seemed. She wondered whether she had experienced, or only imagined, moments of exaltation in what must otherwise have been a horrible travesty of the Partita.

Across the brown lino she trailed to put away her violin. In future she would have the excuse that a string was broken.

Unlike Busby Le Cornu. Nothing need prevent her playing another record. She would too, if she felt it. Just as nobody, not even He, could prevent the cockatoos from coming to her garden if they chose to come.

She played them a record for the first time on an afternoon when, unintentionally, she must have taken the sedative instead. She had dragged out the little table on which the player stood, and there where the shadow of the house cut the sunlight, on the edge of the lawn, she was crouching over what might have been her own lament for a real passion she had never quite experienced.

> *"Mi tradì, quell' alma ingrata,*
> *Infelice, o Dio, mi fa..."*

she all but sang, herself soaring against reason and the tablet she had swallowed.

The cockatoos shot off into the dazzle. She was alone with her alter ego, the voice.

> *"Ma tradita e abbandonata,*
> *Provo ancor per lui*
> *pietà..."*

Cockatoos, two or three of them at least, were rejoining her in vindicating spirals, white-to-sunplashed.

> *"Quando sento il mio tormento,*
> *Di vendetta il cor favella,*
> *Ma se guardo il suo cimento,*
> *Palpitando il cor mi va..."*

Wings aswirl in alighting, the birds were soon striding adventur-
ously back towards the dish she had filled to overflowing. When
suddenly she switched off the machine. It wasn't that she feared
an encounter with the Don; she could not have faced the moonlit
statue by daylight: a pity, because the Commendatore might have
appealed to cockatoos.

•

He had drawn one of the veranda chairs out to where the grass
began. The air was growing chillier with early winter. Never before
had he sat so close to his birds. His wife would probably have
disapproved, but if she was watching from inside the house, he
wasn't aware of it.

By this sharpened light the garden looked a deeper, lusher
green—unnatural. It intensified, the purity of white plumage as
the cockatoos cracked seed or stalked around. They were restless
today, not on account of his presence (in fact they ignored him)
but because possessed with the desire to bash somebody up. Their
flick-knife crests grew sinister against the walls of brooding green.
One bird in particular, old, or disabled (he trailed a wing from
time to time), appeared to offend the majority. Although tough
and stoical, the outsider was chased away at last. A flight took off
after him, undercarts tightly retracted, ailerons reflecting yellow,
wings sawing as they manoeuvred into position, and pursued the
enemy, or so it seemed, over the park.

Davoren did not see how it ended. His eyes were hurting. (He
had his headaches.) Never been the same since that crash-landing.
They got him. He had got the other bastard first; when a formation
swarmed on him out of the cloud. It became a hide-and-seek through
cloud. He threw them off finally, climbed, and dived on their tails.
He pressed the tit and let them have it with the brutality and
desperation the times demanded.

But failed. He was losing height. Down down o Lord ohhh a
leaden feather could not have fluttered so surely. Then he was
bumping over the hummocks of salt bush. Rebound once. Not
much more than a numbness, he slithered free before the flames
took over. He lay in the wadi, sand hissing around him. He listened
to their bullets ricochet off the surrounding rocks. Afterwards, the
silence. He was not—dead.

There were still the times when he had to tell himself he was free. Or was he? The familiar chair in which he was sitting threatened to pitch him out. Those brutal birds, while bashing at one another with their beaks only a few yards away, had given off a stench he hadn't been aware of before. He must get away. Perhaps if he sat awhile alone in a darkened room, he would recover his balance. He was glad nobody had seen. Not in years he hadn't experienced such terror.

Olive Davoren watched her husband drag his chair back to the veranda, away from the scattering cockatoos. She would not have known what to do for him, she thought, even if they hadn't renounced speech. She would never have known her own husband.

From under the hibiscus Tim Goodenough had watched and heard the flap. This old man had frightened the birds, but was himself frightened, you could see. Which in itself was fearful: an old, frightened man! When you had as good as made up your mind to spend the night in the park—on your own—to test your courage.

•

Not long after, the neighbourhood began asking what had become of the cockatoos. For several days, those in whose lives the birds played a part hadn't caught sight of a single one; no longer the dawn screeching, the ribaldry from finial and chimney-pot.

When she could no longer bear it, Miss Le Cornu went down to Mrs. Dulhunty, for whom she didn't altogether care, and called up at her window, "What do you think has happened to them?"

Mrs. Dulhunty left off combing her hair to look down from where she lived above the garage. "He's poisoned 'em. Figgis!" she said in a loud whisper.

"How could he poison a whole mob?"

"Don't ask me," Mrs. Dulhunty replied, dropping a ball of slag-coloured hair into the lane. "It's what they're sayin'. Figgis has been creatin' because 'is magnolia tree is practically de-*nud*-ed."

Miss Le Cornu wondered which side Mrs. Dulhunty would be on if ever it came to a showdown. "I'd have said there were leaves enough left on his tree—privacy on either side of the fence," she answered feebly for her.

Mrs. Dulhunty realized; she knew which side she was on—her own; and minded her own business; so she pursed up, and repeated, "That's what they say." After which, she retreated slightly to pick between the teeth of her comb with a pin.

Busby Le Cornu could only return up ther lane, hoping she wouldn't bump into either Davoren.

•

More than anybody, Davorens had not been able to accept the disappearance of their cockatoos. They milled around their dark rooms, on the brown lino, and were often almost brought face to face. Olive was noticeably distraught. Her distress was aggravated by the smell of chrysanths which had stood too long in their vases and which ought to be thrown out. Friday she meant to turn out the whole place, if she remembered. She didn't, for coming face to face with Mick in the most awkward, the darkest corner, outside the cupboard where she kept the Hoover and the brooms.

They were properly caught. In spite of the dark she could see the light colour of the eyes she thought she had forgotten. He remembered the twitch in a cheek now that met it again, and how it was probably what had decided him to take pity. The cheek had appeared sallow, and only later, after they started writing messages on pads, had it turned, if he ever glanced, yellow.

There they were, trapped, outside the broom-cupboard, where for the obvious reason, there always lingered a smell of dust.

It was her who uttered first, and then only "...the cockatoos?"

He advanced perhaps a step. "Figgis has poisoned um. That's what they say."

Then they were leading each other through such an unfamiliar labyrinth they were bumping into furniture. (She hated her own bruises: they ended up the colour of hard-boiled eggs.)

"Who else?" he asked

"I don't know. Some foreigner could. The Yugo-Slavs shoot the ducks and take them home. Haven't you heard them? In the park? At night?"

He had stopped considering. Stretched on the bed they were trying to comfort each other; memory was becoming this spastic sarabande through which they were staggering together and apart. (Had love been strangled—or worse, deformed, in both of them, at birth?)

Her bruises wouldn't have risen yet; not that it mattered: they had their clothes on. He was mumbling something about his mother: it must have been the dark colour of her dress. She was suddenly ashamed of her long hands for having lost the art of touch, just as her music had left her except in the presence of the cockatoos.

"Do you think it could have been the gas men? Who was flushing pipes all these days. One of them told me we need new burners on the stove. Said he'd come back and put them for me."

"Don't trust um."

"Why?" she asked.

"Too affectionate."

They were laughing mouth to mouth. He was soothing the hands she thought had grown, or perhaps always had been, useless.

They must have fallen into a doze, and might have forgotten the cockatoos if the light hadn't reminded them; it was about the time the birds used to come. Davorens sat up on hinges, and without so much as smoothing the creases out of their clothes, rushed down to put out the seed.

And the sky was awash with cockatoos returning, settling on the gumtrees which grew in the garden. If silent, the birds might have merged with the trees, but they sat there ruffling, snapping at twigs, screeching—cajoling, it sounded; one of them almost succeeded in forming a word.

"Where have they been?" Olive Davoren called recklessly to her husband.

The Irishman shrugged. "Buggered if I know! Woronora— Wyong—Bullabulla—the *Monaro!*" he shouted.

Then when Davorens had turned their backs to drag out their veranda chairs and prepare themselves for the spectacle, their birds descended. Absence had tamed or made them ravenous. Their plumage was smoothed by concentration; the sulphur feathers in their crests were lying together, at peace.

If Davorens did not comment it was because they had discovered in this other silence the art of speech. Once he touched the back of one of her hands with an index finger, pointing out nothing they didn't already share. She hardly breathed for fear her love might make him fearful of being possessed; she must try to make it look nothing more than gratitude.

It was different fears which began possessing them both, before any reason showed itself from behind that hibiscus she had always meant to prune. It was Figgis; more—Figgis with a shotgun.

"The bloody madman!" From up on the rise, Davoren started

bellowing as soon as he recovered from the shock. "Only perverts would dream of shootun at cockatoos!"

"A public menace! Picking at the slates—shitting on the paths—destroying trees—disturbing the ratepayers' sleep!"

After that, Figgis fired. The cockatoos were already rising, a fountain of white fanning out into separate wavelets; all but those who had been hit: a couple were tumbling, flopping, jerking on the grass, as the life inside them broke up.

Tim Goodenough saw, and it was terrible.

He saw Davoren running down the slope, no longer this elderly man, but like a boy with windmill arms.

"Murderer!"

"I was never one to neglect my duty," Figgis was muttering.

He took aim again, at distance.

A whole mob of kids had come running up and were hanging from the park railings to get a better view of what was happening.

Figgis would have fired again—he was that mad—if Miss Le Cornu hadn't run along the street. She would have grabbed him, if Davoren hadn't got there before her. The two men were whirled round together on their heels, and as part of the same whirlwind, the shotgun.

Which went off for the second time.

A bunch of women began screaming. Children giggled.

Lying on the pavement, Davoren was looking shywards, his eyes as still as still water. The blood was running.

"You *sod!*" Miss Le Cornu shouted, it wasn't clear for who.

She and Mrs. Davoren, already on their knees, tugged at first, each trying to raise, or possess Davoren for herself; then began a regular stroking. They might have been easing the life out of him: you could see it had started to leave. At moments the women unavoidably stroked each other's hands, and threatened to knot. But continued at their work. Their faces were equally pale.

"Speak to me," Mrs. Davoren said. "My darling? My husband?"
(My poor habit! You will understand.)

Tim was glad his father had come, to organize. (Because it was the evening of a week-day Dad wasn't showing his varicose veins.)

Figgis refused to give up his weapon; he would wait for the police. He was sitting on the kerb, clinging to the gun, slightly dribbling.

A little girl was whimpering.

Ladies told each other what a shame.

The police, the ambulance arrived.

"Look!" one of the kids called.

Some way up the street half-a-dozen cockies had returned to settle on top of a pole and along the wires. Feathers ruffled, still shocked, they sat offering their breasts to the wind. They were a nasty grey colour, more like hens which have been fluffing themselves on an ash-heap.

The police collared Figgis and shoved him in the van after taking his gun for an exhibit.

The ambulance carried off what must have been by now Mr. Davoren's body.

Ahhh, Mrs. Dulhunty moaned; she was done with it all, and would go to Our Lady of the Snows, Ashfield, where a nun of her acquaintance had promised to take care of her.

So it was over.

Only Mrs. Davoren and Miss Le Cornu, along with most of the kids present, had not yet found they could believe in death. Then the two women seemed to realize they were empty-handed. They let themselves be led, ramshackle, groping, on their separate ways.

Soon after, Tim Goodenough remembered the dead cockatoos. He would have liked them for their yellow crests. But somebody must have already collected them for burial or snitched them as souvenirs.

Darkness gathering made the grass look poisonous. He might have let out a long howl, like a dog hit by a car, if he hadn't glanced down and seen the pool of somebody else's blood. In the last light it glittered so splendidly it stopped him howling, and he was glad, because Dad was still looking important, ordering people back to their houses.

•

Time passes: nothing better can be said of it. All was tidied up: manslaughter established, and the cockatoo murders overlooked. Some said Figgis had been taken north to Taree, and handed over to relatives; while others had it on the best authority that he was locked up in a nut-house—and good riddance.

Tim Goodenough thought the nut-house more likely, from hearing Mum and Dad on nuts. (There's a lot more than you'd believe, and it's only luck if you're not found out.)

On the eve of his ninth birthday he decided he was ready to

carry out the plan he had been chewing over for the last few months: to test his courage by spending a night alone in the park. Just the other day he had drawn a cross on the inside of his left arm with the smallest, sharpest blade of his penknife, and had not flinched— or not much: he ought to survive night in the park.

He would slip out after they had sent him to bed, after messing up the bedding to make them think he had slept in it. He would take provisions in case he felt hungry, and his knife for protection.

When it came to the point, he forgot the provisions: he was that anxious to get away without being heard. Dad had drunk his last nightcap of beer, and Mum more than her usual sherry. They were already otherwise occupied when he crept out and slid between the park railings.

He made first for the storm-water drain in which he had found the animal's skull he kept in the medicine cupboard. Down-and-outs slept in the drains in the park, Mrs. Dulhunty said; it was a wonder the lot of them weren't flushed out like rats. He lay awhile knocking on the sides of the drain which came out near the Moreton Bay fig. The moon was up, already a bit lopsided; it reminded him of oyster shells.

He continued knocking, listening to the reverberations. There was a man got regularly inside the drain, and lay there knocking, Mrs. Dulhunty said; he was no nut: he was in league with the Redfern thieves, telling them in code which of the houses had been vacated by their owners going to the pictures. What if you hit on the crims' code? They could break in while Dad was on top of Mum. Or murder Mrs. Dulhunty before she got round to leaving for Our Lady of the Snows.

Soon after that he climbed down from the drain. He left the park. He would keep to the street for a bit, to the blue lighting which the council put because some of the ladies were afraid they might be indecently assaulted, though the last thing they could expect was rape. He picked up a stick for company and ran it along the railings as he marched.

Some of the houses were in darkness (waiting for the crims) but a light was shining in what must be Mrs. Davoren's bedroom window. There was a light also in Miss Le Cornu's—Buz. (Wasn't it what everyone called her? since Dad came across it ruling the lines through the names on the electoral roll.)

He walked slower, to prolong the street. There was time enough for the bloody park if he was to spend all night in it.

•

Mrs. Davoren was lying in her bed watching the moon balanced on a black pyramid which by day became a holm-oak. She wasn't frightened living alone in their house. She would never be frightened: there was no reason for it. There was no reason.

She lay and stroked the pillow where his head hadn't lain in years. It had lain on the pavement. She didn't cry: she was as far removed as the Bach partita she had played to the cockatoos before they were frightened by the string snapping.

Miss Le Cornu was the one. Mrs. Davoren often wondered how She was coping with her grief.

•

As Busby Le Cornu lay in her bed watching the moon netted in the araucarias she was not coping: she had taken the lot, the stimulants, the sedatives. But would never—she had to laugh—die.

She wondered about the yellow woman down the street, not interminably, because there were times when they got together, and that removed the necessity.

Mrs. Davoren would walk in. "How are you keeping, dear?" was what she was bound to say.

"Not so bad, thanks. And how's yourself?" Busby Le Cornu did not give the expected answer; because almost nothing is altogether expected.

They are leading each other upstairs. Olive's hand has a rough palm, though the bone structure is fine enough.

Olive says, "You'll have to fill in with what you remember scribbled on walls."

"Oh?" Busby does not say.

Ohhh—euhh Olive has begun to whimper.

Knees planted on either side of the skinny body, Busby stoops to lick with strong, regular, vertical strokes, the yellow belly. In particular, the scar in it.

Of course in actual fact they are seated in the garden below, in the shade of Figgis's fully clothed magnolia tree. Busby has dragged out the record player. She is waiting to play it, not so much for Olive as for their historic cockatoos.

Olive gets up and goes in, probably to the loo, from the look on her face when she returns: a pawnbroker's genteel daughter.

"Oh," she says, picking up the record-sleeve, "I would have thought so."

Though it is plain, from the expression on her face, that Olive has always been wondering which music you have in common.

"Such a glorious work!" She sighs with the resignation she has learnt to adopt for any surrender to ecstasy or martyrdom.

Pish!

Busby sets it off—to turn them on.

> *"Mi tradì, quell' alma ingrata,*
> *Infelice, o Dio, mi fa..."*

it has begun to sing, but the voice is a different one today, and there is no descent of cockatoos.

O Dio! Olive is sitting forward in her deck-chair, holding back a grief she may let fall if you are unlucky enough.

> *"Quando sento il mio tormento,*
> *Di vendetta il cor favella,*
> *Ma se guardo il suo cimento,*
> *Palpitando il cor mi va..."*

Busby switches it off: today she could not have borne the Don, and never the Commendatore.

Presently Olive leaves. Which is what Busby has been hoping for.

●

Mrs. Davoren had heard that Miss Le Cornu "adored" music. Lying alone in her bed, she wondered whether they would dare discuss the subject of their common adoration. For her part, she did not think she would wish to. She had never been what you call religious, but there are certain things you can't even write on a pad and leave on the kitchen table for somebody else to read.

For a moment she thought she heard Him bumping around in the next room. It must have been her own heart.

•

At moments his heart beat thunderously, at others it chugged
like suffocating felt. None of these people asleep in the houses
would rise from their beds to rescue him from the terrors in store.
Which by now he couldn't feel he had chosen to face: they were
chosen for him. As far as he could see it was like that day or night
You couldn't call not even to your mother and father in the next
room: they were too busy discussing the price of meat, or whether
the rates would go up, or the Gas Company mend the leak, or
accusing each other, or fucking together.

He slid, thin and sick, between the railings, back inside the park.
(If he had been just that bit fatter, he wouldn't have fitted, and
might have cried off.)

He went first in the direction of the lake where the coot were
shrieking. At least it was a sign of life. But wasn't it the thought of
finding life which was frightening him stiff—the alkies and freaks
and pervs and old women with stockings halfdown and scabs on
their faces?

The moon was streaming light around him. It should have given
him courage. Instead, everything looked less escapable. Trees were
brandishing themselves. Along the lake's edge flashed the steely
blades of reeds. All had a perverse truth you recognized from
thoughts you could scarcely say you thought: it was more as if they
were slipped uninvited into your head. Of cruelty. And death.

He wouldn't think. He began humming to himself, but stopped.
Somebody "undesirable" might hear.

The lake he knew by day as a placid, brown, and finally boring
stretch of water was tingling with moonlight; it almost looked like
frost. He put his hands in his pockets, and was glad to find the
knife there. The moon became temporarily wrapped in a shred of
cloud, which turned the water leaden. The—body? Yes, a naked
one at that, was floating face-down, hidden, though not enough,
by a screen of reeds. He whimpered down his nose and revolved
twice on the spot where he was standing. Big and bulging, the
corpse must be a woman's, which would make it worse.

He had only once seen a woman's body, and then it was Buz Le
Cornu walking starkers down the garden path the evening he
climbed into Figgis's magnolia watching for cockatoos. Anyone who
could walk naked in the garden only a couple of steps from the

street might get herself murdered. Or go bonkers enough to do herself in. Busby Le Cornu!

Of course he needn't let on about what he had found. Nobody would know he had seen it. But he ought to have a look at least. He got a stick and prodded at one of the bulges. It felt neither one thing nor another; but dead. As the cloud slipped past the moon, the body looked so green it must have spent some time in the water.

He prodded again and the thing bobbed. It slid out from amongst the reeds: an old li-lo somebody must have had no further use for, or couldn't be bothered to fish out.

He was so relieved he let out a drop of two of piss. He was glad to feel the warmth in his pants.

If he had felt afraid it was because it happened at night when everything looks exaggerated. He hadn't been afraid at the real thing the evening Figgis murdered Davoren and the cockatoos. It was the mystery of it which made him almost let out a howl at the time. For a conjuring trick which was real.

He walked on. There was a man sitting in the shadow of a clump of flax. "Hi, sonny, what do they call yer?"

"Tom."

"Come 'ere, Tom," the man said. "I got a surprise for yer."

"What?"

He wasn't going to be surprised; he walked on, and the man cursed for quite a while.

He walked and came to a couple of women who had made themselves comfortable for the night wrapped in sheets of newspaper. Their carrier bags standing around them made fat shadows on the grass.

"Come on over, Dick," one of the women invited. "We've got room for a nice little bolster between us. We'll all sleep the cosier for squeezin' up together."

The second woman laughed. Their faces were so tanned the moonlight made them look black.

"Nah. I got a long way ter go."

Even at a distance he could smell their smell: of bodies and spirits.

The first woman advised, "Fuck off then and get fucked."

He could hear them hitting or resettling their newspapers, and grumbling, after he had left.

He roamed around. For something to do, he started jumping up and down on a rock, and his shadow, like the goat it was, jumped beside him in the moonlit grass.

He felt foolish, then fed up. He might be getting sleepy, without a murder, not even a rape, to keep him awake. He flopped down beside some paperbarks, wondering whether he might catch rheumatic fever, that Uncle Kev nearly died of. At Noraville.

He's real sick they're telling him to lie quiet and let the snow they've plastered on his forehead take effect otherwise he might die *but I won't Sister I can't I'm alive aren't I* criminals must expect the consequences *but I'm not a crim I only tapped out messages without even knowing the code* they got the message all right *but I'm innocent like Mr. Davoren who was murdered for being innocent* not even Mr. Davoren himself can tell you can ask him if you're foolish enough it's visiting hour and he's come to see what's left of the criminal patient *I'm not Mr. Dav am I or am I worse than* Davoren can't speak he is bandaged up he is one big white bandage except for the light-coloured eyes which perhaps can't see you for being unless you also *I can see can't I so I'm not yet* Davoren can only make these creaking noises through his bandages can't pass on the message perhaps he doesn't understand the code he is already leaving the crim's beside stomping sideways backwards past the beds the lockers to avoid trampling cockatoos there is a grassful.

Sparkling.

There must have been a heavy dew. The morning was rustling with moisture and small birds. Firetails: he recognized them from the book Mum and Dad had given at Christmas. The finches were picking at something invisible on the underneath of the paperbark leaves. They took him for granted until, in spite of stiffness, numbness, he jumped up. The birds were flicked in all directions.

To throw off whatever was still clinging to him from his nightmare, he ran full tilt at light. It was spinning round him. Above him the whirligig of whirligigs. Under his feet the earth thundered, but held firm. He might have thrown his arms around someone if anybody had showed up—even one of those leathery women of last night, or the man who wanted to show his prick. And run away before complications arose. Today he was fast as light. Zingg! He might have sung if he could have thought what.

In the end he only sang out his name, and it was broken up, to add to the shimmer of the morning.

He was nine years old, he remembered just before catching sight of IT, in the ragged grass, in the paperbark scrub, beside the lake. He thudded to a stop.

It was a cockatoo. Which first screeched, then let out a few rusty squawks, from age perhaps, and dragging through wet grass. Had he been abandoned by the mob? Or couldn't the others run the risk of further human treachery by staying to support what must be an old or sick bird? At any rate, the loner had survived a winter after the mob had flown.

Tim Goodenough made the noises his mother produced for age and sickness, for the "poor old cockie," when suddenly and unexpectedly, desire spurted in him. He jumped high enough to swing on and bring down a small bough. After a bit of a wrestling match, he succeeded in twisting it free.

All the time the cockatoo was eyeing him, beak half open, one wing trailing.

There was no need to pretend: the bird might have been offering himself.

The boy looked round before swiping. The bird squawked once, less in fear or pain, it seemed, than because it was expected of him, and huddled himself against the grass.

Tim hit and hit. It was soon over. The bird's head lolled when he picked it up; the eyes were hidden behind their shutters of grey skin.

The boy looked round again before taking out his knife to scalp the cockatoo in the way he had read Indians do to whites. Very little blood flowed from under the dry skin, before the yellow tuft was lying in the palm of his hand.

He made off, but remembered, and returned, and took the corpse, and pitched it into the waters of the lake, which were beginning to blaze and steam.

He loped. He trotted. He loped. The yellow tuft he was carrying blew around and threatened to escape. He had to close his hand.

He would have liked to throw the thing away, but it sort of stuck to him now that he'd got it. Blowing inside the half-opened cage of his hand, whenever he dared glance, it made his heart beat, his breath whimper.

His talisman!

After running just a little farther, he came out through the park gate. If he hadn't gone in, he might never have discovered what was waiting to burst out of him.

•

Miss Le Cornu was leaning on her gate. If she had been more like those who lead ordered lives, she supposed she might have fetched a broom and swept the pavement in front of her. But for the moment, leaning in the sun, she was inclined to congratulate herself on being what that kind of person considers unstable. Habits were not in her line; though you do crave for one on and off.

Out of one of Miss Le Cornu's eyes trickled a tear. She rubbed it off, because down the street she could see the Goodenough boy coming from the park, and from the other direction Her approaching.

Since the event in their lives Miss Le Cornu had watched Mrs. Davoren, and had sometimes been on the verge of speaking. Then she hadn't, remembering the touch of hands, and the grief they had briefly shared. Besides, Mrs. Davoren seemed to be enjoying her widowhood. That winter she had bought herself a mini-car and learnt to drive it. She had bought the sealskin coat. It was much as if Mrs. Davoren had inherited money from her late husband, when everyone knew the money had always been hers.

At any rate, here she was, a widow in a sealskin coat, but this morning she had left her mini-car in the garage.

Miss Le Cornu clenched her somewhat grubby hands. She was only too aware that her jeans were split (and at the crutch).

"Lovely day, Mrs. Davoren," Miss Le Cornu said; after all, why not celebrate the fact that you are neighbours?

Mrs. Davoren admitted that it was, indeed, a lovely day.

To meet Miss Le Cornu in the flesh as opposed to conversing together in her thoughts was unnerving Mrs. Davoren. She had often thought that if she did come face to face with Her she would introduce the subject of music, and now this idea came into her head, but fortunately she saved herself in time.

"It'll warm up later, though." Mrs. Davoren was quite firm about it.

"Won't you find a fur coat a bit too much?" Miss Le Cornu couldn't resist.

Mrs. Davoren hadn't expected that. "Yes," she gasped, "but the weight," and in her confusion the spit flew out, "the weight is a comfort—even if hot."

Mrs. Davoren was so embarrassed, and Miss Le Cornu grinning her head off. (You had to remember that Busby Le Cornu was mad.)

"Nicely matched skins—altogether beaut," she complimented her widowed neighbour; only the grace of God prevented Miss Le Cornu adding, "if it wasn't for the slaughter of the seals."

But Mrs. Davoren might have heard just that, for the pain showed in her sallow face and transferred itself to Miss Le Cornu's throat, which had knotted itself almost as if she had a goitre.

For a mere instant. Then their eyes cleared. The light was beating gloriously around them. The relief was tremendous.

"Well," Mrs. Davoren said, "I'm off to the city. Thought I'd start early. Walk. Look round the shops while they're still empty."

She did this at least once a week, picking up things and putting them down again.

"Have a good time," Miss Le Cornu recommended.

Mrs. Davoren left on accepting this advice, and Miss Le Cornu had no opportunity for shouting more, because here was the Goodenough boy.

"Why, Tim," she blared, "what have you been up to? Look at your shoes!"

"The grass," he muttered. "It's wet."

Just his luck to run into old Buz Le Cornu.

Miss Le Cornu had left off her moccasins this morning. She liked the feel of moss beneath her bare feet. She would have liked to hang on to the Goodenough boy and show him something; she would have to think what.

But Tim Goodenough barged on. His left shoulder must be looking out of joint because of what he was carrying so carefully in his hand, which no one must guess at, let alone see.

He could still have thrown the thing away, but by now it felt as much a part of him as his guilt.

At Davorens' the blinds were down, which meant nothing; they always were.

On the only occasion he could remember speaking to the dead man, Davoren had just picked up his paper from the path, and was standing reading it at the gate. He said a war had broken out.

"I used to think that if ever another war broke out I would wanter to be in ut." He spoke in the tone of voice he would have used on any passer-by. "A war brings people closer, you know."

"Oh?" Yourself left out of the Irishman's thoughts, your voice sounded such a bleat. "Did you ever kill a man, Mr. Davoren—in the war you was in?"

"Eh?" He couldn't very well help looking at you, but only after a fashion. "Perhaps—yes—a few. 'Kill' is what you'd call ut, I reckon."

Around the two of you the morning was trembling, or so it seemed.

Now on this similar morning of delicate balance, he went straight round to the garage when he got home, climbed behind the Feltex and wire-netting, and opened the door of the wormy old medicine cupboard. He shoved the limp wisp of a crest in amongst the darkness. He did not bother to feel whether his other "talismans" were there. He slammed the door. Probably wouldn't open it again. It would open, though; it was already opening, of its own accord, in his mind.

A gust of breakfast and other things came at him as soon as he entered the kitchen.

"It's early for you, isn't it? And what's come over you, Tim, to have brushed your hair so nice?"

He had, it was true, wet it a bit, and given it a bash or two with the brush; he could feel the wad of wet hair he had slicked across his forehead.

"It isn't for your birthday, is it?" She, too, was coming at him. "Nine! Fancy! Who'd believe it!"

She grabbed him to her apron. He hated this sort of thing: his cheek squashed; his shoulder would be looking more than disjointed—deformed. As she held him, practically suffocated, and him not supposed to resist, any vision he may have imagined having, ever, was splodged into one great, white blur, at the centre of it a smear of sulphur.

When she was at last satisfied, she let him go. "Dad's running late. We'll have the present when he's finished shaving. He went to no end of trouble getting it. You don't realize, Tim, what you mean to your father. He's that proud of you."

He sat down, and ate his porridge lumps and all this morning before his misery returned. He was hard put to it not to blubber when she stooped and opened the oven door, and let out a blast of half-baked cake. He did, in fact, start to blubber, but managed to turn it into a bubble or two.

Saul Bellow

THE GONZAGA MANUSCRIPTS

Nobel Prize 1976

Saul Bellow was born in Lachine, Quebec, in 1915 but moved with his family at the age of nine to Chicago, a city with which he is closely identified. Educated at nearby Northwestern University, he has found the academic world congenial, working as a professor at a number of American institutions of higher learning, including, since 1969, the University of Chicago. Mr. Bellow is a multiple winner of the National Book Award, and has also won the French Prix International de Littérature, the Pulitzer Prize, and the Gold Medal of the American Academy of Arts and Sciences.

His frequently comic novels combine a strong commitment to human values with a strong dose of realism, a combination that can be seen to great effect in novels like The Adventures of Augie March *(1953),* Herzog *(1964),* Mr. Sammler's Planet *(1970), and* Humboldt's Gift *(1975). Although he is a "Jewish writer," Saul Bellow is a* writer *for all people and for all time.*

BUTTONED TO THE THROAT in a long, soft overcoat, dark green, Clarence Feiler got off the Hendaye Express in the Madrid station. It was late afternoon and it was raining, and the station with its throng and its dim orange lights seemed sunken under darkness and noise. The gaunt horselike Spanish locomotives screamed off their steam and the hurrying passengers struggled in the narrow gates. Porters and touts approached Clarence, obviously a foreigner, judging by his small blond beard, blue eyes, almost brimless hat, long coat, and crepe-soled shoes. But he carried his own bag and had no need of them. This was not his first visit to Madrid. An old limousine took him to the Pensión La Granja, where he had a room reserved. This limousine probably had run on the boulevards of Madrid before Clarence was born but it was mechanically still beautiful. In the spacious darkness of the back seat the windows were like the glass of an old cabinet, and he listened happily to the voice of the wonderful old motor. Where could you get another ride like this, on such an evening, through such a place? Clarence loved Spanish cities, even the poorest and barrenest, and the capitals stirred his heart as no other places did. He had first come as an undergraduate, a mere kid, studying Spanish literature at the University of Minnesota; and then he had come again and seen the ruins of the Civil War. This time he came not as a tourist but on a quest. He had heard from a Spanish Republican refugee in California, where he now lived, that there were more than a hundred poems by Manuel Gonzaga somewhere in Madrid. Not a single Spanish publishing house could print them because they were so critical of the Army and the State. It was hard to believe that poems by one of the greatest of modern Spanish geniuses could be suppressed, but the refugee gave Clarence reliable proof that it was so. He showed him letters to one of Gonzaga's nephews from a man named Guzmán del Nido, Gonzaga's friend and literary executor, with whom he had served in North Africa, admitting that he had once had the poems but had given them up to a certain Countess del Camino since most of them were love poems addressed to her. The countess had died during the war, her home had been looted, and he didn't know what had become of the poems.

"Perhaps Guzmán doesn't care, either," said the refugee. "He's one of these people who think everything has come to an end anyway, and they might as well live comfortably. Guzmán del Nido lives very comfortably. He's rich. He is a member of the Cortes."

"Money doesn't have to do that to you," said Clarence, who had a little money himself. He was not exactly a rich man, but he didn't

have to work for a living. "He must have a bad character not to
care about his friend's work. And such work! You know, I was just
killing time in graduate school till I came across Gonzaga. The year
I spent doing my thesis on *Los Huesos Secos* was the first good year
I had had since I was a boy. There hasn't been anything like it
since. I'm not much on modern poetry in English. Some of it is
very fine, of course, but it doesn't express much wish to live. To
live as a creature, that is. As if it were not good enough. But the
first time I opened Gonzaga I read:

> These few bits of calcium my teeth are,
> And these few ohms my brain is,
> May make you think I am nothing but puny.
> Let me tell you, sir,
> I am like any creature—
> A creature.

I felt right away and in spite of this ironical turn that I was in
touch with a poet who could show me how to go on, and what
attitude to take toward life. The great, passionate poems carried
me away, like 'The Poem of Night,' which I still know by heart
from beginning to end and which often seems like the only thing
I really have got—" Clarence was sometimes given to exagger-
ation. "Or take the poem called 'Confession,' the one that goes:

> I used to welcome all
> And now I fear all.
> If it rained it was comforting
> And if it shone, comforting,
> But now my very weight is dreadful....

When I read that, Gonzaga made me understand how we lose
everything by trying to become everything. This was the most valuable lesson of my life, I think. Gosh! There should be someone
trying to find those posthumous poems. They ought not to be given
up. They must be marvelous."

He felt, suddenly, as if he had been thrown into a race, terribly
excited, full of effort, feverish—and profoundly grateful. For Clarence had not found his occupation and had nothing to do. He did
not think it right to marry until he had found something and could
offer a wife leadership. His beard was grown not to hide weaknesses

but as a project, to give his life shape. He was becoming an eccentric; it was all he could do with his good impulses. As yet he did not realize that these impulses were religious. He was too timid to say he believed in God, and he couldn't think that it would matter to anyone what he believed. Since he was weak, it would be said, he must have some such belief. However, he was really enthusiastic about Gonzaga, and to recover this inspired Spaniard's poems was something that mattered. And "Does it really matter?" was always the test question. It filled Clarence with secret pleasure to know that he was not indifferent, at bottom pretending. It *did* matter, and what mattered might save him. He was in Madrid not to perform an act of cultural piety but to do a decent and necessary thing, namely, bring the testimony of a great man before the world. Which certainly could use it.

As soon as he arrived at the Pensión La Granja and the lamps were lit in his room, a comfortable large room with balconies facing the trees of the Retiro, Madrid's biggest park, Clarence called for the porter and sent off two letters. One was addressed to Guzmán del Nido, Gonzaga's comrade-in-arms of the Moroccan War and literary executor, and the other to a Miss Faith Ungar on García de Paredes Street. This Miss Ungar was an art student, or rather student of art history; her fiancé was an airline pilot who brought in cheaper pesetas from Tangiers. Clarence disliked black-marketing, but the legal rate of exchange was ridiculous; he was prepared to pay a lot of money for those manuscripts and at eighteen to one he might spend a small fortune.

His landlady came to welcome him to the *pensión*— a pale big woman with a sort of turban of hair wound spirally to a point. She came also to collect his passport and other travel papers for police inspection and to give him a briefing on her guests. A retired general was the oldest. She had also some people from British Shell and the widow of a Minister and six members of a Brazilian trade delegation, so the dining room was full. "And are you a tourist?" she said, glancing at the *tríptico,* the elaborate police document all travelers have to carry in Spain.

"In a way," said Clarence, guardedly. He didn't like to be thought of as a tourist, and yet secrecy was necessary. Gonzaga's poems, though unpublished, would probably come under the head of national treasure.

"Or have you come to study something?"

"Yes, that's it."

"There's a great deal here to interest people from a country as new as yours."

"There certainly is," he said, his rosy beard-lengthened face turned to her, seeming perfectly sincere. The color of his mouth was especially vivid in the lamplight. It was not yet full evening and the rain was stopping. Beyond the trees of the Retiro the sky was making itself clear of clouds, and a last yellow daylight pierced the water-gray. Trolley sparks scratched green sparks within the locust trees.

A bell rang, an old hand bell, announcing dinner. A maid passed, ringing it proudly, her shoulders thrown back.

The guests were eating soup in the dining room, an interior room, not very airy, with dark red, cloth-covered walls. The Brazilians were having a lively conversation. The old general, feeble-headed, eyes nearly extinct, was bothering the soup with his spoon but not eating. Doña Elvia seated Clarence with a hefty British lady. He knew he must expect to have trouble with her. She was in a bad way. Her face was heavily made up; she thought she was a person of charm, and she did have a certain charm, but her eyes were burning. Tresses of dark-reddish hair fought strongly for position on her head.

"If you came here with the intention of having fun, you won't have it in Madrid. I've been here twenty years and never had any," she said. "By now I'm so tired out I don't even look for any. I don't read any books, I don't go to the cinema, and I can just barely stand to read *Coyote* and look at the funnies. I can't understand why so many Americans want to come here. They're all over the place. One of your bishops was arrested at Santander for bathing without the top of his costume."

"Really?"

"They're very strict in Spain about dress. I suppose if they had known he was a bishop they would have let him alone. However, in the water..."

"It's strange," said Clarence. "Well, anyway, he's not one of *my* bishops. I have no bishops."

"You do have Congressmen, though. Two of those had their pants stolen while taking a nap on the Barcelona Express. They had hung their pants up because of the heat. The thieves reached into the compartment from the roof and pinched them. It happened in broad daylight. They carried about two thousand dollars each. Don't they have wallets? Why do they carry so much money in their pockets?"

Clarence frowned. "Yes, I read about that," he said. "I can't tell you why they carry so much money in their trouser pockets. Maybe that's the custom down South. It's none of my business, though."

"I'm afraid I'm annoying you," she said. She was not afraid at all; a bold look of enjoyment had entered her eyes. She was trying to bait him. Why? he wondered; he found no ready answer.

"You're not annoying me."

"If I am," she said, "it's not absolutely my fault. You know Stendhal once wrote there was a secret principle of unhappiness in the English."

"Is that so?" he said. He looked at her with greater interest. What a busted-up face; full of unhappy vigor and directionless intelligence. Yes, she was astonishing. He felt sorry for her and yet lucky to have met her, in spite of everything.

"Stendhal may have been right. You see, I used to read widely once. I was a cultivated person. But the reason for it was sex, and that went."

"Oh, come, I wouldn't say—"

"I shouldn't be talking like this. It's partly the weather. It's been raining so hard. It isn't supposed to rain like this in the summer. I've never seen so much damned rain. You people may be to blame for that."

"*Who* people? Which people?"

"It could be because of the atom bomb," she said. "The weather has never been normal since the atom thing started. Nobody can tell what this radioactive stuff is doing. Perhaps it's the beginning of the end."

"You make me feel very strange," said Clarence. "But why are the American bombs the dangerous ones? There are others."

"Because one always reads of the Americans exploding them. They do it under water. Holes are torn in the ocean bottom. The cold water rushes in and cools the core of the earth. Then the earth's surface shrinks. No one can tell what will happen. It's affected the weather already."

Clarence's color grew very high and he looked dazed. He paid no attention to his broiled meat and French fried potatoes. "I don't keep up much with science," he said. "I remember I did read somewhere that industry gives off six billion tons of carbon dioxide every year and so the earth is growing warmer because the carbon dioxide in the air is opaque to heat radiation. All that means that the glaciers won't be coming back."

"Yes, but what about Carbon Fourteen? You Americans are filling the air with Carbon Fourteen, which is very dangerous."

"I don't know about it. I am not all Americans. You are not all the English. You didn't lick the Armada, I didn't open the West. You are not Winston Churchill and I am not the Pentagon."

"I believe you are some sort of fanatic," she announced.

"And I believe you're a nasty old bag!" he said, enraged. He left the table and went to his room.

Half an hour later she knocked at his door. "I'm terribly sorry," she said. "I suppose I did go too far. But it's all right, we're friends now, aren't we? It does you so much good to be angry. It really is good." She did, now, look very friendly and happy.

"It's all right. I'm sorry too," he said.

After all, how would feuding with this Englishwoman help him with his quest? And probably there were wrong ways and right ways of going about it. Gonzaga's poems should be recovered in the spirit of Gonzaga himself. Otherwise, what was the use?

Considering it all in his head, he saw that this Miss Walsh, the Englishwoman, had done him a service by baiting him. Unwittingly, she offered a test of his motive. He could not come to Spain and act badly, blindly. So he was deepened in his thought and in his purpose, and felt an increased debt to Gonzaga and to those poems.

He was in a hurry next morning to get to a bookshop and see what Gonzaga items there were in print. Impatiently he turned himself out of the comfortable bed, pulled on his underpants, dealt nervously with his cuff buttons, washed at his little sink with the glass shelves and pointed faucets, and combed his hair and whiskers with his palms. Odors of soil and flowers came from the Retiro across the freshly watered street. The morning was clear, still, and blue. He took one bite of the brick bits of toast the maid brought, sipped from the immense cup of bitter *café au lait,* and then rushed out to find a bookstore.

At Bucholz's he found only a single volume he had not seen before, a collection of letters from Gonzaga to his father. The frontispiece showed Gonzaga in his lieutenant's uniform—a small man, by Clarence's standard—sitting up straight at the keyboard of an old-fashioned piano, his large eyes opened directly into the camera. Underneath he had noted, "Whenever I am lucky enough to come upon a piano in one of these Moroccan towns, I can, after playing for ten or fifteen minutes, discover how I really feel. Otherwise I am ignorant." Clarence's face colored with satisfaction as he stooped and looked. What a man this Gonzaga was—what a personality! On the very first page was an early version of a poem he had always admired, the one that began:

> Let me hear a sound
> Truly not my own;
> The voice of another,
> Truly other....

The book engrossed him entirely until eleven o'clock. With a sort of hungry emotion, he sat at a café table and read it from cover to cover. It was beautiful. He thanked God for having sent the Republican refugee who had given him the idea of coming to Spain.

Reluctantly he left the café and took a cab to García de Paredes Street, where Miss Ungar lived. He hated to do it, but he needed pesetas, and it was unavoidable.

Again he was lucky. She was not at all the kind of person you would have expected a black-marketing art student to be; she was young and unusually attractive with a long, intelligent white face. Her hair was drawn tightly back over her elongated head and tied off in an arched, sparkling tail. Her eyes were extremely clear. Clarence was greatly taken with her. Even the fact that her teeth, because of the contrast with her very fair skin, were not too bright, impressed him. It proved to him that she was genuine. On a ribbon round her neck she wore a large silver medal.

"Is that a religious thing you're wearing?"

"No. Do you want to look at it?" She bent forward so that it swung free. He picked up the warm piece of silver and read: HELENA WAITE AWARD FOR HISTORICAL STUDIES.

"You won it?"

"Yes."

"Then why are you in this kind of business?"

"And what did you come here for?" she said.

"I need pesetas."

"And we need dollars. My fiancé and I want to buy a house."

"I see."

"Besides, it's a way of meeting a lot of people. You'd be surprised how few interesting people an American woman in Madrid can meet. I can't spend all my time in the Prado or at the Library. The embassy people are about as interesting as a plate of cold-cuts. My fiancé only gets here twice a month. Are you on a holiday?"

"Sort of."

She didn't believe him. She knew he had come with a definite purpose. He could not say why, but this pleased him.

"How do you like the Granja?"

"It's all right. An Englishwoman there lammed into me last night, first about the atom bomb and then saying that I must be a fanatic. She thought I was peculiar."

"Everybody has to make it as he can," she said.

"That's exactly the way I feel about it."

He had thought that the kind of woman who became engaged to an airline pilot might look down on him. She didn't, not in the least. Soon he was wondering how that sort of man could interest her.

"If you have no other plans, why don't you come to lunch with me," he said, "and save me from that Miss Walsh?"

They went out to eat. Though the day had grown hot, she stopped in the courtyard to put on a pair of net gloves; women without gloves were considered common in Madrid. For his part Clarence thought the momentary grasp of her fingers as she worked them into the gloves was wonderful; what a lot of life she had! Her white face gave off a pleasant heat. As they walked, she told him she couldn't give him many pesetas just yet; she'd pay whatever rate was quoted in the *Tribune* on the day the money arrived. That day, Clarence reflected, would also be the day on which her pilot arrived; he had no business to be disturbed by that, and yet it did disturb him.

Near the Naval Ministry they were stopped by a procession. Priests with banners led it, and after them came a statue of the Virgin carried by four men. A group of barefooted widows followed in their mourning with black mantillas. Old women passed, carrying tapers. Most of these appeared to be old maids, and the flames made a clear additional light near each face. A band played Beethoven's Funeral March. Above the walls of the ministry trees shot their leaves; there was the same odor of flowers and soil that Clarence had smelled that morning, of graves, of summer pines. Across the square, on the car tracks, a welding arc hummed and scalded. The dazzling mouths of tubas and trombones passed by and the lighted tapers moved off into daylight, but it was the bare white feet of the widows treading on dusty asphalt that Clarence watched, and when they were gone he said to Miss Ungar, "Wasn't that splendid? I'm glad I'm here."

His brows had risen; his face was so lively that Miss Ungar laughed and said, "You take it big. I like the way you take it. You ought to be sure to visit Toledo. Have you ever been there?"

"No."

"I go often. I'm doing a study. Come with me next time. I can show you lots of things there."

"There's nothing I'd like better. When do you go again?"

"Tomorrow."

He was disappointed. "Oh, I'm sorry, I can't make it tomorrow," he said. "I arrived yesterday and I'm going to be very busy for a while. Just give me a raincheck, will you? I'll hold you to this. But there is something special I came to do—you guessed that, I suppose—and I can't take the time to go anywhere now. I'm all keyed up."

"Is this mission of yours a secret?"

"In a way. There's an illegal side to it, probably. But I don't think you'd tell on me, and I'm so full of it I'm willing to talk. Have you ever heard of a poet named Gonzaga?"

"Gonzaga? I must have. But I don't think I ever read him."

"You should. He was very great, one of the most original of modern Spanish poets, and in the class of Juan Ramón Jiménez, Lorca, and Machado. I studied him at school and he means a lot to me. To understand what he did, you have to think first of modern literature as a sort of grand council considering what mankind should do next, how we should fill our mortal time, what we should feel, what we should see, where we should get our courage, how we should love or hate, how we should be pure or great or terrible, evil (you know!), and all the rest. This advice of literature has never done much good. But you see God doesn't rule over men as he used to, and for a long time people haven't been able to feel that life was firmly attached at both ends so that they could stand confidently in the middle. That kind of faith is missing, and for

many years poets have tried to supply a substitute. Like 'the un-
acknowledged legislators' or 'the best is yet to be,' or Walt Whitman
saying that whoever touched him could be sure he was touching a
man. Some have stood up for beauty, and some have stood up for
perfect proportion, and the very best have soon gotten tired of art
for its own sake. Some took it as their duty to behave like brave
performers who try to hold down panic during a theater fire. Very
great ones have quit, like Tolstoy, who became a reformer, or like
Rimbaud, who went to Abyssinia, and at the end of his life was
begging of a priest, *'Montrez-moi. Montrez...* Show me something.'
Frightening, the lives some of these geniuses led. Maybe they assumed too much responsibility. They knew that if by their poems
and novels *they* were fixing values, there must be something wrong
with the values. No one man can furnish them. Oh, he may try, if
his inspiration is for values, but not if his inspiration is for words.
If you throw the full responsibility for meaning and for the estab-
lishing of good and evil on poets, they are bound to go down.
However, the poets reflected what was happening to everyone.
There are people who feel that they are responsible for *everything*.
Gonzaga is free from this, and that's why I love him. Here. See
what he says in some of these letters. I found this marvelous collection this morning."

His long hands shaking, he pressed flat the little book on the
table of the restaurant. Miss Ungar's quiet face expressed more
than intellectual interest. "Listen. He writes to his father: 'Many
feel they must say it all, whereas all has been said, unsaid, resaid
so many times that we are bound to feel futile unless we understand
that we are merely adding our voices. Adding them when moved
by the spirit. Then and then only.' Or this: 'A poem may outlive
its subject—say, my poem about the girl who sang songs on the
train—but the poet has no right to expect this. The poem has no
greater privilege than the girl.' You see what kind of man he was?"

"Impressive—really!" she said. "I see that."

"I've come to Spain to find some of his unpublished poems. I
have some money, and I've never really been able to find the thing
that I wanted to do. I'm not original myself, except in some minor
way. Anyhow, that's why I'm here. Lots of people call themselves
leaders, healers, priests, and spokesmen for God, prophets or wit-
nesses, but Gonzaga was a human being who spoke only as a human
being; there was nothing spurious about him. He tried never to

misrepresent; he wanted to see. To move you he didn't have to do anything, he merely had to be. We've made the most natural things the hardest of all. Unfortunately for us all, he was killed while still young. But he left some poems to a certain Countess del Camino, and I'm here to locate them."

"It's a grand thing. I wish you luck. I hope people will help."

"Why shouldn't they?"

"I don't know, but don't you expect to run into trouble?"

"Do you think I ought to expect to?"

"If you want my honest opinion, yes."

"I may get the poems—why, just like that," he said. "You never can tell."

•

"Started, by God!" he said when he received an answer from Guzmán del Nido. The member of the Cortes invited him to dinner. All that day he was in a state, and the weather was peculiarly thick, first glaring sunshine, then explosive rains. "See what I told you," said Miss Walsh. But when Clarence went out late in the afternoon, the sky was clear and pale again and the Palm Sunday leaves braided in the ironwork of balconies were withering in the sunlight. He walked to the Puerta del Sol with its crowd of pleasure-seekers, beggars, curb-haunters, wealthy women, soldiers, cops, lottery-ticket and fountain-pen peddlers, and priests, humble door-openers, chair-menders, and musicians. At seven-thirty he boarded a streetcar, following directions; it seemed to take him to every other point of the city first. Finally, with his transfer, the wisp of trolley paper still in his hand, he got off and mounted a bare stony alley at the top of which was the del Nido villa. Suddenly there was another cloudburst—*una tormenta* was what the Madrileños called it. No doorway offered cover and he was drenched. At the gate he had to wait a long while for the porter to answer his ring, perhaps five minutes in the hard rain. This would probably give comfort to the Englishwoman with her atomic theories. His nervous eyes seemed to catch some of the slaty blue of the pouring rain cloud; his blond beard darkened, and he pulled in his shoulders. The tall gate opened. The porter held out an umbrella in his brown fist. Clarence walked past him. Too late for umbrellas. The rain stopped when he was halfway up the path.

So he was at a disadvantage when Guzmán del Nido came for-

ward to meet him. He walked clumsily in his sodden wool suit. It
had a shameful smell, like wet dog.

"How do you do, Señor Feiler. What a shame about the rain. It
has ruined your suit but it gives your face a fine color."

They shook hands, and it came over Clarence with a thrill as he
looked at the high-bridged nose and dark, fine-textured skin of
del Nido that he was in touch with Gonzaga himself—this round-
shouldered man in his linen suit, bowing his sloping head, smiling
with sharp teeth, with his hairless hand and big-boned wrist and
his awkward fanny, had been Gonzaga's friend and belonged within
the legend. Clarence at once sensed that del Nido would make him
look foolish if he could, with his irony and his fine Spanish manners.
Del Nido was the sort of man who cut everyone down to size.
Gonzaga himself would not have been spared by him. *"Go away!
You have no holy ones,"* Gonzaga had written.

"The letter I sent you—" Clarence managed to begin. They were
hurrying toward the dining room; other guests were waiting.

"We can discuss it later."

"I understand you gave certain poems to the Countess del Camino," he said.

But del Nido was speaking with another guest. The candles were
lit and the company sat down.

Clarence had no appetite.

He was sitting between an Italian Monsignore and an Egyptian
lady who had lived in New York and spoke very slangy English.
There was a German gentleman, too, who headed some insurance
company; he sat between Señora del Nido and her daughter. From
his end of the table, del Nido with his narrow sleek head and his
forward-curved teeth shining with valuable crowns, dominated the
conversation. About his eyes the skin was twisted in curious laugh
wrinkles. Impressed, appalled, too, Clarence asked himself again
and again how Gonzaga could have trusted such a person. A maker
of witticisms, as Pascal had said, a bad character. When these words
of Pascal came into his head, Clarence turned to the Monsignore
as a man to whom this might make sense. But the Monsignore was
interested mostly in stamp collecting. Clarence was not, so the Monsignore had nothing further to say to him. He was a gloomy, fleshy
man whose hair grew strongly and low over the single deep wrinkle
of his forehead.

Guzmán del Nido kept talking, He talked about modern painting, about mystery stories, about old Russia, about the movies, about Nietzsche. Dreamy-looking, the daughter seemed not to listen; the wife expanded some of his remarks. The daughter stared with close-set eyes into the candle flames. The Egyptian lady was amused by the strong smell of Clarence's rain-shrinking clothes. She made a remark about wet wool. He was grateful for the absence of electric lights.

"An American was arrested in Córdoba," said Guzmán del Nido. "He stole the hat of a *Guardia Civil* for a souvenir."

"Isn't that unusual!"

"He'll find the jail smaller than the jails at home. I hope you won't mind if I tell a story about Americans and the size of things in Spain."

"Why should I mind?" said Clarence.

"Splendid. Well, there was an American whose Spanish host could not impress him. Everything was larger in America. The skyscrapers were bigger than the palaces. The cars were bigger. The cats were bigger. At last his host placed a boiled lobster between his sheets and when the horrified American saw it his host said, 'This is one of our bedbugs.'"

For some reason this fetched Clarence more than it did the others. He uttered a bark of laughter that made the candles flutter.

"Perhaps you'll tell us an American story," said del Nido.

Clarence thought. "Well, here's one," he said. "Two dogs meet in the street. Old friends. One says, 'Hello.' The other answers, 'Cock-a-doodle-do!' 'What does that mean? What's this cock-a-doodle-do stuff?' 'Oh,' says he, 'I've been studying foreign languages.'"

Dead silence. No one laughed. The Egyptian lady said, "I'm afraid you laid an egg." Clarence was angry.

"Is this story told in English or in American?" del Nido asked.

That started a discussion. Was American really a sort of English? Was it a language? No one seemed sure, and Clarence at last said, "I don't know whether or not it is a language, but there is *something* spoken. I've seen people cry in it and so forth, just as elsewhere."

"We deserved that," said del Nido. "It's true, we're not fair to Americans. In reality the only true Europeans left are Americans."

"How so?"

"The Europeans themselves do not have the peace of mind to appreciate what's best. Life is too hard for us, society too unstable."

Clarence realized that he was being shafted; del Nido was satirizing his guest; he undoubtedly meant that Clarence could not comprehend Gonzaga's poems. An ugly hatred for del Nido grew and knotted in his breast. He wanted to hit him, to strangle him, to trample him, to pick him up and hurl him at the wall. Luckily del Nido was called to the phone, and Clarence stared out his rage at the empty place, the napkin, the silver, the crest of the chair. Only Señorita del Nido seemed aware that he was offended.

Once more Clarence told himself that there was a wrong way to go about obtaining the poems, a way contrary to their spirit. That did much to calm him. He managed to get down a few spoonfuls of ice cream and mastered himself.

"Why are you so interested in Gonzaga?" said del Nido to him later in the garden, under the date palms with their remote leaves.

"I studied Spanish literature in college and became a Gonzagian."

"Wasn't that rather strange, though? You must forgive me, but I see my poor old friend Gonzaga, who was Spanish of the Spanish, in that terrible uniform we used to wear, and our hands and faces bruised and baked and chapped by the desert sun, and I ask myself why he should have had an effect..."

"I don't know why. I'd like to understand it myself; but the fact that he did is what you start with."

"I have an interesting observation about poets and their lives. Some are better in real life than in their work. You read bitter poems and then you find the poet is personally very happy and good-tempered. Some are worse in their personality than you would guess from their work. They are luckier, in a way, because they have a chance to correct their faults and improve themselves. Best of all are the ones who are exactly the same inside and out, in the spoken word and the written. To be what you seem to be is the objective of true culture. Gonzaga was of the second type."

"Was he?" It occurred to Clarence that del Nido was trying to make himself more interesting to him than Gonzaga could be and to push Gonzaga out.

"I think I can tell you one reason why Gonzaga appeals to me," said Clarence. "He got away from solving *his* own problem. I often feel this way about it: a poem is great because it is absolutely necessary. Before it came, silence. After it comes, more silence. It begins when it must and ends when it must, and therefore it's not personal. It's 'the sound truly not my own.'" Now he was proving to del Nido that he *could* comprehend; at the same time he knew that he was throwing away his effort. Guzmán del Nido was fundamentally indifferent. Indifferent, indifferent, indifferent! He fundamentally did not care. What can you do with people who don't fundamentally care! "But you know why I came to you. I want to know what became of Gonzaga's last poems. What are they like?"

"They were superb love poems. But I don't know where they are now. They were dedicated to the Countess del Camino and I was supposed to hand them on to her. Which I did."

"There aren't any copies?" said Clarence, trembling as del Nido spoke of the poems.

"No. They were for the Countess."

"Of course. But they were also for everyone else."

"There's plenty of poetry already, for everyone. Homer, Dante, Calderón, Shakespeare. Have you noticed how much difference it makes?"

"It should make a difference. It's not their fault if it doesn't. Besides, Calderón wasn't your friend. But Gonzaga was. Where's the countess now? The poor woman is dead, isn't she? And what happened to those poems? Where do you think they can be?"

"I don't know. She had a secretary named Polvo, a fine old man. A few years ago he died, too. The old man's nephews live in Alcalá de Henares. Where Cervantes was born, you know. They're in the civil service, and they're very decent people, I hear."

"You never even asked them what happened to your friend's poems?" Clarence was astonished. "Didn't you want to find them?"

"I thought eventually I'd try to trace them. I'm sure the countess would have taken good care of her poems."

This was where the discussion stopped, and Clarence was just as glad that it couldn't continue; he sensed that Guzmán del Nido would have liked to give him the dirt on Gonzaga—revelations involving women, drunkenness and dope-taking, bribery, gonorrhea, or even murder. Gonzaga had escaped into the army; that was notorious. But Clarence didn't want to hear del Nido's reminiscences.

•

It's natural to suppose, because a man is great, that the people around him must have known how to respond to greatness, but when these people turn out to be no better than Guzmán del Nido you wonder what response greatness really needs.

This was what Clarence was saying to Miss Ungar several days later.

"He's glad he doesn't have the poems," said Miss Ungar. "If he had them he'd feel obligated to do something about them, and he's afraid of that because of his official position."

"That's right. Exactly," said Clarence. "But he did me one favor anyway. He put me on to the countess's secretary's nephews. I've written to them and they've invited me to Alcalá de Henares. They didn't mention the poems but maybe they were just being discreet. I'd better start being more discreet myself. There's something unpleasant going on, I think."

"What is it?"

"The police have an eye on me."

"Oh, come!"

"I do. I'm serious. My room was searched yesterday. I know it was. My landlady didn't answer one way or another when I asked her. She didn't even bother."

"It's too peculiar for anything," Miss Ungar said, laughing in amazement. "But why should they search? What for?"

"I suppose I just inspire suspicion. And then I made a mistake with my landlady the day after my visit to del Nido. She's a very patriotic character. She has a retired general in the *pensión*, too. Well, she was talking to me the other morning and among other things she told me how healthy she was, strong as a rock—*una roca*—a sort of Gibraltar. And, like a dumbbell, I said, without even thinking, *'Gibraltar Español!'* That was an awful boner."

"Why?"

"During the war, you see, when the British were taking such a pounding there was a great agitation for the return of Gibraltar to Spain. The slogan was *Gibraltar Español!* Of course they don't like to be reminded that they were dying for the British to get it good from Germany. Well, she probably thinks I'm a political-secret-somebody. And she was just plain offended."

"But what difference does it really make, as long as you don't do anything terribly illegal?"

"When you're watched closely you're bound sooner or later to do *something*," he said.

He went out to Alcalá on a Sunday afternoon and met the two nephews of Don Francisco Polvo and their wives and daughters.

They proved to be a family of laughers. They laughed when they spoke and when you answered. You saw nothing in the town but sleepy walls, and parched trees and stones. The brothers were squat, sandy-haired, broad-bellied men.

"We're having tea in the garden," said Don Luis Polvo. He was called "the Englishman" by the others because he had lived in London for several months twenty years ago; they addressed him as "My Lord," and he obliged them by acting like an *Inglés*. He even owned a Scottish terrier named *Duglas*. The family cried to him, "Now's your chance to speak English, Luis. Speak to him!"

"Jolly country, eh?" Luis said. That was about all he could manage.

"Very."

"More, more!"

"Charing Cross," he said.

"Go on, Luis, say more."

"Piccadilly. And that's all I can remember."

The tea was served. Clarence drank and sweltered. Lizards raced in the knotty grapevines and by the well....The wives were embroidering. The laughing daughters were conversing in French, obviously about Clarence. Nobody appeared to believe what he said. Lanky and pained, he sat in what looked to be a suit made of burlap, with his tea. Instead of a saucer, he felt as though he were holding on to the rim of Saturn.

After tea they showed him through the house. It was huge, old, bare, thick-walled and chill, and it was filled with the portraits and the clothing of ancestors—weapons, breastplates, helmets, daggers, guns. In one room where the picture of a general in the Napoleonic Wars was hung, a fun-making mood seized the brothers. They tried on plumed hats, then sabers, and finally full uniforms. Wearing spurs, medals, musty gloves, they went running back to the terrace where the women sat. Don Luis dragged a sword, his seat hung down and the cocked hat sagged broken, opening in the middle on his sandy baldness. With a Napoleonic musket, full of mockery, he performed the manual-of-arms to uproarious laughter. Clarence laughed, too, his cheeks creased; he couldn't explain however why his heart was growing heavier by the minute.

Don Luis aimed the musket and shouted, "*La bomba atómica! Poum!*" The hit he scored with this was enormous. The women shrieked, swiveling their fans, and his brother fell on his behind in the sanded path, weeping with laughter. The terrier *Duglas* leaped into Don Luis's face, fiercely excited.

Don Luis threw a stick and cried, "Fetch, fetch, *Duglas! La bomba atómica! La bomba atómica!*"

The blood stormed into Clarence's head furiously. This was another assault on him. Oh! he thought frantically, the things he had to bear! The punishment he had to take trying to salvage those poems!

As if in the distance, the voice of Don Luis cried, "Hiroshima! Nagasaki! Bikini! Good show!" He flung the stick and the dog bounded on taut legs, little *Duglas,* from the diminished figure of his master and back—the tiny white-and-brown animal, while laughter incessantly pierced the dry air of the garden.

It was not a decent joke, even though Don Luis in that split hat and the withered coat was mocking the dead military grandeur of his own country. That didn't even the score. The hideous stun of the bomb and its unbearable, death-brilliant mushroom cloud filled Clarence's brain.

This was not right. He managed to stop Don Luis. He approached him, laid a hand on the musket, and asked to speak with him privately. It made the others laugh. The ladies started to murmur about him. An older woman said, "*Es gracioso*"; the girls seemed to disagree. He heard one of them answer, "*Non, il n'est pas gentil.*" Proudly polite, Clarence faced it out. "Damn their damn tea!" he said to himself. His shirt was sticking to his back.

"We did not inherit my uncle's papers," said Don Luis. "Enough, *Duglas!*" He threw the stick down the well. "My brother and I inherited this old house and other land, but if there were papers they probably went to my cousin Pedro Álvarez-Polvo who lives in Segovia. He's a very interesting fellow. He works for the *Banco Español* but is a cultivated person. The countess had no family. She was fond of my uncle. My uncle was extremely fond of Álvarez-Polvo. They shared the same interests."

"Did your uncle ever speak of Gonzaga?"

"I don't recall. The countess had a large number of artistic admirers. This Gonzaga interests you very much, doesn't he?"

"Yes. Why shouldn't I be interested in him? You may someday be interested in an American poet."

"I? No!" Don Luis laughed, but he was startled.

What people! Damn these dirty laughers! Clarence waited until

Don Luis's shocked and latterly somewhat guilty laughter ended, and his broad yap, with spacious teeth, closed—his lips shook with resistance to closing, and finally remained closed.

"Do you think your cousin Álvarez-Polvo would know..."

"He would know a lot," said Don Luis, composed. "My uncle confided in him. *He* can tell you something definite, you can count on him. I'll give you a letter of introduction."

"If it's not too much trouble."

"No, no, the pleasure is mine." Don Luis was all courtesy.

After returning to Madrid on the bus through the baking plain of Castile, Clarence phoned Miss Ungar. He wanted her sympathy and comfort. But she didn't invite him to come over. She said, "I can give you the pesetas tomorrow." The pilot had landed, and he thought she sounded regretful. Perhaps she was not really in love with her fiancé. Clarence now had the impression that the black-marketing was not her idea but the pilot's. It embarrassed her. But she was loyal.

"I'll come by later in the week. There's no hurry," he said. "I'm busy anyway."

It would hurt him to do it, but he'd cash a check at the American Express tomorrow at the preposterous legal rate of exchange.

Disappointed, Clarence hung up. *He* should have a woman like that. It passed dimly over his mind that a live woman would make a better quest than a dead poet. But the poet was already *there;* the woman not. He sent a letter to Álvarez-Polvo. He bathed in the sink, and lay reading Gonzaga by a buzzing bulb under the canopy of his bed.

•

He arrived in Segovia early one Sunday morning. It was filled with sunlight, the clouds were silk-white in the mountain air. Their shadows wandered over the slopes of the bare sierra like creatures that crept and warmed themselves on the soil and rock. All over the old valley were convents, hermitages, churches, towers, the graves of San Juan and other mystical saints. At the highest point of Segovia was the Alcázar of Isabella the Catholic. And passing over the town with its many knobby granite curves that divided the sky was the aqueduct, this noble Roman remnant, as bushy as old men's ears. Clarence stood at the window of his hotel and looked at this conjured rise of stones that bridged the streets. It got him, all of it—the ancient mountain slopes worn as if by the struggles of Jacob with the angel, the spires, the dry glistening of the atmosphere, the hermit places in green hideaways, the sheep-bells' clunk, the cistern water dropping, while beams came as straight as harp wires from the sun. All of this, like a mild weight, seemed to press on him; it opened him up. He felt his breath creep within him like a tiny pet animal.

He went down through the courtyard. There the cistern of fat stone held green water, full of bottom-radiations from the golden brass of the faucets. Framed above it in an archway were ladies' hair styles of twenty years ago—a brilliantine advertisement. Ten or so beautiful *señoritas* with bangs, shingles, and windswept bobs, smiling like priestesses of love. Therefore Clarence had the idea that this cistern was the Fountain of Youth. And also that it was something Arcadian. He said, "'Ye glorious nymphs!'" and burst out laughing. He felt happy—magnificent! The sun poured over his head and embraced his back hotly.

Smiling, he rambled up and down the streets. He went to the Alcázar. Soldiers in German helmets were on guard. He went to the cathedral. It was ancient but the stones looked brand-new. After lunch he sat at the café in front of the aqueduct waiting for Álvarez-Polvo. On the wide sloping sidewalk there were hundreds of folding chairs, empty, the paint blazed off them and the wood emerging as gray as silverfish. The long low windows were open, so that inside and outside mingled, the yellow and the somber, the bar brown and the sky clear blue. A gypsy woman came out and gave Clarence the eye. She was an entertainer, but whether a real gypsy or not was conjectural. In the phrase he had heard, some of these girls were *gitanas de miedo,* fear-inspiring, or strictly from hunger. But he sat and studied the aqueduct, trying to imagine what sort of machinery they could have used to raise the stones.

A black hearse with mourners who trod after it slowly, and with all the plumes, and carvings of angels and death-grimacers, went through the main arch to the cemetery. After ten minutes it came galloping back with furious lashing of the horses, the silk-hatted coachman standing, yacking at them. Only a little later the same hearse returned with another procession of mourners who supported one another, weeping aloud, grief pushing on their backs. Through the arch again. And once more the hearse came flying back. With a sudden tightness of the guts Clarence thought, Why all these burials at once? Was there a plague? He looked at the frothy edge of his glass. Not very clean!

But Álvarez-Polvo set his mind at rest. He said, "The hearse was broken all week. It has just been repaired. A weeks' dead to bury."

He was a strange-looking man. His face seemed to have been worked by three or four diseases and then abandoned. His nose swelled out, shrinking his eyes. He had a huge mouth, like Cousin Don Luis. He wore a beret, and a yellow silk sash was wound about his belly. Clarence often had noticed that short men with big bellies sometimes held their arms ready for defense as they walked, but at heart apparently expected defeat. Álvarez-Polvo, too, had that posture. His face, brown, mottled, creased, sunlit, was edged with kinky gray hair escaping from the beret. His belly was like a drum, and he seemed also to have a drumlike soul. If you struck, you wouldn't injure him. You'd hear a sound.

"You know what I've come for?" said Clarence.

"Yes, I do know. But let's not start talking business right away. You've never been in Segovia before, I assume, and you must let me be hospitable. I'm a proud Segoviano—proud of this ancient, beautiful city, and it would give me pleasure to show you the principal places."

At the words "talking business" Clarence's heart rose a notch. Was it only a matter of settling the price? Then he had the poems! Something in Clarence flapped with eager joy, like a flag in the wind.

"By all means. For a while. It is beautiful. Never in my life have I seen anything so gorgeous as Segovia."

Álvarez-Polvo took his arm.

"With me you will not only see, you will also understand. I have made a study of it. I'm a lover of such things. I seldom have an opportunity to express it. Wherever I take my wife, she is interested only in *novelas morbosas*. At Versailles she sat and read Ellery Queen. In Paris, the same. In Rome, the same. If she lives to the end of time, she will never run out of *novelas morbosas*."

From this remark, without notice, he took a deep plunge into the subject of women, and he carried Clarence with him. Women, women, women! All the types of Spanish beauty. The Granadinas, the Malagueñas, the Castellanas, the Cataluñas. And then the Germans, the Greeks, the French, the Swedes! He tightened his hold on Clarence and pulled him close as he boasted and complained and catalogued and confessed. He was ruined! They had taken his money, his health, his time, his years, his life, women had—innocent, mindless, beautiful, ravaging, insidious, malevolent, chestnut, blond, red, black....Clarence felt hemmed in by women's faces, and by women's bodies.

"I suppose you'd call this a Romanesque church, wouldn't you?" Clarence said, stopping.

"Of course it is," said Álvarez-Polvo. "Just notice how the Renaissance building next to it was designed to harmonize with it."

Clarence was looking at the pillars and their blunted faces of humorous, devil-beast humanities, the stone birds, demon lollers and apostles. Two men carried by a bedspring and a mattress in a pushcart. They looked like the kings of Shinar and Elam defeated by Abraham.

"Come, have a glass of wine," said Álvarez-Polvo. "I'm not allowed to drink since my operation, but you must have something."

When would they begin to talk about the poems? Clarence was impatient. Gonzaga's poems would mean little if anything to a man like this, but in spite of his endless gallant bunk and his swagger and his complaints about having broken his springs in the service of love and beauty, he was probably a very cunning old fuff. He wanted to stall Clarence and find out what the poems were worth to him. And so Clarence gazed, or blinked, straight ahead, and kept a tight grip on his feelings.

In the *bodega* were huge barrels, copper fittings, innumerable bottles duplicated in the purple mirror, platters of *mariscos,* crawfish bugging their eyes on stalks, their feelers cooked into various last shapes. From the middle of the floor rose a narrow spiral staircase. It mounted—who-knew-where? Clarence tried to see but couldn't. A little torn-frocked beggar child came selling lottery tickets. The old chaser petted her; she wheedled; she took his small hand and laid her cheek to it. Still, talking, he felt her hair. He stroked his fill and sent her away with a coin.

Clarence drank down the sweet, yellow Malaga.

"Now," said Álvarez-Polvo, "I will show you a church few visitors ever see."

They descended to the lower part of town, down littered stairways of stone, by cavelike homes and a vacant lot where runty boys were butting a football with their heads, and dribbling and hooking it with their boots.

"Here," Álvarez-Polvo said. "This wall is of the tenth century and this one of the seventeenth."

The air inside the church was dark, cool, thick as ointment. Hollows of dark red and dark blue and heavy yellow slowly took shape, and Clarence began to see the altar, the columns.

Álvarez-Polvo was silent. The two men were standing before a harshly crowned Christ. The figure was gored deeply in the side, rust-blooded. The crown of thorns was too wide and heavy to be borne. As he confronted it, Clarence felt that it threatened to scratch the life out of him, to scratch him to the heart.

"The matter that interests us both..." Álvarez-Polvo then said.

"Yes, yes, let's go somewhere and have a talk about it. You found the poems among your uncle's papers. Do you have them here in Segovia?"

"Poems?" said Álvarez-Polvo, turning the dark and ruined face from the aisle. "That's a strange word to use for them."

"Do you mean they're not in that form? What are they then? What are they written in?"

"Why, the usual legal language. According to law."

"I don't understand."

"Neither do I. But I can show you what I'm talking about. Here. I have one with me. I brought it along." He drew a document from his pocket.

Clarence held it, trembling. It was heavy—glossy and heavy. He felt an embossed surface. Yes, there was a seal on it. What had the countess done with the poems? Had them engraved? This paper was emblazoned with a gilt star. He sought light and read, within an elaborate border of wavy green, *Compañia de Minas, S.A.*

"Is this—It can't be. You've given me the wrong thing." His heart was racing. "Put it back. Look in your pocket again."

"Why the wrong thing?"

"It looks like shares of stock."

"It's what it's supposed to be, mining stock. Isn't that what you're interested in?"

"Of course not! Certainly not! What kind of mine?"

"It's a pitchblende mine in Morocco, that's what it is."

"What do I want with pitchblende?" Clarence said.

"What any businessman would want. To sell it. Pitchblende has uranium in it. Uranium is used in atom bombs."

Oh dear God!

"Claro. Para la bomba atómica."

"What have I to do with atom bombs? What do I care about atom bombs! To hell with atom bombs!" said Clarence.

"I understood you were a financier."

"Me? Do I look like one?"

"Yes, of course you do. More an English than an American financier I thought. But a financier. Aren't you?"

"I am not. I came about the poems of Gonzaga, the poems owned by the Countess del Camino. Love poems dedicated to her by the poet Manuel Gonzaga."

"Manuel? The soldier? The little fellow? The one that was her lover in nineteen twenty-eight? He was killed in Morocco."

"Yes, yes! What did your uncle do with the poems?"

"Oh, that's what you were talking about. Why, my uncle did nothing with them. The countess did, herself. She had the poems buried with her. She took them to the grave."

"Buried! With her, you say! And no copies?"

"I doubt it. My uncle had instructions from her, and he was very loyal. He lived by loyalty. My uncle—"

"Oh, damn! Oh, damn it! And didn't he leave you anything in that collection of papers that has to do with Gonzaga? No journals, no letters that mention Gonzaga? Nothing?"

"He left me these shares in the mine. They're valuable. Not yet, but they will be if I can get capital. But you can't raise money in Spain. Spanish capital is cowardly, ignorant of science. It is still in the Counter Reformation. Let me show you the location of this mine." He opened a map and began to explain the geography of the Atlas Mountains.

Clarence walked out on him—ran, rather. Panting, enraged, he climbed from the lower town.

●

As soon as he entered his room at the hotel he knew that his valise had been searched. Storming, he slammed it shut and dragged it down the stairs, past the cistern, and into the lobby.

He shouted to the manager, "Why must the police come and turn my things upside down?"

White-faced and stern, the manager said, "You must be mistaken, *señor.*"

"I am not mistaken. They searched my wastebasket."

A man rose angrily from a chair in the lobby. In an old suit, he wore a mourning band on his arm.

"These Englishmen!" he said with fury. "They don't know what hospitality is. They come here and enjoy themselves, and criticize our country, and complain about Spanish police. What hypocrisy! There are more police in England than in Spain. The whole world knows you have a huge jail in Liverpool, filled with Masons. Five thousand Masons are *encarcelados* in Liverpool alone."

There was nothing to say. All the way to Madrid Clarence sat numb and motionless in his second-class seat.

As the train left the mountains, the heavens seemed to split. Rain began to fall, heavy and sudden, boiling on the wide plain.

He knew what to expect from that redheaded Miss Walsh at dinner.

Isaac Bashevis Singer

YENTL THE YESHIVA BOY

NOBEL PRIZE 1978

Isaac Bashevis Singer was born in Radzymin, Poland, in 1904, came to America in 1935, and became a United States citizen in 1943. He worked as a journalist for the Jewish Daily Forward *of New York for many years, and won the National Book Award (in the children's literature category) in 1970.*

Singer writes in Yiddish and frequently translates his own work into English, although it should be pointed out that there are important differences in content and style between the originals and the translations in some cases. He had a large body of work completed in Yiddish before 1950. Mr. Singer is a master of the old and the new, the traditional and modern, and the transition (often painful) from one to the other. In many ways he is a "Third World" writer. It should also be noted that Singer incorporates considerable mysticism and fantasy into his work; in fact, he has been a Guest of Honor at the International Conference on the Fantastic, which is held each spring at Florida Atlantic University. He is truly a man for all seasons.

I

AFTER HER FATHER'S DEATH, Yentl had no reason to remain in Yanev. She was all alone in the house. To be sure, lodgers were willing to move in and pay rent; and the marriage brokers flocked to her door with offers from Lublin, Tomashev, Zamosc. But Yentl didn't want to get married. Inside her, a voice repeated over and over: "No!" What becomes of a girl when the wedding's over? Right away she starts bearing and rearing. And her mother-in-law lords it over her. Yentl knew she wasn't cut out for a woman's life. She couldn't sew, she couldn't knit. She let the food burn and the milk boil over; her Sabbath pudding never turned out right, and her *challah* dough didn't rise. Yentl much preferred men's activities to women's. Her father Reb Todros, may he rest in peace, during many bedridden years had studied Torah with his daughter as if she were a son. He told Yentl to lock the doors and drape the windows, then together they pored over the Pentateuch, the Mishnah, the Gemara, and the Commentaries. She had proved so apt a pupil that her father used to say:

"Yentl—you have the soul of a man."

"So why was I born a woman?"

"Even heaven makes mistakes."

There was no doubt about it, Yentl was unlike any of the girls in Yanev—tall, thin, bony, with small breasts and narrow hips. On Sabbath afternoons, when her father slept, she would dress up in his trousers, his fringed garment, his silk coat, his skullcap, his velvet hat, and study her reflection in the mirror. She looked like a dark, handsome young man. There was even a slight down on her upper lip. Only her thick braids showed her womanhood— and if it came to that, hair could always be shorn. Yentl conceived a plan and day and night she could think of nothing else. No, she had not been created for the noodle board and the pudding dish, for chattering with silly women and pushing for a place at the butcher's block. Her father had told her so many tales of yeshivas, rabbis, men of letters! Her head was full of Talmudic disputations, questions and answers, learned phrases. Secretly, she had even smoked her father's long pipe.

Yentl told the dealers she wanted to sell the house and go to live in Kalish with an aunt. The neighborhood women tried to talk her out of it, and the marriage brokers said she was crazy, that she was more likely to make a good match right here in Yanev. But Yentl was obstinate. She was in such a rush that she sold the house to the first bidder, and let the furniture go for a song. All she realized from her inheritance was one hundred and forty rubles. Then late one night in the month of Av, while Yanev slept, Yentl cut off her braids, arranged sidelocks at her temples, and dressed herself in her father's clothes. Packing underclothes, phylacteries, and a few books into a straw suitcase, she started off on foot for Lubin.

On the main road, Yentl got a ride in a carriage that took her as far as Zamosc. From there, she again set out on foot. She stopped at an inn along the way, and gave her name there as Anshel, after an uncle who had died. The inn was crowded with young men journeying to study with famous rabbis. An argument was in progress over the merits of various yeshivas, some praising those of Lithuania, others claiming that study was more intensive in Poland and the board better. It was the first time Yentl had ever found herself alone in the company of young men. How different their talk was from the jabbering of women, she thought, but she was too shy to join in. One young man discussed a prospective match and the size of the dowry, while another, parodying the manner of a Purim rabbi, declaimed a passage from the Torah, adding all sorts of lewd interpretations. After a while, the company proceeded to contests of strength. One pried open another's fist; a second tried to bend a companion's arm. One student, dining on bread and tea, had no spoon and stirred his cup with his penknife. Presently, one of the group came over to Yentl and poked her in the shoulder:

"Why so quiet? Don't you have a tongue?"

"I have nothing to say."

"What's your name?"

"Anshel."

"You *are* bashful. A violet by the wayside."

And the young man tweaked Yentl's nose. She would have given him a smack in return, but her arm refused to budge. She turned white. Another student, slightly older than the rest, tall and pale, with burning eyes and a black beard, came to her rescue.

"Hey, you, why are you picking on him?"

"If you don't like it, you don't have to look."

"Want me to pull your sidelocks off?"

The bearded young man beckoned to Yentl, then asked where she came from and where she was going. Yentl told him she was looking for a yeshiva, but wanted a quiet one. The young man pulled at his beard.

"Then come with me to Bechev."

He explained that he was returning to Bechev for his fourth year. The yeshiva there was small, with only thirty students, and the people in the town provided board for them all. The food was plentiful and the housewives darned the students' socks and took care of their laundry. The Bechev rabbi, who headed the yeshiva, was a genius. He could pose ten questions and answer all ten with one proof. Most of the students eventually found wives in the town.

"Why did you leave in the middle of the term?" Yentl asked.

"My mother died. Now I'm on my way back."

"What's your name?"

"Avigdor."

"How is it you're not married?"

The young man scratched his beard.

"It's a long story."

"Tell me."

Avigdor covered his eyes and thought a moment.

"Are you coming to Bechev?"

"Yes."

"Then you'll find out soon enough anyway. I was engaged to the only daughter of Alter Vishkower, the richest man in town. Even the wedding date was set when suddenly they sent back the engagement contract."

"What happened?"

"I don't know. Gossips, I guess, were busy spreading tales. I had the right to ask for half the dowry, but it was against my nature. Now they're trying to talk me into another match, but the girl doesn't appeal to me."

"In Bechev, yeshiva boys look at women?"

"At Alter's house, where I ate once a week, Hadass, his daughter, always brought in the food...."

"Is she good-looking?"

"She's blond."

"Brunettes can be good-looking too."

"No."

Yentl gazed at Avigdor. He was lean and bony with sunken cheeks. He had curly sidelocks so black they appeared blue, and his eyebrows met across the bridge of his nose. He looked at her sharply with the regretful shyness of one who has just divulged a secret. His lapel was rent, according to the custom for mourners, and the lining of his gaberdine showed through. He drummed

restlessly on the table and hummed a tune. Behind the high fur-
rowed brow his thoughts seemed to race. Suddenly he spoke:
"Well, what of it. I'll become a recluse, that's all."

II

It was strange, but as soon as Yentl—or Anshel—arrived in
Bechev, she was allotted one day's board a week at the house of
that same rich man, Alter Vishkower, whose daughter had broken
off her betrothal to Avigdor.

The students at the yeshiva studied in pairs, and Avigdor chose
Anshel for a partner. He helped her with the lessons. He was also
an expert swimmer and offered to teach Anshel the breast stroke
and how to tread water, but she always found excuses for not going
down to the river. Avigdor suggested that they share lodgings, but
Anshel found a place to sleep at the house of an elderly widow
who was half blind. Tuesdays, Anshel ate at Alter Vishkower's and
Hadass waited on her. Avigdor always asked many questions: "How
does Hadass look? Is she sad? Is she gay? Are they trying to marry
her off? Does she ever mention my name?" Anshel reported that
Hadass upset dishes on the tablecloth, forgot to bring the salt, and
dipped her fingers into the plate of grits while carrying it. She
ordered the servant girl around, was forever engrossed in story-
books, and changed her hairdo every week. Morever, she must
consider herself a beauty, for she was always in front of the mirror,
but, in fact, she was not that good-looking.

"Two years after she's married," said Anshel, "she'll be an old
bag."

"So she doesn't appeal to you?"

"Not particularly."

"Yet if she wanted you, you wouldn't turn her down."

"I can do without her."

"Don't you have evil impulses?"

The two friends, sharing a lectern in a corner of the study house,
spent more time talking than learning. Occasionally Avigdor
smoked, and Anshel, taking the cigarette from his lips, would have
a puff. Avigdor liked baked flatcakes made with buckwheat, so
Anshel stopped at the bakery every morning to buy one, and
wouldn't let him pay his share. Often Anshel did things that greatly
surprised Avigdor. If a button came off Avigdor's coat, for ex-

ample, Anshel would arrive at the yeshiva the next day with needle and thread and sew it back on. Anshel bought Avigdor all kinds of presents: a silk handkerchief, a pair of socks, a muffler. Avigdor grew more and more attached to this boy, five years younger than himself, whose beard hadn't even begun to sprout. Once Avigdor said to Anshel:

"I want you to marry Hadass."

"What good would that do *you*?"

"Better you than a total stranger."

"You'd become my enemy."

"Never."

Avigdor liked to go for long walks through the town and Anshel frequently joined him. Engrossed in conversation, they would go off to the water mill, or to the pine forest, or to the crossroads where the Christian shrine stood. Sometimes they stretched out on the grass.

"Why can't a woman be like a man?" Avigdor asked once, looking up at the sky.

"How do you mean?"

"Why couldn't Hadass be just like you?"

"How like me?"

"Oh—a good fellow."

Anshel grew playful. She plucked a flower and tore off the petals one by one. She picked up a chestnut and threw it at Avigdor. Avigdor watched a ladybug crawl across the palm of his hand. After a while he spoke up:

"They're trying to marry me off."

Anshel sat up instantly.

"To whom?"

"To Feitl's daughter, Peshe."

"The widow?"

"That's the one."

"Why should you marry a widow?"

"No one else will have me."

"That's not true. Someone will turn up for you."

"Never."

Anshel told Avigdor such a match was bad. Peshe was neither good-looking nor clever, only a cow with a pair of eyes. Besides, she was bad luck, for her husband died in the first year of their marriage. Such women were husband-killers. But Avigdor did not answer. He lit a cigarette, took a deep puff, and blew out smoke rings. His face had turned green.

"I need a woman. I can't sleep at night."

Anshel was startled.

"Why can't you wait until the right one comes along?"

"Hadass was my destined one."

And Avigdor's eyes grew moist. Abruptly he got to his feet.

"Enough lying around. Let's go."

After that, everything happened quickly. One day Avigdor was confiding his problem to Anshel, two days later he became engaged to Peshe, and brought honey cake and brandy to the yeshiva. An early wedding date was set. When the bride-to-be is a widow, there's no need to wait for a trousseau. Everything is ready. The groom, moreover, was an orphan and no one's advice had to be asked. The yeshiva students drank the brandy and offered their congratulations. Anshel also took a sip, but promptly choked on it.

"Oy, it burns!"

"You're not much of a man," Avigdor teased.

After the celebration, Avigdor and Anshel sat down with a volume of the Gemara, but they made little progress, and their conversation was equally slow. Avigdor rocked back and forth, pulled at his beard, muttered under his breath.

"I'm lost," he said abruptly.

"If you don't like her, why are you getting married?"

"I'd marry a she-goat."

The following day Avigdor did not appear at the study house. Feitl the Leatherdealer belonged to the Hasidim and he wanted his prospective son-in-law to continue his studies at the Hasidic prayer house. The yeshiva students said privately that though there was no denying the widow was short and round as a barrel, her mother the daughter of a dairyman, her father half an ignoramus, still the whole family was filthy with money. Feitl was part-owner of a tannery; Peshe had invested her dowry in a shop that sold herring, tar, pots and pans, and was always crowded with peasants. Father and daughter were outfitting Avigdor and had placed orders for a fur coat, a cloth coat, a silk capote, and two pair of boots. In addition, he had received many gifts immediately, things that had belonged to Peshe's first husband: the Vilna edition of the Talmud, a gold watch, a Chanukah candelabra, a spice box. Anshel sat alone at the lectern. On Tuesday when Anshel arrived for dinner at Alter Vishkower's house, Hadass remarked:

"What do you say about your partner—back in clover, isn't he?"

"What did you expect—that no one else would want him?"

Hadass reddened.

"It wasn't my fault. My father was against it."

"Why?"

"Because they found out a brother of his had hanged himself."

Anshel looked at her as she stood there—tall, blond, with a long neck, hollow cheeks, and blue eyes, wearing a cotton dress and a calico apron. Her hair, fixed in two braids, was flung back over her shoulders. A pity I'm not a man, Anshel thought.

"Do you regret it now?" Anshel asked.

"Oh, yes!"

Hadass fled from the room. The rest of the food, meat dumplings and tea, was brought in by the servant girl. Not until Anshel had finished eating and was washing her hands for the Final Blessings did Hadass reappear. She came up to the table and said in a smothered voice:

"Swear to me you won't tell him anything. Why should he know what goes on in my heart!..."

Then she fled once more, nearly falling over the threshold.

III

The head of the yeshiva asked Anshel to choose another study partner, but weeks went by and still Anshel studied alone. There was no one in the yeshiva who could take Avigdor's place. All the others were small, in body and in spirit. They talked nonsense, bragged about trifles, grinned oafishly, behaved like shnorrers. Without Avigdor the study house seemed empty. At night Anshel lay on her bench at the widow's, unable to sleep. Stripped of gaberdine and trousers, she was once more Yentl, a girl of marriageable age, in love with a young man who was betrothed to another. Perhaps I should have told him the truth, Anshel thought. But it was too late for that. Anshel could not go back to being a girl, could never again do without books and a study house. She lay there thinking outlandish thoughts that brought her close to madness. She fell asleep, then awoke with a start. In her dream she had been at the same time a man and a woman, wearing both a woman's bodice and a man's fringed garment. Yentl's period was late and she was suddenly afraid...who knew? In *Medrash Talpioth* she had read of a woman who had conceived merely through desiring a man. Only now did Yentl grasp the meaning of the Torah's prohibition against wearing the clothes of the other sex. By doing so one deceived not only others but also oneself. Even the soul was perplexed, finding itself incarnate in a strange body.

At night Anshel lay awake; by day she could scarcely keep her eyes open. At the houses where she had her meals, the women complained that the youth left everything on his plate. The rabbi noticed that Anshel no longer paid attention to the lectures but stared out the window lost in private thoughts. When Tuesday came, Anshel appeared at the Vishkower house for dinner. Hadass set a bowl of soup before her and waited, but Anshel was so disturbed she did not even say thank you. She reached for a spoon but let it fall. Hadass ventured a comment:

"I hear Avigdor has deserted you."

Anshel awoke from her trance.

"What do you mean?"

"He's no longer your partner."

"He's left yeshiva."

"Do you see him at all?"

"He seems to be hiding."

"Are you at least going to the wedding?"

For a moment Anshel was silent as though missing the meaning of the words. Then she spoke:

"He's a big fool."

"Why do you say that?"

"You're beautiful, and the other one looks like a monkey."

Hadass blushed to the roots of her hair.

"It's all my father's fault."

"Don't worry. You'll find someone who's worthy of you."

"There's no one I want."

"But everyone wants you...."

There was a long silence. Hadass's eyes grew larger, filling with the sadness of one who knows there is no consolation.

"Your soup is getting cold."

"I, too, want you."

Anshel was astonished at what she had said. Hadass stared at her over her shoulder.

"What are you saying!"

"It's the truth."

"Someone might be listening."

"I'm not afraid."

"Eat the soup. I'll bring the meat dumplings in a moment."

Hadass turned to go, her high heels clattering. Anshel began hunting for beans in the soup, fished one up, then let it fall. Her appetite was gone; her throat had closed up. She knew very well she was getting entangled in evil, but some force kept urging her on. Hadass reappeared, carrying a platter with two meat dumplings on it.

"Why aren't you eating?"

"I'm thinking about you."

"What are you thinking?"

"I want to marry you."

Hadass made a face as though she had swallowed something.

"On such matters, you must speak to my father."

"I know."

"The custom is to send a matchmaker."

She ran from the room, letting the door slam behind her. Laughing inwardly, Anshel thought: "With girls I can play as I please!" She sprinkled salt on the soup and then pepper. She sat there lightheaded. What have I done? I must be going mad. There's no other explanation.... She forced herself to eat, but could taste nothing. Only then did Anshel remember that it was Avigdor who had wanted to marry Hadass. From her confusion, a plan emerged: she would exact vengeance for Avigdor, and at the same time, through Hadass, draw him closer to herself. Hadass was a virgin: what did she know about men? A girl like that could be deceived for a long time. To be sure, Anshel too was a virgin but she knew a lot about such matters from the Gemara and from hearing men talk. Anshel was seized by both fear and glee, as a person is who is planning to deceive the whole community. She remembered the saying: "The public are fools." She stood up and said aloud: "Now I'll really start something."

That night Anshel didn't sleep a wink. Every few minutes she got up for a drink of water. Her throat was parched, her forehead burned. Her brain worked away feverishly of its own volition. A quarrel seemed to be going on inside her. Her stomach throbbed and her knees ached. It was as if she had sealed a pact with Satan, the Evil One who plays tricks on human beings, who sets stumbling blocks and traps in their paths. By the time Anshel fell asleep, it was morning. She awoke more exhausted than before. But she could not go on sleeping on the bench at the widow's. With an effort she rose and, taking the bag that held her phylacteries, set out for the study house. On the way, whom should she meet but Hadass's father. Anshel bade him a respectful good morning and received a friendly greeting in return. Reb Alter stroked his beard and engaged her in conversation:

"My daughter Hadass must be serving you leftovers. You look starved."

"Your daughter is a fine girl, and very generous."

"So why are you so pale?"

Anshel was silent for a minute.

"Reb Alter, there's something I must say to you."

"Well, go ahead, say it."

"Reb Alter, your daughter pleases me."

Alter Vishkower came to a halt.

"Oh, does she? I thought yeshiva students didn't talk about such things."

His eyes were full of laughter.

"But it's the truth."

"One doesn't discuss these matters with the young man himself."

"But I'm an orphan."

"Well...in that case the custom is to send a marriage broker."

"Yes...."

"What do you see in her?"

"She's beautiful...fine...intelligent...."

"Well, well, well....Come along, tell me something about your family."

Alter Vishkower put his arm around Anshel and in this fashion the two continued walking until they reached the courtyard of the synagogue.

IV

Once you say "A," you must say "B." Thoughts lead to words, words lead to deeds. Reb Alter Vishkower gave his consent to the match. Hadass's mother Freyda Leah held back for a while. She said she wanted no more Bechev yeshiva students for her daughter and would rather have someone from Lublin or Zamosc; but Hadass gave warning that if she were shamed publicly once more (the way she had been with Avigdor) she would throw herself into the well. As often happens with such ill-advised matches, everyone was strongly in favor of it—the rabbi, the relatives, Hadass's girl friends. For some time the girls of Bechev had been eyeing Anshel longingly, watching from their windows when the youth passed by on the street. Anshel kept his boots well polished and did not drop his eyes in the presence of women. Stopping in at Beila the Baker's to buy a *pletzl,* he joked with them in such a worldly fashion that they marveled. The women agreed there was something special about Anshel: his sidelocks curled like nobody else's and he tied his neck scarf differently; his eyes, smiling yet distant, seemed always fixed on some faraway point. And the fact that Avigdor had become bethrothed to Feitl's daughter Peshe, forsaking Anshel, had endeared him all the more to the people of the town. Alter Vishkower had a provisional contract drawn up for the betrothal, promising Anshel a bigger dowry, more presents, and an even longer period of maintenance than he had promised Avigdor. The girls of Bechev threw their arms around Hadass and congratulated her. Hadass immediately began crocheting a sack for Anshel's phylacteries, a *challah* cloth, a matzoh bag. When Avigdor heard the news of Anshel's betrothal, he came to the study house to offer his congratulations. The past few weeks had aged him. His beard was disheveled, his eyes were red. He said to Anshel:

"I knew it would happen this way. Right from the beginning. As soon as I met you at the inn."

"But it was you who suggested it."

"I know that."

"Why did you desert me? You went away without even saying goodbye."

"I wanted to burn my bridges behind me."

Avigdor asked Anshel to go for a walk. Though it was already past Succoth, the day was bright with sunshine. Avigdor, friendlier than ever, opened his heart to Anshel. Yes, it was true, a brother of his had succumbed to melancholy and hanged himself. Now he too felt himself near the edge of the abyss. Peshe had a lot of money and her father was a rich man, yet he couldn't sleep nights. He didn't want to be a storekeeper. He couldn't forget Hadass. She appeared in his dreams. Sabbath night when her name occurred in the Havdala prayer, he turned dizzy. Still it was good that Anshel and no one else was to marry her....At least she would fall into decent hands. Avigdor stooped and tore aimlessly at the shriveled grass. His speech was incoherent, like that of a man possessed. Suddenly he said:

"I have thought of doing what my brother did."

"Do you love her *that* much?"

"She's engraved in my heart."

The two pledged their friendship and promised never again to part. Anshel proposed that, after they were both married, they should live next door or even share the same house. They would study together every day, perhaps even become partners in a shop.

"Do you want to know the truth?" asked Avigdor. "It's like the story of Jacob and Benjamin: my life is bound up in your life."

"Then why did you leave me?"

"Perhaps for that very reason."

Though the day had turned cold and windy, they continued to walk until they reached the pine forest, not turning back until dusk when it was time for the evening prayer. The girls of Bechev, from their posts at the windows, watched them going by with their arms round each other's shoulders and so engrossed in conversation that they walked through puddles and piles of trash without noticing. Avigdor looked pale, disheveled, and the wind whipped one side-lock about; Anshel chewed his fingernails. Hadass, too, ran to the window, took one look, and her eyes filled with tears....

Events followed quickly. Avigdor was the first to marry. Because the bride was a widow, the wedding was a quiet one, with no musicians, no wedding jester, no ceremonial veiling of the bride. One day Peshe stood beneath the marriage canopy, the next she was back at the shop, dispensing tar with greasy hands. Avigdor prayed at the Hasidic assembly house in his new prayer shawl. Afternoons, Anshel went to visit him and the two whispered and talked until evening. The date of Anshel's wedding to Hadass was set for the Sabbath in Chanukah week, though the prospective father-in-law wanted it sooner. Hadass had already been betrothed once. Besides, the groom was an orphan. Why should he toss about on a makeshift bed at the widow's when he could have a wife and home of his own?

Many times each day Anshel warned herself that what she was about to do was sinful, mad, an act of utter depravity. She was entangling both Hadass and herself in a chain of deception and committing so many transgressions that she would never be able to do penance. One lie followed another. Repeatedly Anshel made up her mind to flee Bechev in time, to put an end to this weird comedy that was more the work of an imp than a human being. But she was in the grip of a power she could not resist. She grew more and more attached to Avigdor, and could not bring herself to destroy Hadass's illusory happiness. Now that he was married, Avigdor's desire to study was greater than ever, and the friends met twice each day: in the mornings they studied the Gemara and the Commentaries, in the afternoons the Legal Codes with their glosses. Alter Vishkower and Feitl the Leatherdealer were pleased and compared Avigdor and Anshel to David and Jonathan. With all the complications, Anshel went about as though drunk. The tailors took her measurements for a new wardrobe and she was forced into all kinds of subterfuge to keep them from discovering she was not a man. Though the imposture had lasted many weeks, Anshel still could not believe it: How was it possible? Fooling the community had become a game, but how long could it go on? And in what way would the truth come to the surface? Inside, Anshel laughed and wept. She had turned into a sprite brought into the world to mock people and trick them. I'm wicked, a transgressor, a Jeroboam ben Nabat, she told herself. Her only justification was that she had taken all these burdens upon herself because her soul thirsted to study Torah....

Avigdor soon began to complain that Peshe treated him badly. She called him an idler, a schlemiel, just another mouth to feed. She tried to tie him to the store, assigned him tasks for which he hadn't the slightest inclination, begrudged him pocket money. Instead of consoling Avigdor, Anshel goaded him on against Peshe. She called his wife an eyesore, a shrew, a miser, and said that Peshe had no doubt nagged her first husband to death and would Avigdor also. At the same time, Anshel enumerated Avigdor's virtues: his height and manliness, his wit, his erudition.

"If I were a woman and married to you," said Anshel, "I'd know how to appreciate you."

"Well, but you aren't...."

Avigdor sighed.

Meanwhile Anshel's wedding date drew near.

On the Sabbath before Chanukah Anshel was called to the pulpit to read from the Torah. The women showered her with raisins and almonds. On the day of the wedding Alter Vishkower gave a feast for the young men. Avigdor sat at Anshel's right hand. The bridegroom delivered a Talmudic discourse, and the rest of the company argued the points, while smoking cigarettes and drinking wine, liqueurs, tea with lemon or raspberry jam. Then followed the ceremony of veiling the bride, after which the bridegroom was led to the wedding canopy that had been set up at the side of the synagogue. The night was frosty and clear, the sky full of stars. The musicians struck up a tune. Two rows of girls held lighted tapers and braided wax candles. After the wedding ceremony the bride and groom broke their fast with golden chicken broth. Then the dancing began and the announcement of the wedding gifts, all according to custom. The gifts were many and costly. The wedding jester depicted the joys and sorrows that were in store for the bride. Avigdor's wife, Peshe, was one of the guests but, though she was bedecked with jewels, she still looked ugly in a wig that sat low on her forehead, wearing an enormous fur cape, and with traces of tar on her hands that no amount of washing could ever remove. After the Virtue Dance the bride and groom were led separately to the marriage chamber. The wedding attendants instructed the couple in the proper conduct and enjoined them to "be fruitful and multiply."

At daybreak Anshel's mother-in-law and her band descended upon the marriage chamber and tore the bedsheets from beneath Hadass to make sure the marriage had been consummated. When traces of blood were discovered, the company grew merry and began kissing and congratulating the bride. Then, brandishing the sheet, they flocked outside and danced a Kosher Dance in the newly fallen snow. Anshel had found a way to deflower the bride. Hadass in her innocence was unaware that things weren't quite as they should have been. She was already deeply in love with Anshel. It is commanded that the bride and groom remain apart for seven days after the first intercourse. The next day Anshel and Avigdor took up the study of the Tractate on Menstruous Women. When the other men had departed and the two were left to themselves in the synagogue, Avigdor shyly questioned Anshel about his night with Hadass. Anshel gratified his curiosity and they whispered together until nightfall.

V

Anshel had fallen into good hands. Hadass was a devoted wife and her parents indulged their son-in-law's every wish and boasted of his accomplishments. To be sure, several months went by and Hadass was still not with child, but no one took it to heart. On the other hand, Avigdor's lot grew steadily worse. Peshe tormented him and finally would not give him enough to eat and even refused him a clean shirt. Since he was always penniless, Anshel again brought him a daily buckwheat cake. Because Peshe was too busy to cook and too stingy to hire a servant, Anshel asked Avigdor to dine at his house. Reb Alter Vishkower and his wife disapproved, arguing that it was wrong for the rejected suitor to visit the house of his former fiancée. The town had plenty to talk about. But Anshel cited precedents to show that it was not prohibited by the law. Most of the townspeople sided with Avigdor and blamed Peshe for everything. Avigdor soon began pressing Peshe for a divorce, and, because he did not want to have a child by such a fury, he acted like Onan, or, as the Gemara translates it: he threshed on the inside and cast his seed without. He confided in Anshel, told him how Peshe came to bed unwashed and snored like a buzz saw, of how she was so occupied with the cash taken in at the store that she babbled about it even in her sleep.

"Oh, Anshel, how I envy you," he said.

"There's no reason for envying me."

"You have everything. I wish your good fortune were mine— with no loss to you, of course."

"Everyone has troubles of his own."

"What sort of troubles do *you* have? Don't tempt Providence."

How could Avigdor have guessed that Anshel could not sleep at night and thought constantly of running away? Lying with Hadass and deceiving her had become more and more painful. Hadass's love and tenderness shamed her. The devotion of her mother- and father-in-law and their hopes for a grandchild were a burden. On Friday afternoons all of the townspeople went to the baths and every week Anshel had to find a new excuse. But this was beginning to awake suspicions. There was talk that Anshel must have an unsightly birthmark, or a rupture, or perhaps was not properly circumcised. Judging by the youth's years, his beard should certainly have begun to sprout, yet his cheeks remained smooth. It was already Purim and Passover was approaching. Soon it would be summer. Not far from Bechev there was a river where all the yeshiva students and young men went swimming as soon as it was warm enough. The lie was swelling like an abscess and one of these days it must surely burst. Anshel knew she had to find a way to free herself.

It was customary for the young men boarding with their in-laws to travel to nearby cities during the half-holidays in the middle of Passover week. They enjoyed the change, refreshed themselves, looked around for business opportunities, bought books or other things a young man might need. Bechev was not far from Lublin and Anshel persuaded Avigdor to make the journey with her at her expense. Avigdor was delighted at the prospect of being rid for a few days of the shrew he had at home. The trip by carriage was a merry one. The fields were turning green; storks, back from the warm countries, swooped across the sky in great arcs. Streams rushed toward the valleys. The birds chirped. The windmills turned. Spring flowers were beginning to bloom in the fields. Here and there a cow was already grazing. The companions, chatting, ate the fruit and little cakes that Hadass had packed, told each other jokes, and exchanged confidences until they reached Lublin. There they went to an inn and took a room for two. On the journey, Anshel had promised to reveal an astonishing secret to Avigdor in Lublin. Avigdor had joked: what sort of secret could it be? Had Anshel discovered a hidden treasure? Had he written an essay? By studying the Cabala, had he created a dove?... Now they entered the room and while Anshel carefully locked the door, Avigdor said teasingly:

"Well, let's hear your great secret."

"Prepare yourself for the most incredible thing that ever was."

"I'm prepared for anything."

"I'm not a man but a woman," said Anshel. "My name isn't Anshel, it's Yentl."

Avigdor burst out laughing.

"I knew it was a hoax."

"But it's true."

"Even if I'm a fool, I won't swallow this."

"Do you want me to show you?"

"Yes."

"Then I'll get undressed."

Avigdor's eyes widened. It occurred to him that Anshel might want to practice pederasty. Anshel took off the gaberdine and the fringed garment, and threw off her underclothes. Avigdor took one look and turned first white, then fiery red. Anshel covered herself hastily.

"I've done this only so that you can testify at the courthouse. Otherwise Hadass will have to stay a grass widow."

Avigdor had lost his tongue. He was seized by a fit of trembling. He wanted to speak, but his lips moved and nothing came out. He sat down quickly, for his legs would not support him. Finally he murmured:

"How is it possible? I don't believe it!"

"Should I get undressed again?"

"No!"

Yentl proceeded to tell the whole story: how her father, bed-ridden, had studied Torah with her; how she had never had the patience for women and their silly chatter; how she had sold the house and all the furnishings, left the town, made her way disguised as a man to Lublin, and on the road met Avigdor. Avigdor sat speechless, gazing at the storyteller. Yentl was by now wearing men's clothes once more. Avigdor spoke:

"It must be a dream."

He pinched himself on the cheek.

"It isn't a dream."

"That such a thing should happen to me...!"

"It's all true."

"Why did you do it? *Nu,* I'd better keep still."

"I didn't want to waste my life on a baking shovel and a kneading trough."

"And what about Hadass—why did you do that?"

"I did it for your sake. I knew that Peshe would torment you and at our house you would have some peace...."

Avigdor was silent for long time. He bowed his head, pressed his hands to his temples, shook his head.

"What will you do now?"

"I'll go away to a different yeshiva."

"What? If you had only told me earlier, we could have..."

Avigdor broke off in the middle.

"No—it wouldn't have been good."

"Why not?"

"I'm neither one nor the other."

"What a dilemma I'm in!"

"Get a divorce from that horror. Marry Hadass."

"She'll never divorce me and Hadass won't have me."

"Hadass loves you. She won't listen to her father again."

Avigdor stood up suddenly but then sat down.

"I won't be able to forget you. Ever...."

VI

According to the law Avigdor was now forbidden to spend another moment alone with Yentl; yet dressed in the gaberdine and trousers, she was again the familiar Anshel. They resumed their conversation on the old footing:

"How could you bring yourself to violate the commandment every day: 'A woman shall not wear that which pertaineth to a man'?"

"I wasn't created for plucking feathers and chattering with females."

"Would you rather lose your share in the world to come?"

"Perhaps...."

Avigdor raised his eyes. Only now did he realize that Anshel's cheeks were too smooth for a man's, the hair too abundant, the hands too small. Even so he could not believe that such a thing could have happened. At any moment he expected to wake up. He bit his lips, pinched his thigh. He was seized by shyness and could not speak without stammering. His friendship with Anshel, their intimate talk, their confidences, had been turned into a sham and delusion. The thought even occurred to him that Anshel might be a demon. He shook himself as if to cast off a nightmare; yet that power which knows the difference between dream and reality told him it was all true. He summoned up his courage. He and Anshel could never be strangers to one another, even though Anshel was in fact Yentl....He ventured a comment:

"It seems to me that the witness who testifies for a deserted woman may not marry her, for the law calls him 'a party to the affair.'"

"What? That didn't occur to me!"

"We must look it up in Eben Ezer."

"I'm not even sure that the rules pertaining to a deserted woman apply in this case," said Anshel in the manner of a scholar.

"If you don't want Hadass to be a grass widow, you must reveal the secret to her directly."

"That I can't do."

"In any event, you must get another witness."

Gradually the two went back to their Talmudic conversation. It seemed strange at first to Avigdor to be disputing holy writ with a woman, yet before long the Torah had reunited them. Though their bodies were different, their souls were of one kind. Anshel spoke in a singsong, gesticulated with her thumb, clutched her sidelocks, plucked at her beardless chin, made all the customary gestures of a yeshiva student. In the heat of argument she even seized Avigdor by the lapel and called him stupid. A great love for Anshel took hold of Avigdor, mixed with shame, remorse, anxiety. If I had only known this before, he said to himself. In his thoughts he likened Anshel (or Yentl) to Bruria, the wife of Reb Meir, and to Yalta, the wife of Reb Nachman. For the first time he saw clearly that this was what he had always wanted: a wife whose mind was not taken up with material things.... His desire for Hadass was gone now, and he knew he would long for Yentl, but he dared not say so. He felt hot and knew that his face was burning. He could no longer meet Anshel's eyes. He began to enumerate Anshel's sins and saw that he too was implicated, for he had sat next to Yentl and had touched her during her unclean days. *Nu*, and what could be said about her marriage to Hadass? What a multitude of transgressions there! Willful deception, false vows, misrepresentation!—Heaven knows what else. He asked suddenly:

"Tell the truth, are you a heretic?"

"God forbid!"

"Then how could you bring yourself to do such a thing?"

The longer Anshel talked, the less Avigdor understood. All Anshel's explanations seemed to point to one thing: she had the soul of a man and the body of a woman. Anshel said she had married Hadass only in order to be near Avigdor.

"You could have married me," Avigdor said.

"I wanted to study the Gemara and Commentaries with you, not darn your socks!"

For a long time neither spoke. Then Avigdor broke the silence:

"I'm afraid Hadass will get sick from all this, God forbid!"

"I'm afraid of that too."

"What's going to happen now?"

Dusk fell and the two began to recite the evening prayer. In his confusion Avigdor mixed up the blessings, omitted some and repeated others. He glanced sideways at Anshel who was rocking back and forth, beating her breast, bowing her head. He saw her, eyes closed, lift her face to heaven as though beseeching: You, Father in Heaven, know the truth.... When their prayers were finished, they sat down on opposite chairs, facing one another yet a good distance apart. The room filled with shadows. Reflections of the sunset, like purple embroidery, shook on the wall opposite the window. Avigdor again wanted to speak but at first the words, trembling on the tip of his tongue, would not come. Suddenly they burst forth:

"Maybe it's still not too late? I can't go on living with that accursed woman.... You...."

"No, Avigdor, it's impossible."

"Why?"

"I'll live out my time as I am...."

"I'll miss you. Terribly."

"And I'll miss you."

"What's the sense of all this?"

Anshel did not answer. Night fell and the light faded. In the darkness they seemed to be listening to each other's thoughts. The law forbade Avigdor to stay in the room alone with Anshel, but he could not think of her just as a woman. What a strange power there is in clothing, he thought. But he spoke of something else:

"I would advise you simply to send Hadass a divorce."

"How can I do that?"

"Since the marriage sacraments weren't valid, what difference does it make?"

"I suppose you're right."

"There'll be time enough later for her to find out the truth."

The maidservant came in with a lamp but as soon as she had gone, Avigdor put it out. Their predicament and the words which they must speak to one another could not endure light. In the blackness Anshel related all the particulars. She answered all Avigdor's questions. The clock struck two, and still they talked. Anshel told Avigdor that Hadass had never forgotten him. She talked of him frequently, worried about his health, was sorry—though not without a certain satisfaction—about the way things had turned out with Peshe.

"She'll be a good wife," said Anshel. "I don't even know how to bake a pudding."

"Nevertheless, if you're willing...."

"No, Avigdor. It wasn't destined to be...."

VII

It was all a great riddle to the town: the messenger who arrived bringing Hadass the divorce papers; Avigdor's remaining in Lublin until after the holidays; his return to Bechev with slumping shoulders and lifeless eyes as if he had been ill. Hadass took to her bed and was visited by the doctor three times a day. Avigdor went into seclusion. If someone ran across him by chance and addressed him, he did not answer. Peshe complained to her parents that Avigdor paced back and forth smoking all night long. When he finally collapsed from sheer fatigue, in his sleep he called out the name of an unknown female—Yentl. Peshe began talking of a divorce. The town thought Avigdor wouldn't grant her one or would demand money at the very least, but he agreed to everything.

In Bechev the people were not used to having mysteries stay mysteries for long. How can you keep secrets in a little town where everyone knows what's cooking in everyone else's pots? Yet, though there were plenty of persons who made a practice of looking through keyholes and laying an ear to shutters, what happened remained an enigma. Hadass lay in her bed and wept. Chanina the herb doctor reported that she was wasting away. Anshel had disappeared without a trace. Reb Alter Vishkower sent for Avigdor and he arrived, but those who stood straining beneath the window couldn't catch a word of what passed between them. Those individuals who habitually pry into other people's affairs came up with all sorts of theories, but not one of them was consistent.

One party came to the conclusion that Anshel had fallen into the hands of Catholic priests, and had been converted. That might have made sense. But where could Anshel have found time for the priests, since he was always studying in the yeshiva? And apart from that, since when does an apostate send his wife a divorce?

Another group whispered that Anshel had cast an eye on another woman. But who could it be? There were no love affairs conducted in Bechev. And none of the young women had recently left town— neither a Jewish woman nor a Gentile one.

Somebody else offered the suggestion that Anshel had been car-

ried away by evil spirits, or was even one of them himself. As proof
he cited the fact that Anshel had never come either to the bathhouse
or to the river. It is well known that demons have the feet of geese.
Well, but had Hadass never seen him barefoot? And who ever heard
of a demon sending his wife a divorce? When a demon marries a
daughter of mortals, he usually lets her remain a grass widow.

It occurred to someone else that Anshel had committed a major
transgression and gone into exile in order to do penance. But what
sort of transgression could it have been? And why had he not
entrusted it to the rabbi? And why did Avigdor wander about like
a ghost?

The hypothesis of Tevel the Musician was closest to the truth.
Tevel maintained that Avigdor had been unable to forget Hadass
and that Anshel had divorced her so that his friend would be able
to marry her. But was such friendship possible in this world? And
in that case, why had Anshel divorced Hadass even before Avigdor
divorced Peshe? Furthermore, such a thing can be accomplished
only if the wife has been informed of the arrangement and is
willing, yet all signs pointed to Hadass's great love for Anshel, and
in fact she was ill from sorrow.

One thing was clear to all: Avigdor knew the truth. But it was
impossible to get anything out of him. He remained in seclusion
and kept silent with an obstinancy that was a reproof to the whole
town.

Close friends urged Peshe not to divorce Avigdor, though they
had severed all relations and no longer lived as man and wife. He
did not even, on Friday night, perform the kiddush blessing for
her. He spent his nights either at the study house or at the widow's
where Anshel had found lodgings. When Peshe spoke to him he
didn't answer, but stood with bowed head. The tradeswoman Peshe
had no patience for such goings-on. She needed a young man to
help her out in the store, not a yeshiva student who had fallen into
melancholy. Someone of that sort might even take it into his head
to depart and leave her deserted. Peshe agreed to a divorce.

In the meantime Hadass had recovered, and Reb Alter Vishkower let it be known that a marriage contract was being drawn
up. Hadass was to marry Avigdor. The town was agog. A marriage
between a man and a woman who had once been engaged and
their betrothal broken off was unheard of. The wedding was held
on the first Sabbath after Tishe b'Av, and included all that is cus-

tomary at the marriage of a virgin: the banquet for the poor, the canopy before the synagogue, the musicians, the wedding jester, the Virtue Dance. Only one thing was lacking: joy. The bridegroom stood beneath the marriage canopy, a figure of desolation. The bride had recovered from her sickness, but had remained pale and thin. Her tears fell into the golden chicken broth. From all eyes the same question looked out: why had Anshel done it?

After Avigdor's marriage to Hadass, Peshe spread the rumor that Anshel had sold his wife to Avigdor for a price, and that the money had been supplied by Alter Vishkower. One young man pondered the riddle at great length until he finally arrived at the conclusion that Anshel had lost his beloved wife to Avigdor at cards, or even on a spin of the Chanukah *dreidl*. It is a general rule that when the grain of truth cannot be found, men will swallow great helpings of falsehood. Truth itself is often concealed in such a way that the harder you look for it, the harder it is to find.

Not long after the wedding, Hadass became pregnant. The child was a boy and those assembled at the circumcision could scarcely believe their ears when they heard the father name his son Anshel.

Translated by Marion Magid
and Elizabeth Pollet